Meghan's Beads

*Love &
Blessings
Angela*

Meghan's Beads

Angela Rush

First Edition
July 2019, Burlington ON

Printed by: Virtual Impact Marketing VIMI Corp.

Editor: Fred Ouimette
Email: Fredoui@rogers.com
Artist: Samantha Teagan Le Grand

: Meghans Beads
: @meghansbeads
Email: missmeghansbeads@gmail.com

ISBN 978-0-9958455-0-3 paper back
ISBN 978-0-9958455-1-0 eBook

Dedication

This book is first and foremost dedicated to my love of God. I believe His love was a constant through this journey, and it was His love that had carried me through it. Secondly, to my beautiful daughters Meghan and Caitlin.

Meghan - this is your story, but it belongs to the world. You were chosen, and never forget it. One special evening, you said to me. "Mom, it's not about how long you live, it's about how you live your life." How true, how wise, and how admirable, words I will live by. I shall never forget that lesson, thank you.

Caitlin - you are a sweetheart, my soul mate and wise beyond your years. My sweet youngest daughter who had to grow up fast, and sometimes alone through this journey; you were always in my heart and never forgotten. Please know that this book is so much a part of you also. You gave me strength and courage whenever God knew I needed it. Your love for me and your sister is truly from your heart, and I couldn't even write this book if you didn't constantly remind me of what being strong and having faith was all about.

Finally this book has to be dedicated to all the children who fight and struggle to live. Whether you are battling an illness, whether you are abused, abandoned, or whatever the fight you are fighting; no child should ever have to fight to live. So I dedicate this book to all of you, the children, and our future. You all inspire me. Remember above all you are loved.

Author's Note

I am a single mom and a Christian who believes that God works through all of us. It is my belief that every choice we make in life impacts the lives of others and that our choices determine the path of every journey. Life can be simple or complicated; it is our actions and reactions that reveal the path. Through decisions life becomes a series of journeys. This book reflects the painful yet inspiring journey of my daughter Meghan. This journey began in 2005 but truly is timeless. Travel with love and light in your heart. Always have faith my friend always have faith.

About the editor: Fred Ouimette

Fred is a licensed Spiritual Practitioner with Centres for Spiritual Living and is currently studying to be a Minister. He agreed to work on this book as editor because of his relationship to me as a friend, and his love for moving people through the healing process.

Editor's Note

This book is a mother's testament to the love for her daughter whose resilience and desire for life prove that love conquers all no matter what. A powerful moving journey that will remind you to appreciate your life, especially in the simplest moments.

Introduction

Meghan's Beads

". . *Why me, why me, why me* . . ." she cried. Life wasn't about being popular; it wasn't about the so many things that Meghan thought it was, and she was about to discover for herself what truly mattered most in life. Her journey would take her to death's doorstep and back more than once, while becoming the young woman that God had intended her to be, a perfect picture of His grace.

Meghan's Beads, a true story, told from my heart, the aching heart of her mother as I journeyed with my daughter through something so difficult, and yet so inspiring that the words were almost impossible for me to put together. Thank you God for taking us all into your loving arms and for carrying us through this journey and teaching us through Meghan, that love is love is love. Also, thank you for giving me the words, courage and inspiration to share her story. Together, with love holding onto all of us we would continue this journey day by day. Fear often took a hold of our hearts as we spun out of control in our minds afraid of what may happen. Yet as we travelled this journey together, we discovered that courage is one step ahead of fear, and that love was and is more powerful than anything.

Contents

Chapter 1 – Where it all began

As I stood with Randy in the parking lot of McMaster Children's Hospital, using a lamppost to hold me up, I felt the life and strength in my body about to leave. My feet were anchored to the ground. As I dug my heels in hard I could feel the pressure in the soles of my feet; afraid to move even an inch for the fear of collapsing. With my back pressed firmly against the cold hard concrete I could feel the chill of the icy post right through my coat. I wanted to press harder against it, to feel something, anything; even if it was the rigid frozen pillar, anything was more bearable than the fear that grew inside my heart and took over me moment by moment.

It was bright outside, the sun shone, but I didn't. Using Randy's cell phone I dialed numbers, not even truly aware of whom I called until a person picked up the receiver on the other end and answered. My fingers seemed to search the keypad, and felt as lost as I was. *What am I doing?* I thought to myself, yet the numbers just seemed to come to me. They would just appear from nowhere in my mind as I placed call after call to anyone and everyone. *The next 48 hours were going to be critical,* were words of terror that ran through my mind like a racehorse.

It was only a few hours earlier that Randy, Gerry, Meghan and I arrived here at McMaster Children's Hospital for what I thought would be a simple visit to get Meghan on the proper treatment for some sort of infection, or at least that was what I had hoped. Confused is what I felt now.

I had met Gerry, my ex-husband, earlier that morning as we were ushered quite quickly into examination room five of the oncology clinic and waited for Dr. Posthma to arrive. I walked quickly through the main area of the clinic. My heart felt heavy with so much pain as I looked upon all the children here that were clearly very sick. Meghan still had a fever, but no other complaints. Strict instructions were given to me by Dr. Chad, whom we saw two days prior, to have Meghan medication free so that a proper exam and tests could be conducted on her. Dr. Chad was adamant that the doctors didn't want any symptoms to be masqued by medication. "Do not treat her fever prior to your appointment" were his instructions.

Meghan sat quietly as she swung her legs off the edge of the examination table, back and forth, like a pendulum. It was almost hypnotic to stare at them. Her running shoes were loose with the laces tucked inside and her heel would occasionally pop in and out of the shoe. She had on her pink tartan flannel pajama pants, an oversized sweatshirt, and her multi-toned blue ski jacket. Her hair was pulled back and tied in a ponytail that was long enough that it hung over her left shoulder. She looked so beautiful; I always loved that blue jacket on her. Tears began to fill my eyes so I shifted my gaze and looked around the exam room, nothing but beige, typical hospital beige.

"Will I have to stay overnight?" Meghan asked. It broke my heart because she was so sad and afraid.

"Probably a couple of days" her dad reassured her.

Meghan was always daddy's little girl, even more so after our divorce when she was only eight years old. She had his blue eyes and warm smile. Gerry hadn't changed much from when we were married, a little less hair and a few more pounds, but overall, the years had been good to both of us. I was so glad that he was here with us today, she needed him, and I must admit that I did too.

Doctors, students, nurses, and interns, they all took turns as they would enter and exit our simple beige room to meet with Meghan and to discuss amongst each other their findings. There was hustle and bustle going on in the hallway. Hustle and bustle, I never quite pictured what the phrase would look like, but this hallway was definitely hustle and bustle. Their voices meshed together, so that I could only hear and comprehend a few words; a remix of medical terminology that I could not quite understand. I felt that things just didn't look good, that quite possibly it could be something more than an infection. Meghan had rarely ever been sick; sure she caught the odd cold, but never anything like this. For the most part she was a perfectly healthy 15 year old girl. As the doctors, nurses, and interns conversed I caught bits and pieces of information, and pieced enough together that I knew something very significant and quite serious was definitely going on. A feeling of complete discomfort overwhelmed me. I felt out of place not knowing what they talked about and this conversation was all about my daughter. I had never even been inside a hospital like this one. Actually, besides giving birth, I had never had reason to attend a hospital with either of my girls and I was scared.

My poor Meghan was poked and prodded and I wondered just how much blood they had to take to run these tests, *what are they looking for,* I thought. Shortly after the tests were started and blood was drawn, Dr. Posthma had entered the room to deliver her initial findings. She was a petite woman with short black hair. She seemed like a force, a get it done kind of person. I knew that if she wanted answers, she would definitely get them. She wore a white lab coat and had a light blue stethoscope draped around her neck. Her hands were shoved deep into the outer pockets of her crisp white coat. I could see the shape of fists inside her pockets and knew this lady meant business.

"You are a very sick little girl and you will be here for more than a day or two" she informed Meghan. She was calm that bellowed over with concern. Gerry and I looked at each other; neither of us had anticipated that at all. I rose from my form fitted hard plastic chair and walked out into the hallway. My eyes met hers and she immediately followed me.

"Can I ask something" I pleaded as we were out of the room where the innocent ears of my daughter could not hear me. I didn't even have to finish my statement, she knew I needed to talk and get some answers.

"Her first round of tests appeared as if it was an infection, but now it looks like a malignancy." She was certain.

"Cancer", that's all I could say and then just froze. *Cancer,* it echoed softly in my mind that was wrapped in fear.

"We are going to have a few more doctors look at her, she is very sick; we will then determine if she is going to ICU, or to a ward."

I stood there and looked at this tiny woman; my eyes were fixed onto the fists in her pocket. I thought to myself, *how angry she must get when she has to deliver this type of news to a family.* This news, this time was for my family. *This just can't be,* I thought. "How can we go from being just at home, with fevers, and now this? It's too much, you must be wrong." I questioned her with the hope that she would give me a new answer. My thoughts now went straight to Meghan, *oh God she is going to be so scared.*

Gerry came out to join the conversation and then he took a deep breath and went back to see his daughter. He took control at that moment. "They have to run lots of tests." He sounded so calm and reassuring. "So we may as well just stay and get the tests done and over with and just be here for as long as the doctors need to determine what's next. Okay peanut." Her beautiful blue eyes became grey with sadness and fear. Her legs stopped swinging and without a word, she lowered her gaze to the floor.

What came next was something neither of us expected. I know there's a typical saying, *never in a million years,* but in this case it's so true. I overheard something that *never in a million years* did I expect to hear. Dr. Nora, the ICU pediatric resident who came to look at Meghan earlier, said to Dr. Posthma as they met in the hallway outside, "she is a very sick little girl who is in septic shock. She is going to ICU." *ICU,* I knew that ICU meant something very serious as it stood for Intensive Care Unit. I had no clue what septic shock was, it just went in one ear and out the other, much like the rest of the medical remix I listened to. But what stuck with me was that my baby, who thought that she had just come in to have some tests done, was going to the intensive care unit. *Oh God, this can't be happening,* my mind raced *all the tests before for the past weeks, doctors kept assuring me it was a virus. What on earth was going on?*

The voice on the other end of the line snapped my mind back to the present moment. I got through to my younger brother Jeff and I could barely get the words out. "Jeff, I'm at McMaster Children's Hospital, Meghan is in pediatric ICU." Jeff was always the strong one, at least I have always thought of him that way, strong and calm, and I knew I had to call him first. He stood up with me when I gave the eulogy at my dad's funeral, and I remembered his firm hand on my

14

back as I felt support in more ways than one so he was first on my list of loved ones to call.

"What?" he said completely shocked. A moment frozen in time for both of us.

I couldn't believe the words that were being formed and then spoken from my own lips; but there they were. As each breath formed yet another painful sentence, the words could not be contained; they exploded out of me as I choked back tears. I never understood until this moment how much pain, fear and heartache can be held in just a single moment. Time seemed to stand still and let you wade in it as if you were in a pool of your own words.

I continued to speak again, "Meghan had to come in for some blood work, she has been sick, as you know, for the past few weeks."

"What?" he echoed, as I choked back even more salty tasting tears, I could sense that Jeff felt the same heaviness in his chest that I did.

Randy, my boyfriend, stood beside me and kept his hand always firmly on my back so that I knew he was always there. In those moments he was my gift; perfectly placed and perfectly timed, in my life. Was it the lamppost that I leaned against that held me up or was it my faith that I felt in the comfort of the hand of someone special? Perhaps a bit of both. As I held onto this love and strength I was able to get the rest out.

"Jeff, Meghan was put into a drug induced coma, they still have so many tests to run, and it could be leukemia or something completely different. The doctors have told us that Meghan is in septic shock and that the next few days would be critical."

Once again I stood there in that wading pool of my words and thoughts. I felt like I was being pulled underwater as I sank into a terrible darkness within my own words. I pressed hard against that lamppost as my thoughts were so painful. *Was it possible, was my baby going to die?* This was my thought that hid deep inside my pain, suppressed under the strong faith that I tried so hard to show. I took a deep breath. "The next few days would be critical." Those words just echoed into my very soul and I couldn't believe that they came from me and that they were about my baby girl.

Rhythmically, with each beating thud of my heart, the thought would come into my mind but I couldn't say it; I could not say that Meghan was going to die, my faith would not allow it, fear wanted to scream it out; but faith maintained focus on the positive. I stated to everyone, "Meghan has to fight for her life now."

"I'll be right over" and before I could even get out a thank you, the phone went silent.

Call after call, brought all my loved ones and all of Meghan's family to her bedside. I had no emotion left in me and the words just spilled out. I was drained. I can't even remember how many calls were made. Gerry made all of his calls also. I could feel his pain and worry. He tried to maintain his composure, as he always did, but I knew inside he hurt and he was terrified but he knew he had to remain so strong for both Meghan and myself. I knew he ached for his wife Lanette. She arrived shortly after as did all of their family. It seemed strange in a way to have such a mix of family together, but we were all there for one reason, and one very important reason, love; for the love for a 15-year-old girl who now had to fight for her life.

ICU allowed very short visits. These would consist of parents, siblings, and grandparents, and only two at a time. *ICU* I thought, *Meghan, my Meghan, always healthy, how on earth could she now be in a coma in ICU?* My mind wandered in every direction and I had no ability to clearly focus on anything. In pairs we visited this precious girl, sometimes it was Gerry and I, sometimes Lanette and I; whatever the combination, we would be by Meghan's side. Caitlin, my youngest daughter, would go in with either her dad or me. We all developed a new found closeness and respect for each other, all in the name of love.

One by one my family arrived, each with a look that I had never seen before and hoped to never see again. I couldn't explain it. It felt like they were afraid to look at me, but at the same time I could sense that they wanted to hold me so tight that I would beg to be let go. Mom arrived first, I don't know how or with whom, probably one of my brothers. Todd, my older brother, arrived with his wife Leighann. Jeff arrived with his wife Karen and shortly after my sister Pam. Pam's husband Brian made it to the hospital a little later. Rev'd

Sue arrived in what seemed only a few short moments.   Mom must have made some calls for me as I don't remember having talked to everyone, but this news traveled fast and people just arrived.   I was pretty sure there were also people there that I don't even remember being there as I felt like I was in a thick fog, unaware of my surroundings. Meghan's ICU room was all I could focus on. People would appear and disappear in and out of my fog as I would go from ICU to the waiting area.   I couldn't bear to be away from her bedside so I would hug my friends and family quickly, not knowing what to say or do, and then head back into room 13 through the thick sliding glass door.   We were all lost in this whole scene, as if we played parts but didn't know the lines. How were we to act out a scene that had never before even graced our stage called life. Every time I had to enter ICU I would stand in front of the double glass doors, push the red button and wait for them to part. The doors would open much like the curtain opens on stage. With a brave step that was unsteady, yet had to be taken, I would enter ICU and become part of a scene that unfolded before me.   My baby now had to fight for her life and there wasn't anything I could do but pray and hang on to my faith. So, I did just that, I prayed. I prayed over and over again.

Randy took me aside in order to step away from it all for a moment so that I could collect my thoughts. I had been there for many hours and the whole time I was numb to everything. It wasn't until I was in her room alone with Randy that I looked at my sweet baby that the reality of everything caused me to collapse into his arms. Randy held me tight as I cried and broke down. There were so many machines and so many sounds. Things hummed and buzzed and beeped; lights flashed and my mind was filled with all of it at once. My ears rang loud and I didn't even know from where the sound came. Meghan was hooked up to a heart monitor and as I watched the line jump about and as numbers flashed I shivered with fear. A tube was inserted into her mouth and taped down to her cheek; her lungs were not able to function on their own due to being in a coma so she required the aid of a mechanical lung. I will never forget the way she looked, her chest rose and fell with such force with each and every breath.

"Why does her chest heave so deeply?" I asked her nurse Christine that was close by. Christine had shoulder length dark hair, beautiful bright eyes. She showed a deep genuine compassion.

"It's because of the respirator as it breathes for her". Her voice was sweet and comforting. Meghan had so many IV's hooked up to her and I was scared, but the voice of this wonderful nurse brought me peace. "It is a good thing you got her here when you did" she continued. "I don't think Meghan would have lived to see tomorrow if you hadn't brought her in." I knew in that moment that my fears were real, confirmed by an angelic nurse, that Meghan was now fighting for her life. Oh God she looked so fragile. I was afraid I would never see her beautiful smile and her big blue eyes again.

Dr. Doyll entered through the large sliding glass door that kept her in isolation. He was a handsome man, tall and slender, with very short brown hair that he likely kept shaved close due to thinning. Gerry also came in at that moment with Caitlin. Randy went to meet his daughters Courtney, Brittany, Lindsay and Zoe, who had just arrived.

"She is stable, but things will get worse before they get better" Dr. Doyll said. "The next few days will be very difficult for her, she is in septic shock, as you know, and we have had to put her into a drug induced coma."

Get worse I thought, *what on earth could be worse than this*. Just as thunder clouds crash hard in a stormy sky it hit me and my mind, body and spirit froze. I was thunderstruck. *Worse means death* I thought. *He had just told us she could die very easily and that she was going to get very close to that point, or was quite possibly there already.* Was I in denial? Probably. In shock? Definitely. Faith is what I had to cling to now. "She has to fight for her life now."

Tears could not be stopped, my heart broke a little more with every single breath and thought. Prayer was my tool, the only thing I could use to do my part was to pray, to beg with everything in me from a desperate pleading mother to God. This prayer was short and to the point, "God please don't let my baby die."

I felt like the whole room began to buzz and things were somewhat spinney. I heard all of the machines at once and the sting of the thoughts in my mind created a frightening hum. I just couldn't take my eyes off Meghan, to watch her in such a state and not know if she would ever open her eyes again. *How could all this be happening? It's simply insane, this just can't be real; the doctors have made some sort of mistake. We were told to come for blood tests and now she is here dying; I mean fighting, and in a coma.* My disbelief of all of this caused horrible thoughts to constantly play in my mind, faster and faster, over and over. I simply couldn't believe it was all happening, nothing made sense. The depth of my confusion and my fear were equal. My prayer now became a scream, a cry from deep inside my soul, did He hear my cry?

We took turns being by Meghan's side and waited patiently for the word from the doctors to tell us what on earth was wrong with her; to give to us a confirmed diagnosis. It was quite late at night when Dr. Doyll and Dr. Winthrope came to talk to Gerry and I. "Follow us, we need to talk quiet and private" one of them said. Together, we took a walk down a long hall and into a private room. For the first time in years Gerry took my hand and we walked together, mom and dad, hand in hand, as we followed the doctors to be given the news.

"Be strong, be positive" Gerry said, "She'll be okay" he tried to assure me as he squeezed my hand so tight I felt my fingers begin to go numb.

I tried to crack a joke, "gee you're holding my hand, this is quite a picture." I just didn't want to face any bad news, so I took my mind to a completely different place, if even for just a moment. I didn't want to take this walk; I wanted to wake up from this horrible nightmare. But I wasn't sleepwalking; it was real. So I held his hand tightly as we walked together mom and dad; a walk we would never forget.

The door was held open for us as we entered this little room. The walls were painted a soft green and were adorned with paintings of birds, beautiful birds and butterflies just scattered about; not just one or two but a room full of winged creatures of all types. For some strange reason a feeling of peace and calm poured over me. God sure did appear in the strangest of forms sometimes. In this moment, to me, He appeared as peaceful birds and butterflies on the wall that calmed my racing heart and stormy being. The room's colours were similar to what you would find in a peacock's feather, blues, greens, and a hint of lilac and gold; it felt warm, safe and had a power to heal. Of course, butterflies for me symbolized new beginning. It gave me peace for a moment. This room instantly became very special and hope is what I felt here within the walls of the butterfly room. I was also able to find a thread of peace and hang onto it. This little bit of hope and peace helped me to understand the doctors as it quieted the buzz that had been going on in my mind for hours and hours.

Then the conversation began. "She doesn't have cancer," both doctors said in unison.

'Well that's great" I said. Boy what a relief that was, the dreaded C word that we didn't want to hear again.

Gerry asked, "Okay, what does she have and what do we do?" He showed me in that moment a type of take charge strength that I never encountered before.

In that very same moment of question, however, both Dr. Doyll and Dr. Winthrope remained focused. They had a look. It was not good. We felt they had just given us great news, yet they still looked grim. I knew what Meghan was about to face was not good.

"She has a very rare blood disorder that is called Hemophagocytic Lymphohistiocytosis, or in short terms, HLH." Gerry and I looked at each other and then he spoke up.

"Okay, but it's not cancer, so what is the treatment, we have never heard of this disease, fill us in." Neither doctor really had any answers for us, except that it was extremely rare and could affect approximately one in 2.6 million. To the best of what I can recall there are were two types, primary and secondary. One is genetic and one is induced by a virus. Meghan was believed to have had the viral induced type. We all have a particular cell called the histio. It is produced in the bone marrow and released into the blood. When a person is sick, its job is to fight the infection. Well somehow Meghan's histio cells had become reprogrammed to kill everything and they were succeeding. She now had an overactive immune system that acted like Pacman. Her body and organs were being attacked and destroyed cell by cell and there was a strong possibility that it could attack the brain. A lot of the conversation was a blur in my mind, all I could focus on were some simple facts, it was rare, it was life threatening and that they had really no idea of how she would respond to the treatment that was being set out before her, nor did we know how far it had progressed and what damage had been done. In one day my vocabulary was about to expand into the medical field. A lot of new words were being thrown at me and I would find myself telling people what was wrong and at the same time I would listen to myself and think, *how strange was it that I was now used words to form phrases like, it will be an eight week protocol.* The team of doctors at McMaster had consulted with a children's hospital in Cincinnati where they specialized in HLH. The eight week protocol would arrive shortly and we would then have a plan of attack set in place.

As I sat and listened to both doctors, I continued to ask myself the same question over and over. *How on earth did we get to this place? What on earth was going on?* and deeply sighed *God please keep me strong, please God stay by Meghan's side and in our hearts from this moment on.*

We were all in this butterfly room for what seemed to be hours and hours. I would constantly shift my focus to a bird or a butterfly on the wall and try to regain that peace that I felt when I entered the room. There was this part of me that wanted to bolt out of the door, run down the hallway and scream at everyone. I was so worried, so frightened and felt so terribly alone. I couldn't do it; I couldn't face this new reality that we had been dealt. Hell no, I just didn't want it. Please take it from me. Is this how Jesus felt in the garden of Gethsemane when He had to face his fear? *Help me please, help me,* was the cry in my heart.

Gerry and I remained in the butterfly room and collected our thoughts as best as we could. Both of the doctors headed back to ICU to have Lanette and Randy to come and speak with us. As our significant partners we needed to tell them first before we talked to any of the other family members about what had been laid out before us. When Randy came in he saw the look of despair in my eyes, he sat beside me and I leaned my head onto his shoulder and kept silent while tears rolled down my cheeks. My tears were warm on my skin and left a trail that somewhat burned as they slowly travelled down each cheek and under my chin. Once again I could taste the salty tears as they rolled past my lips.

Gerry spoke, and reiterated the same speech that we were just given. "She doesn't have cancer" was all I could say. I just lay there with my head on Randy's shoulder. The salt of my tears would never be forgotten by this mother who felt like her daughter was about to be taken from her completely.

Together the four of us then headed back to the ICU waiting room to fill in the rest of the family members on Meghan's diagnosis. I knew I would probably spit something out backwards, because this whole situation just didn't make any sense; still we had to tell them what was discovered and what Meghan now faced. HLH. For some strange reason, the only way I could remember the actual name of this hideous disease was to sing, in my mind, the Mary Poppins song – supercalifragilisticexpialidocious -I would replace the words with the same tune, Hemo Phagocytic Lympho Histio Cytosis, and for some reason they fit perfectly to the tune and I was able to say the actual name, or sing it to people.   This new tune played over and over in my head. It wasn't a happy tune by any means but it was the only way I could remember its horrible name.

Gerry started to explain to everyone her diagnosis the way we heard it. "She doesn't have cancer" and as expected everyone was relieved until we told them the rest. The future from this point on was in God's hands and we asked for His presence and blessings upon everyone that was to be a part of Meghan's journey from this moment on. Rev'd Sue spoke up and asked for our attention as she gathered us all in. She said a very special prayer for Meghan and all those who would help her through this journey. Rev'd Sue is such a gentle peaceful soul. She is fairly new to our church and I really like her style. She openly accepts anyone and everyone.   I believe she had a nursing background also, which was perfect, as she could help me understand most of this.

Feeling the need to pray over Meghan, Rev'd Sue and I went into Meghan's room, she asked if she could anoint Meghan with oil and recite some special healing prayers for her, "Absolutely," I said without hesitation.

I was alone by Meghan's bedside, it was very late in the evening, or perhaps early in the morning, I can't quit remember. I softly stroked Meghan's cheek; her skin was pale with a slight blush in her cheeks likely because of her fevers. *Could she hear me*, I wondered. *Could she feel the brush of my hand against her beautiful soft cheek?* Oh how I hoped that she could "Does she even know I am here?" I asked the Lord in a silent prayer as I reached and held her hand. As my fingers encircled Meghan's delicate hand, a silent stranger appeared by my side. I did not know who this man was, *was he a doctor* I thought, and then pushed that thought aside, *of course he is a doctor if he is in the room with her now.*

In a soft gentle tone, his words penetrated my wall of thought and confusion. "She is going to be alright; I will take this journey with her" he said.

I must have looked completely puzzled and frazzled because he then said, "Oh, pardon me, I am Dr. Meado, I specialize in HLH along with the doctors in Cincinnati and I will be one of her physicians, she's in God's hands now, and mine."

How blessed were we, to know that a specialist for this HLH just happened to now be at the hospital and had taken on Meghan's case and who happens to be a very Godly man himself. Are you asking yourself now if he was called in specifically to see Meghan, well the answer was no. Dr. Meado was not called in, he was placed there and it was a true tell-tale sign to me that the Lord had definitely taken over. Dr. Meado gently placed his hand with mine and Meghan's and said "you are both in my prayers," as he walked away. I wasn't always so open with my faith, I kept it to myself, but now it was being pulled at and stretched so I just gave in and let it guide me.

I don't know how long everyone stayed at the hospital. I seemed to wander in and out of the waiting room, then back into the butterfly room, and then through the hallways to find Caitlin. Time was something that I hated right now and that I wanted to speed it up and rewind all at the same time. I wanted to be past the eight weeks, fast. I wanted to go back to before she was sick. I wanted to run from time so that it didn't continually scare me to death.

I went back to be by my baby's side. I can't remember anything other than the desperate pleading prayers in my heart that she be saved. My mind became muddled, facts clouded by emotion. *I can't possibly remember all of this*, I thought, so I took a quick trip to the gift shop to find a journal to keep notes in. My intention was to try to write it all down in my new journal and try to keep clear what the doctors would tell me and what I needed to know, medical wise, about this HLH. Well, what we intend and what actually happen are often completely different. So I began my journal as letters to Meghan as she lay in that comatose state which only God could control. I wrote about the things that I overheard, about things that I felt, and about things that I knew Meghan would want to know as she wouldn't remember a lot of this due to her medication. What started as letters to Meghan soon became my lifeline and comfort. Right now, the road appeared long and dangerous and as I wrote down my fears I was able see things in a calmer light. I felt God in my pen, as He would guide the words from my mind and calm them into my heart and then deliver them on paper. He was with me in thought and word and deed as my first entry was a prayer.

"Dear Lord,

This road looks and feels like the scariest place that my feet have ever been placed upon. Please Lord, guide each step. Be my strength, be my shoulder, I need You to get me through this. Alone I can't, with You I can, and I will.

Please Lord, heal my baby girl. I am so afraid, more afraid than I have ever been in my entire life. This is a storm, that I feel is going to get even worse, please calm it, and bring us all into a sense of peace.

I pray this in the name of Jesus. Amen"

"So don't worry, because I am with you. Don't be afraid, because I am your God. I will make you strong and will help you; I will support you with my right hand that saves you" Isaiah 41:10

24

Chapter 2 – The Butterfly Room

Day after day, hour after hour and moment by moment I relied on my faith. As pen hit paper, usually at the strangest of hours, I would ask Him for advice and clarity on what I would hear from the doctors and nurses and ask to have my hand divinely guided. I would feel Him constantly as I would pray over Meghan's bedside. I would feel the gentle loving spirit comfort me and give me that special knowing that everything would be okay. For those of you who have never felt God, this probably all seems way out there, but it's not, it's very real, and very close to each and every one of us, in whatever we go through and at whatever moment we choose to find it. I pray that you are touched by something and that you can feel the love and hope in Meghan's journey as I do my best, with God, to share with you Meghan's Beads.

So, on April 9, 2005 I began my journal writing:

"Dear Meghan

My precious baby girl. You have gone through so much so fast, so many doctors, nurses, people, such a scary time for you and for all of us that love you so very much. At this very moment, it is almost 2:30 early Saturday morning on April 9th. Since I haven't gone to bed, for me it's still April 8th.

For the past few hours, I sat by your bedside watching you in your sleep state, and I have seen with my own eyes all the prayers being answered. We have all been by your side since the moment you walked through the doors here at McMaster Hospital.

Tonight I have been talking with a really nice nurse named Julia. All the doctors and nurses here are so amazing and it's like you have your own angels in hospital scrubs all sent from God above to help you get better. When I picked out this notebook to keep with me here while I am at your side, originally it was to ask questions, write down a bunch of medical stuff and all that. But after talking with Julia, and this real cute respiratory doctor, (Courtney would call him a hottie for sure, haha), well they told me that you probably won't remember what has happened that got you here. You probably won't even remember anything that you have heard or had done, you are in a drug induced coma, and are being given some amnesia type of drugs also so that you don't remember. So it was then that I decided to write to you about things I thought you might like to know. This is something you will have after this is all over and will know special moments that we all shared. You will know about promises people have made. Yep I said promises. It's kind of funny what people promise when they are looking over a person in such a state as you are. I will get to those promises in a bit. Well Meghan this is my first journal entry and now I need to get back to your bedside........ much love mommy."

I would take refuge for a few hours at a time in my butterfly room. Even though this was the room where we were given such horrific news, it became my room to find peace and truly connect with the power of love. I would take my mind away from the fear of each present moment; then refuel with hope and positive energy enabling me to rekindle the faith inside that I found so very difficult to hold on to at times. Moment by moment, as I watched Meghan in this comatose state, my insides screamed. I would reach a point inside where I needed to escape from the attack of fears and the butterfly room became my solace.

My thoughts would continually jolt me back to that frightening constant reality. Meghan was in ICU and we could only take this one moment at a time, she may die. Every moment was spent by her bedside and with prayer and hope with God we would get through it all. We were bedside in pairs, mixed and matched between Gerry, myself, Randy and Lanette; there were always two people with Meghan. Often, I became an observer as I watched and listened as each person had a different demeanor with Meghan; their own special way to fill her with hope. In time additional immediate family members were soon allowed to visit with Meghan, if they were with one of the parents or step parents. So, we paired up and took turns so that we could all share our love and support with Meghan.

It was our belief that she could in fact hear us, even though she was in a coma, so whoever was in the room with her would just talk and talk, always keeping her aware that she had family with her. Meghan needed to feel the power of love and prayer and family. I couldn't even begin to imagine what it was like for her, to be in a coma and cut off from the world in a way that was so terrifying. We had to let her know we were all here, she was never left alone.

Her dad and her Aunt Linda spent so much time with her. Linda was Gerry's dad's younger sister, so really she was Meghan's great aunt, but she would never want to be called that. She was a beautiful person who had always reached out to others. Linda worked as an education assistant and helped special need children, a true testament to her character. I remembered being with Linda at one point, I didn't know what more to say to Meghan, so Linda just took over the conversation and talked to her. I was so glad that she was there and that she continued to talk when I just couldn't go on. She gave Meghan an update on her own daughters, Kyla and Liane, and talked about school and some of her students and of course about shopping. I didn't want Meghan to hear the background noise, which consisted of the hum of machines, the beeping of monitors and the distant conversation of surgeons and specialists. She needed to hear family and to be given hope and most important she needed to feel the power of love. Love was the most powerful gift that we could all give her. We all had our special way of showing her love. She was promised so much, she just had to continue to fight and stay with us.

God's promise to us is His love, and to never forsake us. I knew that He was with Meghan. We all made promises fed by faith. My sister Pam would encourage Meghan to fight and get well so she could take her shopping. We all knew how much Meghan loved to shop, what 15 year old girl didn't. My mom talked to her of foot massages, of special lunches, she just wanted to pamper her granddaughter.   Jeff, my younger brother, whom I made that very first call to, well he promised a pool party. Jeff and Karen had just bought a gorgeous new home with an amazing in ground pool. He promised a pool party for Meghan and all her friends this summer. We all had a good laugh about that, did he truly know what he was promising? I knew that Meghan would smile at the promise of a pool party, and she would hold her Uncle Jeff to it also.   Jeff then took the promise to the next step. "No parents allowed," he assured with a slight chuckle at the end of it. To have a brief moment of laughter and fun in what we all shared was a welcomed feeling. We had hope, we had promise and most importantly we had love.

Mom had called the prayer chain at St. Philip's (my church) and a few members of our church had then called other prayer chains. Prayers were being sent heaven bound to Jesus by the hundreds.

Our prayers were once again being answered. We were told that Meghan would no longer have to rely on life support and that she had gained enough strength and had turned that corner of this journey in a direction that we all had prayed for. My baby was going to wake from a horrible slumber and together with God she would make it.

Three days later her beautiful blue eyes opened, a moment that I feared I would never experience again. Eyes, so beautiful, a soft shade of blue that I call heaven's sky blue.

Poor Meghan was so confused. "Did I have my tests yet?" Her voice was scratchy and shaken. So many things ran through my mind. *What exactly was the last thing she remembered? Does she even remember being up in the 3F clinic?* Meghan spoke again, with a look of complete confusion and fright. "I was supposed to come to the hospital for some tests, I don't get it, and my throat is sore and how come I have a sore on my mouth?"   I just fixed my eyes on hers and let her feel my love.

Gerry took over and comforted her in his joking manner. "Hey Peanut, yep, your tests are done and they figured out a lot of stuff also. You don't remember things because they gave you a drug to make you have a deep sleep and said you would probably not remember much." He smiled at her as he assured her he was there to make it okay. "Ya think they will have drugs to help me remember stuff I forget, you know what your dad is like Peanut." She giggled a bit but I could see the storm of tears about to pour out like a heavy rainfall. My heart broke a little more with each tear that trailed down her cheek. How could I keep my composure, yet it seemed that with every thought, Gerry was able so sense my pain and would lighten things up. Gerry was good for her in many ways. I was glad that he was my ex-husband in this situation, as he could focus completely on his daughter and I had someone else, Randy, that I could lean on for support. And most important of all, we all had faith that kept us together. Four parents meant four times the love and strength in this situation.

I kissed her cheek, stroked her hair and got as humanly close to my baby as I could at that moment. I wanted to breathe her in and keep her with me. It was the most beautiful moment that I can remember. Meghan was awake. Meghan was alive. Thank you Jesus, my heart had never felt such joy, God had answered all of our prayers.

In that moment of gratefulness reality gave me a jolt. Also, I felt so much inside that I had to control so that Meghan wouldn't sense my fears. As I looked at her beautiful face, I knew that she too was frightened. Meghan didn't have any idea of why she was in ICU, or of what had happened to her. The last thing she remembered was being told she had come to the hospital to have tests done, she didn't even remember being up in the clinic. It was like time had just passed by and she missed an entire part of her life. *Did she have any recollection of being in a coma?* I wondered. How strange and frightening it must have felt for her if she had heard the hum of machines, the sound of distant beeps from other rooms and the business of doctors and nurses as they would come in and out of her room. Nothing could break the trance that the drugs induced her into, but did she hear and feel while sedated. Here we were mother and daughter, an unbreakable bond; our eyes would not let each other go. Meghan's eyes cried out in fear and I knew in an instant the sense of invasion she felt as she noticed tubes and IVs; I knew what frightened her as she motioned with her eyes to the catheter.

"It's okay sweetie that will come out real soon." All I could think of was how completely violated she must have felt and in such a delicate and private way for a young woman. It broke my heart to feel this with her. Meghan woke to a room full of doctors and machines. "I assure you it will be fine, and they will take it out and it won't hurt. My poor baby, how could she possibly absorb all the news that would soon come to her; here she was in a hospital bed in ICU and with each moment she would become more and more aware of everything. Her fears and anxieties were about to become so very real and her confusion set in hard. Meghan had never before even set foot into a hospital and now here she was a patient herself. We decided earlier that we would wait to tell her about her diagnosis and that the four of us would all talk first and decide on the best way to explain her diagnosis in the most delicate manner possible. Faith filled my heart.

How do we even tell her that it involved chemotherapy, this HLH would take eight weeks, where would I begin to find all the words to best let her know what was going on. I thought.

My prayer was answered in an instant, before I even finished thinking about it. I suppose our prayers are heard before they even become formed. Gerry was the answered prayer, he knew exactly what to say and I was pleasantly surprised that the one man that for years drove me nuts had the answers. I listened for a bit as Gerry continued to chit chat with Meghan while I just struggled to find my composure. I sat beside Meghan and held her hand while he smiled at her and explained a few things; enough so she got a sense of her surroundings and he managed to even make her laugh a few times. I didn't hear all of what they talked about, but I trusted that God would direct Gerry as He had done more than once these past few days. I knew Gerry felt that if I spoke too much that I might just fall apart, so he stepped up to the plate and did a fine job. I felt weak and I knew Meghan would see through anything that wasn't real. Meghan and I had that special connection; I couldn't get anything past her without her knowing the truth. Gerry, however, could stay strong when he had to, I guess that's what dads do when the moms feel like they are about to crumble.

Nurse Christine had said to me that they would soon move Meghan to 3B, the ward where she would likely spend the next few weeks. Meghan would rest, and then they would do a fair bit of

30

bloodwork and get her settled in. "She will sleep a lot, maybe you need to do the same," with her hand on my shoulder. Christine and I were similar in size, which is a polite way saying that she was a full figured woman. She had thick dark hair that rested just above her shoulders, a beautiful complexion, and deep brown caring eyes. She was to me what a nurse should represent, compassion and gentleness with an inner strength also that could tackle the situations that ICU would bring about.

I took a deep breath, "okay and you are right, I do feel exhausted." I took a walk down the hallway, gathered my belongings out of the butterfly room then returned to hand her back the keys and kiss my angel. "I will go rest a bit, and come back in a couple of hours." I made my way to the underground parking lot. The stench hit me right away, the mix of car exhaust, oil and damp made my stomach turn. I had become so use to the medical smell of my surroundings in ICU that I had completely forgotten how horrible the underground parking smelt. I found my white Ford Escort, entered the driver's side, took a deep breath once inside and put it into drive as I headed to my mom's. I had to see Caitlin and mom; I had to share the news that Meghan was being moved out of ICU. I needed to lay my head down, pray, and give thanks now that she was *out of the woods* as the saying goes. Caitlin had spent so many days with Nannie and she desperately just wanted to hold onto her mom; I needed her too. Caitlin and I have always been very close; we connect with each other even when we were not together. I knew she needed me, and she knew I would be there soon. I also felt in my heart that she was silently telling me with her love that it was okay. I didn't need to worry about her; she was going to be fine and strong for me. She, my little CJ, was giving me strength and she probably didn't even know it. However, I so desperately needed to hold on to my baby girl and rest and in some way as I held on to her I also held on to her sister. So off I went to mom's house to catch up on my journaling and some rest. When I arrived at my moms, Caitlin had a gift for me. She was always quite the artist and she painted me a beautiful picture. Out of her creative mind and on canvas she created a painting of arms that came out of the sky, big strong arms that stretched into a forest to embrace a small child that was wrapped in gold. At the bottom of her painting she wrote "God helping Meghan out of the woods." I suppose Caitlin must have heard one of the doctors say, "she isn't out of the woods yet." This beautiful painting spoke to me of all the prayers that were answered. It spoke to me about how we can't, as humans, even come close to comprehending what it is to be in God's arms. His power and His might, the glory of it all. I looked at the painting and was at a loss for words. What she painted and how her heart saw this whole journey just took my breath away and still does to this very day.

I placed the painting on the ledge of the window in mom's spare room so that it would be the last thing I would see when I fell asleep and the first thing I would see when I woke. It was my reminder of just whose arms we are all in. As Caitlin drifted off to sleep beside me I just lay there and looked at her beautiful sleeping face. Her lashes were long and curled and reminded me of those of a porcelain doll. She had chestnut brown hair that fell just below her shoulders and softly brushed across her cheek as she slept; I gently pushed it past her face and kissed her on the cheek where she said the angels kiss her. Caitlin has a birthmark, a tiny little blush of red on her right cheek that looks like a tiny rosebud lip and one day many years ago she said to me as she pointed to her cheek, "you see this mommy, this is where the angels kiss me." What some girls might see as an imperfection and try to hide with makeup, my girl sees as something so beautiful that it takes your breath away. I touched her rosebud birthmark and smiled, and thought to myself *it definitely is where the angels kiss you."* I lay my head down beside Caitlin, and held on to her never wanting to let go. I decided that I would wait until early morning to journal, right now I just wanted to sleep beside my baby.

Chapter 3 – Frogs

"Hi Sweetie   April 12/2005

     "Well it's been 4 days since I have even had a chance to write, and right now it's about 6:30 in the morning. I am just waking up at Nannies from a short nap. You were so much better yesterday. We were all so thankful to God and so happy to see you alert and with no tubes in you. It was a very strange day for you yesterday because you don't remember much of the past few days at all. You woke, and asked me if your tests were done yet. So, I guess the last thing you remember is you had to come here for a few tests. Maybe we should start there, save a few pages for each day in my journal, and write things down so as they come to me, to catch us up on things. So sweetie it all begins......"

"The Day Before Your Hospital Stay, April 7th 2005.
    Hi Sweetie

I will just make a brief note on this time because I think you will remember most of it. For about three weeks before you came to McMaster Hospital, you were very sick at home. Fevers that would not go away, the flu, the runs and a sore throat, you had it all. You had a lot of doctor's appointments with Dr. Tony. Do you remember the ultrasound, chest x-rays, and so much more? We kept going to the doctors, getting blood tests, bringing in samples, and everything looked ok, except for your ferritin level; which is something to do with the iron and blood counts. Dr. Tony set up an appointment with Dr. Chad. I call him the "frog man."

Dr Chad had an idea something serious was going on, and it was he that sent us to the 3F Clinic. So, here we are Wednesday, the day before your hospital stay."

Randy picked Meghan and me up early to go Dr. Chad. I was nervous and relieved at the same time. Finally we were going to find out what was going on with Meghan. I had never taken either of my girls to a pediatrician before; we always just attended our family physician, Dr. Tony. He delivered both of my girls and he was so much more than just a family doctor. However, Meghan's blood results puzzled him and Dr. Tony knew when it was time to have someone else step in. The pediatrician he selected was for a reason. Dr. Chad's wife was a hematologist so I knew Dr. Tony chose him, or who was kidding who, God made the choice, Dr. Tony made the call.

We sat in the waiting area, and then Dr. Chad called us into his office. It was the strangest doctor's office I had ever sat in; even for a pediatrician it was odd; frogs, frogs, and more frogs. There were frog figurines, stuffed frogs, frogs of every colour, shape, and size. There were frog books, frogs that played sports, anything and everything was frog. Hundreds upon hundreds. So, the first thing I said was "Oh, I guess you collect frogs."

"Not anymore," and he chuckled.

For me F.R.O.G. had always meant Fully Reliant On God, so I smiled and knew that we were definitely where we were supposed to be.

The doctor began with the usual questions of history and medical stuff. We then moved to an exam room where he performed an exam on Meghan and requested that I remain in the room for it. He asked if she was pregnant and I replied "no."

"Let the young lady answer the questions please."

"No way," Meghan replied, "not a chance of that." As he felt her he had a worried look upon his face. At the end of the exam we reentered the frog room and a referral was made for us to see a hematologist at the 3F clinic at McMaster Children's Hospital tomorrow, Thursday April 7, 2005. Strict instructions were given that

Meghan was not to have any medications, not even if she had a fever. The clinic wanted her system clean and clear for a thorough exam. I had Meghan go and sit with Randy in the waiting room while I went back to ask Dr. Chad some questions.

"Is this just a virus or something significant?" I asked.

"Oh, it's very significant" he said.

"Are you thinking Leukemia?" I asked, hoping for a different answer, but knew full well that one was about to come that I would not want to hear.

"It could be, and I am also thinking of something called Gaucher Syndrome. Now don't go home and look it up on the internet or anything," he said. I suppose he knew that as soon as I would hear a diagnosis like that that I would go and search. It's just the way things are now. We look up what we don't know and then we worry ourselves crazy over it.

We shook hands, I held back tears, and walked out to meet up with Randy and Meghan. *Keep yourself composed; don't show signs of worry, keep it together,* I kept thinking to myself.

"You're worried I can tell by the look on your face," Meghan blurted. "What did he say? Tell me" she insisted.

"He just said that they will do more blood work at the hospital tomorrow and have an answer for us."

"Ya right" Meghan added. Somehow Randy managed to say something goofy to quickly change the topic. He knew I was lost in my worry and didn't know what to say next.

When we got home, the sun was still nice and bright, fairly warm for an early spring day in April. I called Gerry, and spoke with him from the front porch so that Meghan wouldn't overhear our conversation; thank goodness for cordless phones.

"Gerr, you need to come over, we can order pizza, but we need to talk about Meghan."

"Why, is she still sick?" he asked.

"Yes" I told him "you know we have been getting test after test and that today she saw Dr. Chad" I continued.

"Yes I remember you said that you and Randy were going to take her, how did it go?"

35

"Well, that's what we need to talk about." I could barely keep from crying on the phone. "Gerr, he said it could be leukemia, or some other weird thing called Gaucher Syndrome or disease or something like that, I'm gonna google it in a bit, even though the doctor said not to." He let me know that he would be right over. "We aren't supposed to give her any medications, so she will probably end up spiking a fever every four hours like she has been doing" I told him.

"We can't even give her Tylenol?" he questioned and I could sense the concern and fear.

"Nope," I replied.

He arrived in about 20 minutes. Meghan was so happy to see her dad. It peaked her interest though, because it was not a usual occurrence for me to ask him over, let alone have him stay for pizza. I was so glad Randy was there as Meghan was less suspicious of things when Randy was being goofy, and he always knew the right thing to say or do to smooth out the wrinkles. So, while Randy goofed around with Meghan, Gerry and I were able to talk about tomorrow's trip to the hospital. McMaster was one of the best hospitals for sick children in the world and it was only 20 minutes away so we were blessed with this for sure as children from all over the world come to this hospital.

"I'm really scared," I said to Gerry, as I stepped outside so that no one knew I was crying. "Leukemia, good golly, what is going on, and what is this Gaucher disease?" I mumbled as I wandered out onto the porch.

"She will be fine," he assured me. "Just let the doctors do what they need to do to find out what is going on." My mind was not going to let me relax tonight. I was glad that Gerry was over, he could now see the cycle of Meghan's illness. Previously I was able to give her Tylenol for the fever, however I wasn't going to be able to give her anything tonight, doctor's orders, and it scared me.

Heather, Meghan's best friend for many years, had called to see how she was feeling. "How's Meegs?" she asked in a soft sweet voice. Heather was the brunette version of Meghan, long hair, big blue eyes and a knockout.

"Not good pookey, we are taking her to the hospital tomorrow for even more tests." Pookey was my nickname for Heather.

"What, OMG, well that's good because she is really sick and it's not going away, let me know what they say, k love you." I sensed her love and concern.

"Love you too, and yes I will" I said as we both hung up. They knew how to fight like best friends do and they knew how to forgive; their bond was strong and lifelong for sure.

I never slept that night. Meghan was by my side all night as she lay in my bed. Her fevers spiked up to almost 105°F and I was terrified and felt that I had to do whatever I could to get it down. I used a cold compress on her forehead and gave her a cool bath to keep her temperature down. It did come down to about 103, but I was still so very afraid. *Oh God let us get through tonight and get our answers tomorrow*, I thought and prayed. I was so tempted to give Tylenol, but refrained, after all, doctor's orders. I lay by her side and continually replaced the cool cloth on her forehead as I flipped it over you could feel the heat of her fever absorb into the cloth. My heart raced with fear, I had only one task, to keep her cool through the night. Her fevers would climb with each cycle. The cool bath seemed to knock it down a fair bit, and Meghan did manage to get some sleep. My sleep didn't happen, I constantly changed the cloths, and by morning her fever was considerably lower, around 101 when we got to hospital, but it did not break completely.

Randy picked us up early to take us in to McMaster where Gerry would meet us. Randy then had to leave for a jobsite, as an electrician who worked for himself he needed to keep his work going. We shared a kiss and a hug, he assured Meghan that everything would be fine, and that he would come back to be with us in a couple of hours, if we weren't done by then. We were dropped off at the front door and together Meghan and I made our way up to the third floor where the clinic was located. It felt strange being in this place, and to be honest, I am not a fan of hospitals at all. I tend to deal with a lot of anxiety over things; it's just something I've always dealt with, even as a teenager myself I would get panic attacks from time to time. So in the next moments to follow I would definitely have to deep breath and keep it calm inside, as much as I could. "Oh God take control, please calm my heart and keep me focused, this is my baby and I need strength." I mumbled to myself.

As we approached the clinic reception I felt a calm envelop me and I knew my prayers were heard. In life we are always given signs when we are conscious. Maybe it's in something we see or in something we say or a song; but signs are always given to us. Sometimes I think my Lord has a sense of humor. Frogs perhaps!

As a woman of faith, which has deepened over the years, I have learned to listen and watch as there were so many instances when I missed my sign and therefore may have missed the boat, (so to speak) or got the message completely ass backwards. Now I pay attention to signs.

As we approached the reception area of the 3F clinic, on the morning of Thursday April 7th there it was – my sign. A definite undisputable sign that solidified to me that we were exactly where we were supposed to be. The reception desk was completely covered with – you guessed – frogs. I introduced Meghan and myself and said we had an appointment that Dr. Chad had booked. However, I could definitely not let this frog thing go by without saying something to the receptionist. My mind was fixated on all these frogs.

"Does Dr. Chad work here also?" Of course she had had no idea of whom I referred to.

"No Dr. by that name here, he was just the Dr. who referred you; he doesn't work out of here" she replied.

"Really?" I was confused because it would appear to anyone who had been into Dr. Chad's office that this clearly must be an extension of his very office. "Well why are there so many frogs then"?

"Because I like frogs" and she smiled. Well I just grinned inside. I knew that it was a sign, a message for me that deepened my faith. I told the receptionist all about Dr. Chad's office and how he had just as many, if not more, frogs; but it didn't really mean anything to her. The message was meant for me. Yes, the Lord does speak through frogs.

Chapter 4 – A Need to Know

   The drive to the hospital had become a part of my regular routine. When most people got up they got ready for work and sent their children off to school. Well my morning routine had become quite different. I would get up, quickly check my email for work and send an update to my boss Frank on Meghan's progress and also on my work progress. I would then get Caitlin off to school, gather my laptop, journal, and personal items needed for Meghan, and then head off to 3B.   This drive was always so hard. I wanted Meghan home; I wanted her well. It was two weeks now since she had pulled through ICU and Meghan had now begun her treatments – the eight week protocol. I still couldn't get use to that word, protocol. My mind would wander each morning as I remembered bits and pieces of things that happened over the past few weeks. I guess I was putting together a puzzle in my mind about this whole horrible ordeal, and how we got to where we were and what would come next.

   I remembered that sometime last week Gerry and I had met with a couple of the specialists that would be on Meghan's team of doctors. We went over this *protocol*, and what exactly it involved. Meghan would be on some heavy duty medication and also chemotherapy, which I dreaded terribly. The chemotherapy would be administered through what is called a pic line and also through lumber punctures.   The lumber punctures (LPs) were going to be done regularly at first to see if the disease had progressed into the spinal column as HLH can and usually does attack the brain. The chemo they used for this was called Methotrexate; it would be administered in the LP. If no HLH was found in her spinal fluid after a few tests she would not need this particular chemo again. What a relief that would be; one less drug in her body. So far her spinal fluids had all been clear of histio activity.   Praise God!   The other list of medications would include, Dexamethasone, (we nick named it Dex) which was to be used to suppress the immune system so that the HLH stayed inactive, while the chemo did its job. We would soon discover that Dex also made one eat like a horse and crave anything and everything constantly. This I loved, because it meant that Meghan would eat and nourish her body. There's something you feel as a parent when you see your sick child eat. It gave relief. We had hope for sure now, I felt it.

Another drug that would be induced into her system was called VP16 – the dreaded powerful chemotherapy that would be given twice a week for the first two weeks then once a week. This was the chemo that would be constant for the full eight weeks. The lists of side effects were not pretty at all. Cyclosporine was another horrible drug that she would have to take. We quickly and appropriately named them *skunk pills*, because they smelled like a skunk, good golly they stunk.

"These are nasty" Meghan would say, "nasty." It was a very powerful immune suppressant and was also used in transplant patients to prevent organ rejection. Meghan would have to take the skunk pills daily and the side effects could potentially be very serious. Blood work was constantly being done to monitor Meghan's drug levels in her body. On top of the *protocol* medications, there were of course other drugs to take to help with the side effects of the chemotherapy and the whole protocol treatment. Septra – an antibiotic was given to help with the lungs, to protect them from things like pneumonia as when the blood counts go down; the risks of illness would increase. Apparently this was normal for the kids to become quite sick with many things when counts were down. Nystatin –an anti-fungal that helped with the mouth, throat, gut, and kept bacteria down, as with chemotherapy one would develop mouth sores. It had quickly become one of my quests, to familiarize myself with everything that was going into Meghan. I had to know the whos, whats, whys, whens and hows of each drug, and what the potential side effects would be that each drug produced. As her mom, I felt I had to learn this, because to take care of my baby, I had to know everything possible and always be alert. I needed to know about all the medications and anything that would interact with them so that when my baby was home I would be equipped to take care of her to the very best of my ability. I needed to feel confident that I was able to give her the best care she needed. One of the first things we learned was that there were certain common pain medications that could not be given because they destroy platelets and other things in the blood. So I had now stepped into the phase of the journey that I called Protocol 101.

Our hospital was very fortunate that Meghan's doctor, one in particular, was quite familiar with this rare blood disorder. Dr. Meado, the specialist who knew of this dreaded HLH. His first words ever spoken to me were "She is a very sick little girl, with God we will make her well, she will be okay" I remembered his soft soothing tone, which calmed me then and now.

Imagine, if you can, a mom, me, who was constantly trying to piece together a puzzle that didn't fit or make sense. It was as if a handful of three different puzzles were put into a box and I was to piece it together. It just didn't make sense. Impossible, but that was how this all felt to me.

The stagnant smell of the underground parking lot snapped my mind back to the present moment. As I pulled into the underground parking; the horrible smell of gas and oil spills mixed with dirt burned my nostrils and immediately erased all my wondering thoughts. This stench had become too familiar. I found a place to park somewhere in the red zone so that I was close to the wing of the hospital that I needed to be in. I then made my way up to 3B to see Meghan. I smiled at a few familiar faces as I made my way towards the red zone elevator. I arrived in front of the elevator where a few others also stood and waited; even though the light was already lit indicating that the elevator had been called, I pushed the button anyway, and stood there with my eyes fixed on the directional arrow that pointed up. *Hmm, keep my mind focused on what is up and above* I thought, somehow for a brief moment that simple up arrow said God. Again I felt that inner strength. Always look for that sign my friends; always look for it in your own lives. Let me tell you that no matter how big or small look for the sign, and be blessed.

I looked forward to today, it was a day to relax, no chemo, and no procedures. I smiled inside as I thought about the up arrow and then stepped inside the elevator to go be with Meghan. I was just going to spend time with my sweetie to have somewhat of a calm ordinary day.

There is no such thing as an ordinary relaxing day at the hospital. Maybe that is why the arrow gave me that burst of strength. When there were no tests scheduled, or procedures happening, time was found for something else. I met with one of her nurses outside her room and she expressed to me that "Meghan was quite weepy today, as she had noticed her hair has started to thin." *Hair loss, holy crap* I thought, as the lump in the pit of my stomach grew. I had completely forgotten about that aspect of this whole ordeal. Chemotherapy does cause hair loss.

"So soon," I said to Rochelle, the on duty nurse, as I stopped just outside Meghan's room. I remembered the doctors in ICU told us that her dosage of chemo was not quite the same as that of a cancer patient, so her hair may not completely fall out, but it will continue to become thinner and thinner, eventually being so thin that she will have to decide what to do about it. Well today it all began. As I went in to her room Meghan was in deep conversation with Anna, her social worker assigned to her case, about hair loss and wigs. Anna was a fairly tall woman; I would guess her age to be around 28 or early 30's. She was soft spoken, with dark deep brown eyes, and a very short haircut, very stylish, the type of cut that not everyone could pull off, but she could and did. I thought to myself, *what is worse, to lose it slowly and feel that horrible loss a girl or woman must feel over a long period of time; or having the shock of it go all at once.* There was no easy outcome in this at all, her hair was going to disappear and Meghan chose to just let it happen, slowly and daily.

"What about a wig?" I asked.

"No mom, I don't want to talk about wigs" she insisted. There was a sadness that I have never heard from her before. Meghan wanted to hang on to something of herself for as long as she could, her hair, her beautiful long blonde hair; oh how my heart broke for her. I can't tell you that I knew how she felt, because I truly didn't know. This was not something that any 15 year old girl would ever want to face.

Meghan's hair was her claim to fame at school. She was beautiful, one of the most popular girls in school. Her beauty was far beyond skin deep, she radiated from the inside out and all her *peeps*, as she would call them, loved her. She looked at me with her big beautiful blue eyes that were behind tears, and said "mommy, it's not fair, it's just not fair, why me, why me, why me" she cried and let the tears flow. Meghan could not contain her tears any longer and she had every right to cry and cry hard.

"No it sure isn't" as I cried with her, "none of this is fair or easy, but together we can do it" I assured her.

"Just don't be one of those cancer moms who shaves their head to make a point, don't be that mom, I don't want you shaving your head mom, promise." So I promised her and I didn't. Part of me felt guilty for feeling relieved that she said that. I truly did not want to shave my head, but I would have if Meghan didn't say what she did, I would have shaved it all off. I guess God spoke through her also, to let me know that He would be in control of everything including hair loss. I curled up beside her as she fell asleep in my arms. She laid there sound asleep against the pounding of my heart. I thought of all that was being laid before the feet of my little girl. So much to deal with; so much pain and at what point would it end. With so many thoughts I reached carefully into my bag for my journal; now seemed to be the perfect time to write down all that was going on in my mind.

Wednesday April 20th

Today, at this moment, I am beside you. Its 10am. It's cool and raining outside. We are watching a movie, Down with Love. I tried to catch up with my journaling from time to time, but it has been hard. I have either been here at the hospital or home with Caitlin, or catching up with some work, or sleep. When I get to Nannies, I start to write, then I end up just tossing and turning, or I cuddle up with Caitlin as she needs me so much, and then I fall asleep for a bit, and wake up startled and worried with my heart racing, praying for you to get better. I sure know the powers of prayer.

It's still Wednesday April 20th, Pam just called and said she would be coming up early in the afternoon, I will leave then and go do some cleaning at home, hoping you will be coming home soon. Meghan is sound asleep and looking so peaceful, answered prayers for sure. I was talking with mom last night about how grateful I am to God for answering so many prayers. I watched my daughter and knew that prayers were being heard and answered. I see it and am witness to it all. It's incredible the spirit in this little girl who has fought for her life and with God's blessings she is winning this battle.

Discharge day April 27th; twenty days of being in hospital and this day had finally arrived; Meghan was good to come home. However, before we could leave we had one more procedure to go through, the pic line. So I guess you could say that today we would crossed the picket line. Her line needed to be inserted and it was decided that they would do it today rather than wait until the first clinic visit.

Meghan and I headed over to the 3F clinic and met up with her dad. Gerry and I were with her in the clinic and hoped it would all go smoothly and we would be on our way home soon. A specially trained IV nurse was on her way up to do the insertion. I could feel my heart begin to race. "Oh God help my queasy stomach, I am not good with blood and needles, keep me strong," I prayed.

The 3F clinic was quite large and decorated like a playroom for kids, with another larger area off to the side where the older kids sat in cozy recliners. Those teens would watch movies while IV poles were situated nearby. This was the treatment area where Meghan would sit when she came for her weekly visits.

As my eyes gazed upon some of the kids having treatments of one type or another, careful to not look obvious in my glances, I couldn't help but notice these long strands of beads threaded on leather and tied to IV poles or hung around tiny frail necks; all the kids seemed to have them.

There was another area at the far end of the clinic where there were four beds that could be draped off by one of those circular ceiling curtains. This was where Meghan sat with her dad and waited for the pic line nurse to arrive. While we waited I noticed a little girl in the bed across from Meghan. This little girl was so brave.

She said to Meghan, "Are you getting your pic line in?"

"Yes" Meghan answered in a voice that was quite shaky. She was frightened.

"Piece of cake" the girl said, "piece of cake, doesn't hurt at all; I've had a couple in."

My insides were squeamish. I didn't know how well I would hold up if I watched this procedure. Gerry started to talk with this little angel and her mom. I tapped his shoulder. "You got this one, okay? I am gonna go grab us something to drink and nibble on." He knew I wasn't good with anything that involved needles and blood.

"Sure, no problem, I'll have a coke and a bagel if they have them."

"Iced tea for me and cookies" Meghan hollered to me.

Off I went, while Gerry sat with Meghan as the nurse prepared her tray to begin the procedure. I guess I didn't take long enough down in the cafeteria because when I returned the nurse wasn't quite finished yet. I let Gerry sit by Meghan's side while they inserted the line; I got a bit queasy and fought to compose myself, the last thing I needed was for Meghan to see me faint, so I sat off in the distance a bit, sipped my diet coke and tried to do some slow deep breathing so that no one would even suspect I was having such an issue. The ringing in my ears started to ease up and I didn't feel that sensation of fainting so much.

"Oh, I forgot the bagel." I said to Gerry, which I didn't, but knew I would hold up better if I got some air. I stood up, said the Lord's Prayer silently in my mind to keep my focus. "Oh, God, please don't let me go down, don't let me faint here and now, keep me up, Lord, keep me upright." I mumbled as I headed out of the clinic back to the cafeteria.   It was going to take some getting used to, all these tests and procedures, because I was never good with blood at all.

I would get there and God would help me step by step.   I discovered that faith is stronger than fear, if you truly believe.   My faith continued to grow and I knew it was my responsibility not only as a mom, but as a woman of faith, to show this to everyone, especially Meghan.   She needed to know the power of prayer, the awesomeness of the Lord, and that miracles do happen.

When I re-entered the clinic about 15 minutes later the procedure was complete, finally we could leave; the pic line was inserted.   Meghan was so brave.   I was the chicken hearted one once again, but it's done now and she now had this tube that was inserted into her vein in her arm and it ran into a main artery near the heart.   It was securely taped down and then a stretch covering was put over like a sleeve.   My mind kept thinking of what could happen if it got pulled or tugged.   Ughhhh even now just thinking of it makes me queasy.

We met Randy at the hospital pharmacy, filled all the prescriptions and had print outs of each drug with our instructions.   We were now officially discharged. Woohoo.   I was ecstatic.   We took Meghan to my mom's, aka Nannie's, because it would be easier for Meghan to get around at her place.

Our assigned clinic day was set for Friday; it would be our first of many weekly clinic appointments.   It sure felt good to be going home; I can only imagine how great it must have felt for Meghan.   I never thought that this day would ever arrive, and yet here it was. Meghan was so frail and needed a lot of assistance.   It amazed me how fast your muscle strength left your body, especially your legs, when you didn't use them.   Meghan would need assistance to walk up and down the stairs and also getting in and out of the car.

Along with the handouts of each medication, we had a folder of information that contained her protocol, telephone numbers, what to do if a fever spiked and what to expect with the drastic changes that occur in blood cell counts from chemo.   Meghan had already had a few rounds of chemo; her blood counts had started to drop and had become quite low; likely Meghan would become neutropenic.   Simply put, grans are cells that fight infection and would fall below 0.5.

When Meghan was neutropenic she would need to be very careful, no sick individuals were to be around her and any ventures out in public were a definite no no. We were strictly instructed that she was never to go to any other hospital other than McMaster and to simply call the ward.

Meghan's counts were good enough for her to be allowed to go home, but still they were not that high and given the fact that she had a round of chemo just days ago, she was likely going to be neutropenic. But for now we were taking her home, and that was the best feeling you could imagine for all of us.

"I can do this mom, I can and I will, but I am scared," she said to me.

"I know you can do it, and you won't be doing it alone, I will be with you and so will God, trust that, prayers are being answered," I assured her.

As we pulled into mom's driveway, I remember the smile on Meghan's face.

Gleefully she asked "I wonder what Nannie will have to eat?" *Yes, the steroids have kicked in,* I thought, it was great to see her enjoy food again.

Randy and I helped Meghan out of the back seat of his truck and guided her to the porch. I held onto her arm and could feel the soft muscle; she just felt so frail. I didn't want to hold on too hard for fear of hurting her delicate arm. As she was about to step unto that one step she buckled and bumped her knee. We both had a hold of her but she slipped just ever so slightly and bumped her knee. To this day I truly don't know how it happened as it was only one step.

"Relax mom, it's just a bump on my knee," Meghan said.

"Well I am still going to have a look at it inside," I assured her. We got inside and went straight upstairs to her room. I rolled up her pant leg, and saw a tiny little skinned knee, no blood, but the skin was scrapped, just a touch. Immediately I got out the alcohol swabs and the Polysporin and cleaned the wound. It was the tiniest of scrapes, but I had to clean it. Randy and Meghan laughed at me. "What? I am being overprotective, I know but I am going to clean it, so don't mess with me," I insisted as I got everything out and ready.

47

"Ok, Ok mom, but I am fine" she said as she giggled, "I didn't even fall, you are being dramatic mom."

We had a wonderful lunch. Nannie had fruit and a special pasta salad that Meghan loved so much; macaroni with tuna, french dressing and corn all mixed together.

Meghan's Aunt Karen, (Gerry's sister), and Grandma and Grandpa (Gerry's parents) came by for a short visit. We didn't want many visitors as it was her first day home and she needed to rest. Meghan slept well that night. I slept beside my mom in her room and Caitlin had the pullout couch. We woke to another beautiful day, the sun was out and it was warmer than normal for late April. Breakfast was like a gourmet buffet, whatever Meghan wanted, Nannie made. We had strawberries that were deep red in colour so you knew that their taste would be out of this world and of course they were prepared with a special touch. Mom could not just serve simple regular strawberries; she washed them, cut them in quarters, and sprinkled a little sugar on them. On the menu were also pancakes, and french toast or cereal if you preferred something simple. I think Meghan had a bit of everything, and a yogurt. By late afternoon all our visitors had gone and now it was just my girls and my mom.

"I want to sit on the porch" Meghan said.

"What? You want to go outside, but you" I stopped myself and took a breath, and said "ya, let's go on the porch its beautiful outside." I wanted to keep her inside away from the world, away from harm, but I had to let go a bit. So, mom found an old fisherman style hat of dads and it became Meghan's new hat for the day. I gently placed it on her head and brought her thin long braids over her shoulders. As I looked at her sweet adorable face, my heart melted. Meghan's hair started to thin so much that we kept it braided as it was the only way to keep it from falling out before her eyes, we dressed her warm as to not catch any kind of chill, put pillows on the porch bench to soften it for her and brought out a blanket to wrap around her shoulders if she needed it.

Mom and I then helped her out onto the front porch where she then sat on the old wooden bench with her iced tea. Mom sat beside her and this picture was one that I would cherish forever,

Meghan and her nannie in a sweet moment shared side by side. The love that this moment held was incredibly powerful. *Oh my gosh, she is really home, she looks so beautiful in her pajamas and dad's fisherman's hat* I thought. The most beautiful picture etched in my mind for eternity. My silent prayer went to heaven, "thank you Jesus for bringing her home."

Chapter 5 – Tears and Fears

Remember that bump on the knee? Well, I sure remember that moment. As soon as her knee hit that patio step, my heart felt terror. Meghan had left for her dad's on Friday to spend the weekend there as it was his time with girls. He called me later that Friday night somewhere between 7p.m. and 8p.m.

"Meghan had spiked a fever" he said. Our conversation was brief. My heart was hit with that zap of fear again. I knew what that meant; it was on the list, that list of things to watch for and when we saw them we were to call the hospital, ask for 3B and speak to the oncologist on call. Meghan was going back to McMaster and would once again be admitted. *Too soon* I thought, as I drove towards McMaster. I felt so terribly guilty and felt that it was because I didn't hold her up enough. I felt like a failure, but Gerry assured me that it was likely to happen even just by her being outside for the first time in weeks. He handled things amazingly and I was proud of him for having such calm and collectiveness. I took the winding York Road all the way through the town of Dundas. It was longer, but more comfortable for me as I was not a fan of highway driving. I arrived shortly after 9:00 pm, and met Gerry in the lounge while they admitted Meghan.

"Here we go again" I mumbled to myself, and I didn't like it one bit, neither did Meghan, but she was relieved. She was so very weak and tired. Meghan knew most of the nurses and we were stepping back into a comfort zone for her. I was the one who had more trouble with it than anyone else. It felt like I was going to lose her all over again. After I talked with another mom in the parents lounge, I felt a bit of relief, apparently it is *completely normal* to come in and out and in and out when the kids are on chemo.

"What kind of cancer does she have?" she asked.

"Oh, she doesn't have cancer", I felt relief and confusion at the same time. I thought to myself, *why the heck does she have to receive chemo if she doesn't have cancer.* Here I was confused, puzzle pieces. "Um, she has something called HLH, it's like leukemia, so they treat it with chemo."

"Oh, interesting," she said. "Well, it's normal in this cancer world, for the kids to come in and out when they are neutropenic," she assured me.

Those strands of beads appeared again and again, some longer than others, and this time this mom wore one.

"May I please ask what it is that you are wearing, the necklace of little coloured wooden beads? I have seen them in the clinic and some of the kids wear them, I've seen them everywhere. I hope you don't mind, but I just had to ask." I was eager to know.

"What, this?" she replied as she ran her hand over it so gently and I could see the tears build.

"Yes, please, what are they?" I pleaded. "I am sorry if it upset you to ask."

"They are called bravery beads, the kids collect them but in order to collect them they have to go through things, horrible things" she said as she wiped her tears.

"Oh, I'm sorry," I said again and simply let the subject drop as I knew it was simply not the right time to ask any more.

Neutropenic, that new word that continued to pop up that I am sure I will hear a lot of. It's the low white cell thing I told you about earlier when infections occur. That bump on the knee, it caused a staph infection. A type of infection that you and I could handle with ease and was the most common bacteria on any surface, but for Meghan, just that tiny bump on the knee was enough to produce a neutropenic fever and it all began again. Perhaps it wasn't the bump; the doctors said it could have simply been touching a surface like a door handle or table, or even a car door. Regardless, Meghan was admitted into 3B again and routine bloodwork was drawn. Results would come back quickly as they always do; they are quite amazing here with how fast they get things done.

Bloodwork did come back positive for infection, Grand Positive Coci I believe it was called. But it meant that ultimately Meghan we would be in here for a few days. IV antibiotics were started on Friday night, and I was told by the nurse that they were using the right one; that they had begun the round with the correctly anticipated drug.

Every morning we went through the same routine here where bloodwork was drawn and we would then wait for that count sheet; the key indicator of how things progressed; or if you look at it differently how messed up things were. It was hard to stay positive when my worries overpowered me. It's then that I would lean on God or as my wonderful mom would say "let go and let God."

Sometimes I felt like I was in my own version of medical school. I overheard things, and then I would go and Google them. It could be both good and bad I suppose, but I did it anyhow, even though I was told not to, the internet was right there, at my fingertips and I just couldn't relinquish the curiosity. I made sure I ran things by the doctors that I found out to make sure that I understood them correctly. A lot of tests had been done on Meghan again, they carefully and diligently watched her liver as she was somewhat jaundice. Meghan also had a lot of pain in her side, around the area where she had her chest tube in while in ICU. If ICU was an earthquake, then we were now in the midst of the aftershocks. Her x-rays from today were good, nothing to worry about. *Worry about*, I thought, everything in this world was something to worry about.

Tonight Grandma and Grandpa Rush were coming up for a visit. Grandma planned a sleepover. The small blue imitation leather chair that sat in the corner of each room unfolded and resembled a bobsled. Tonight Grandma Rush was going to bobsled beside Meghan. Apparently Meghan was a chatter box all night. What a cute picture I was able to paint in my mind, Meghan and Grandma chatting through the night while Grandma was confined to her bobsled bed.

I tried to stay some nights and bobsled myself. Repeatedly we were told by the nurses "It's better for Meghan to adjust to not having mom or dad in her room at night". This was so hard for me, as it would be for any mom or dad. Whether it was Gerry or myself, or Randy, we all took our turns and stayed as late as we could, usually until 11 p.m. Mom, and my sister Pam have been wonderful; they came here with me and sat with Meghan many times while I wandered

53

to the lounge to connect to the Internet which enabled me to still get some work done.

There were days that I feel like Gumby, being pulled in so many directions. You know that green little stretch and bend toy. I cried a lot, mostly when I made that drive home, after having left Meghan for the night. My heart was torn because all I wanted to do was just curl up beside her and hold her close. Then I thought of Caitlin, my precious little one, who needed her mommy so much. I didn't know how to cope. How do I keep going on? This was so much for a single mom, so much for any parent. Even though I had Randy, and my family, the reality hit hard in the lonely drive home, the reality that I was in fact a single mom who felt the weight of the world upon her. I had responsibilities with a home, a job, and two children. So tonight, like many, I kissed her goodbye, gave her a big cuddle, we both teared up. I tried to hold mine back to be strong for Meghan, and reminded her that I am in her heart and just a few minutes drive away assuring her that she could pick up the phone at any time and that I would be right back in the morning.

I had to remind Meghan sometimes that I have to be home for Caitlin, I couldn't leave her with family all the time, she also needed me and that we were all in this together. Then I would take that horrible walk out the doors of 3B. As I walked I kept my eyes somewhat downward with the hopes that my tears would go unnoticed by anyone I passed. My silent cry was held within as I headed toward the elevators and made my way to the stench drenched underground parking. That familiar smell of damp dirt and leaked automotive fuel once again filled my nostrils; this time I could almost taste the dirt. I entered the driver's seat of my little white Ford Escort and I reached for one of my favorite CD's, inserted and pushed play. This was the drive that ripped into my soul every single day or night when I left her bedside. My hands placed at ten and two as my heart pounded with a sad steady beat. It usually worked out that I was a complete mess for the 15 minute drive home, then when I saw my little Caitlin, we would cuddle and I felt a sense of normal return to my being.

I soaked in a bath either at home or moms, wherever I happen to sleep that night. A good soak helped with my worries and calm washed over me. In the tub is where I tended to do a lot of my praying.

"Jesus said, "don't let your hearts be troubled. Trust in God and trust in me." John 14:1

Today was a tough day for our family, as it was the anniversary of my dad's passing. Dad died on May 9, 2003. I won't ever forget that night. I got a call from my mom; she was frantic, confused, and distraught. My phone rang very late in the evening.

"Ang, its mom, its dad, I think he's gone, the firemen are here, come." I woke up, stood up, and completely forgot what to do. I actually froze right there in my bedroom and didn't even remember how to dress. It was very difficult to put into words how overwhelmed I felt. Powerlessness in everything but standing. I woke Meghan for a moment, she was 13 at the time, and I said "Meghan, Nannie needs me. Poppie is sick, so I will be back in a bit, just go back to sleep."

I drove to mom's house, a brown brick side split that was only three blocks away. The streets were completely bare and the world was still asleep except for a few birds that chirped sweetly in their nests as the young begged for their early morning feed. A fire truck was parked in front of the neighbor's home and an ambulance was in mom's driveway. I stepped onto the small square concrete porch that had a few chips out of the corners just as my dad was being wheeled out on a stretcher by a couple of firefighters and paramedics.

"He is VSA," one of them said to me. I knew what he meant; vital signs absent. I looked at my dad; the heart monitor displayed a flat line and the look on my dad's face was one of complete peace. I could only think of my mom now, a woman whom I have never heard cry or complain, was in tears just a few steps away and my heart was broken.

"Your mom needs you now" spoke one of the firemen. The living room table was pushed aside, dad's false teeth were on the side table and the feeling in the home was of complete sadness. I went upstairs to find mom and let the ambulance attendants and firemen do what they needed to do.

"I can't find matching socks and I need my lipstick," my mom tried to compose herself she mumbled things that sounded normal on any other day, but today just seemed to be so out of place. *Who cares if your socks don't match, who cares if you don't have on your lipstick* were my thoughts, but instead I just helped her find what she needed and held her hand as we walked down to the living room. "They forgot Bill's teeth" she cried as she brushed her hand over them. "I have to put them in a jar to soak" mom insisted as she went to the kitchen to get a cup filled with water. She placed the teeth in the jar to soak.

Soon my brothers and sister arrived. Jeff said to me, "Your clothes are inside out."

"I know" I said, "I got dressed in the dark." This wasn't completely true, I had forgotten how to function in the moment of that phone call, so I guess I put my clothes on inside out.

Now with Meghan's situation inside out was how I felt most days.

Dad was in a place now that he could give me a different kind of strength and so as I looked at her bloodwork I asked him for just that. "Dad, help me sort through this." Today's bloodwork showed yet another fungus, similar to that of a yeast infection, but in the blood and a new antibiotic would be administered today. Meghan was so upset about this.

"I'm not getting better mommy, I keep getting sicker, I want to go home" she begged. I assured her that she wasn't getting sicker, that she would be better, and that she needed to stay in the hospital until all the infections cleared up. Trying to explain to her that this was somewhat normal seemed completely *inside out*.

Sonia, Meghan's nurse practitioner came in to speak with Meghan to help her understand. Sometimes to hear it from someone other than me helped to put her mind at ease. She assured Meghan that she wasn't getting sicker, that this was what would happen when the grans (white cells) were low, infections happen and the only place to properly look after them was in the hospital. The nurses and doctors here were truly amazing and constantly showed such care and compassion, I did feel blessed.

After a few days of improvement we got a day pass and I had Meghan out for the day, it was May 10, 2005. We went for a nice drive with the car windows open and we cried as we were both so happy. I watched as Meghan held her hand out the window; she would bend it up and down like the wing of the airplane so that she could feel the power of the breeze against her hand and skin.

"Look at my wiggly skin on my arm mommy, freaky" she said to me as the wind current blew strong against her fragile skin. "Mommy, I don't want to go in our house, not if I am only allowed a day pass. Let's just drive by, and then go to nannies."

I understood, and said "OK sweetie, today is your day, whatever you want."

She cried, "I want to go home, and to stay there, so I can't do that today because I will have to go back to the hospital after dinner, so let's just go to nannies." It took everything in me not to cry, *be strong* I thought, *be strong*. So I smiled, and we went to see nannie.

We had a beautiful visit, and hopefully another day pass tomorrow, and then we would have our discharge by the end of this week. I thought *praise God for getting us through yet another hurdle.*

Six o'clock came too quick and it was time to go. Our drive back to McMaster was a sad one for sure. Meghan and I held hands; she just reached out and grabbed my hand.

"I don't want to let go mommy" she said, and so I held her hand tightly in mine and we enjoyed the deep connection in that moment. Just when we were in our moment of holding hands thinking of home, a song came on that reminded Meghan of the one thing she longed for, home. It's heartbreaking and we so often take for granted the aspect of home and what it truly means. For me, I will never lose sight of the value of home and family.

We arrived back at the hospital by 6 p.m., and got settled in. I hoped that someone would come to visit tonight to take away some of the sadness Meghan had being back in here, if only for one night, tonight was going to be a hard night. Linda and Kyla came up to see her and I left so that she could have a visit with her aunt and cousin. We parted ways with a kiss and a love.

"A kiss and a love," Meghan said as she turned her soft cheek towards me for her kiss. So I gave her a *"kiss and a love"* and then headed home sad and happy, sad to be leaving, but happy that she would be given another day pass tomorrow, and we would spend it with family and friends again. I popped in some uplifting Christian tunes and cried my way home. How can one heart hold so much pain, the same way a puddle holds so much rain, one drop at a time?

Today I was actually looking forward to my drive in. Why? Because I was going to bring Meghan home on another day pass. I would remember this day, Wednesday May 11 and cherish it. How absolutely amazing it felt to know that we will hold hands and drive home again. I dropped Caitlin off at school, and headed into the hospital. Just as I drove into the underground parking, my cell phone rang. It was Randy.

"Where are you?" he said in a tone of complete urgency.

"I am just pulling into the underground parking at the hospital and bringing Meghan home on a day pass. Why, what's up?" I reached through the open window and retrieved the parking pass that I would later have to punch on the way out. I found a spot near the red zone and parked.

"Ok, when you get in, go to ICU, they have been trying to call you at home, they called a Code Blue on Meghan, she is in ICU." I felt my heart in my throat.

"What, what, what?" was all I could think or say. I began to feel for a moment the way I did when I got that call from my mom about my dad. I felt like I couldn't drive, think, or react. I put the car into park, took a breath and a moment to collect myself and literally ran to ICU.

It didn't take Gerry long to get there either, he was on day shift at Ford and the nurses reached him there. I met Randy down in ICU and we found out that Meghan had a full blown seizure, what they call a Grand Mal Seizure. I didn't know what to think or say as I looked at Meghan once again, in a drug induced coma I had no idea what was going on. She lay on her back, her head slightly off to the right, her tube taped down on her right cheek, IVs in her hands and legs. A pink paper blanket, puffed up like a pillow with air lay on top of her; it looked like a floating pink air mattress. It was to keep her body cool and it matched the pink flush in her cheeks. *How, why, what, why, why and why* were the thoughts that ran through my mind and I needed answers.

"She was out on a day pass with me yesterday, and we were going to do the same today" I said to Randy, *holy crap* I thought, *what if it happened while we were out.* Why did she have the seizure, what was going on?

Tests, tests, and more tests. ICU was running CT scans, bloodwork was being done, bone marrow tests, and lumbar punctures were ordered and reordered. Dr. Doyll met us just outside of Meghan's room.

"We are looking at a few causes of her seizure; one possibility could be that the HLH has now entered the spinal column and was in her brain." I felt my feet tingle, and the sensation ran completely through me. It was as if all feeling and blood flow in me stopped. A single fraction of a moment was felt in every fiber of my being.

Dr. Doyll had actually given us five possible causes, and the tests now being done would determine the cause. 1- Infection causes the seizure from the blood, 2 - Blood pressure high could set it off, or blood sugar low, 3 - Reaction to the Cyclosporin medication she was prescribed, 4 - HLH in the brain or 5 -Chemotherapy could have caused it.

My mind went frantic as I would imagine it over and over, a code blue being called as Meghan was in a full blown Grand Mal Seizure. *What if she had been with me at home, or in the car* I thought.

All of the initial tests came back normal, there was no HLH activity, nothing showed up on the CT scan, her bone marrow tests and lumbar puncture showed that there was no HLH in the brain. Also, the infection had cleared up, so what caused this horrific grand mal seizure? It could be the chemotherapy, or the Cyclosporine.

Cyclosporine is one of the medications that Meghan took daily; the one we nicknamed the "skunk" pill. It is used to suppress the immune system in her because of the HLH. It was a very nasty medication to be on and on May 13th 2005 we got some results back. Her level of cyclosporine in her body was 581. It was about 3x what it should be, and most likely, this was what caused the seizure. Her levels were now going to be monitored very closely.

"Will she have any brain damage or anything permanent from this?" I asked.

"No, she will be fine" I was reassured; *Fine* I thought, what on earth is fine? I have to be honest with you, a part of me was so very angry over this, that I wanted to go on a rampage and I definitely muttered a few not so pretty four letter words under my breath. However, anger never solved anything and the most important thing to me was to get Meghan out of ICU and back on the road to recovery. This poor girl was already on so many drugs and now she had another one added, Dylantin, an anti-seizure medication. So I just bit my tongue, and focused on Meghan. My mission now was to know all about her medications, what they could possibly do, and what to look for. She was on so many drugs, Septra, Magnesium, Dexamethasone, Cyclosporine, Ranitidine, Marvelon, Ondansetron, Morphine, and now Dylantin. These were just a few that I could recall, but there were many, some anti biotics, some anti fungals; but all in all, too many for any person to have to take.

Meghan was finally moved out of ICU, and up to 3B. She was about to become tubeless, no feeding tube, no IV's and no breathing tube. She was still not very coherent and wondered why she was back in ICU. She didn't remember much of anything and the morphine did not help her to clear her mind. I noticed something strange with her skin. Meghan had developed these horrible bright red stretch marks. She had not gained weight to cause them; they just appeared, around the knees, abdomen, arms, chest, and sides.

"Mommy, what's happening to me?" she asked a few times as she looked at her arms and legs while touching the skin.

"Meghan, let's just listen to the doctors, they said they can fix all that later, and they will, let's just get you better and home" I tried to sound comforting and calm but felt I had failed at it terribly. She still spiked fevers on and off, and her Fluconosol medication was going to be increased to help with the yeast infection in the blood that was still a cause for concern. A Neurologist came to see Meghan, how she hated to have new faces appear. His findings confirmed what ICU felt, that it was the medication, or the chemotherapy that induced the seizure.

I listened politely, but I had an instinct it was the "skunk" pills. Of this I was so sure and it was not going to happen again. Not on my watch.

Saturday morning I brought in a special visitor for Meghan; one of my close friends who had known Meghan since she was five, Glenn. Glenn was a firefighter in Toronto. He had wanted to see her and today now that she was out of ICU he came in tonight to surprise her. Meghan was so excited and definitely not herself. As Glenn and I entered the room we both looked at each other and felt concern. Meghan's eyes actually bounced in their sockets. She wasn't rolling them, or moving them on purpose, they literally bounced is the only way I can explain it.

She was also completely out of it from the morphine that she was so loopy. "Mommy, you and Glenn keep moving," she said and giggled. When the nurse came in, Glenn asked her about the Dylantin. The nurse explained to me that it was the Dylantin that made her dizzy and her eyes bounce. I insisted that she be taken off it because the results indicated the only reason she had the seizure was due to the cyclosporine level. I am and always will be an advocate for my children. I felt Meghan had too many drugs in her system and this one wasn't needed. Doctors agreed, and she was taken off it and never took another seizure. The morphine was also going to be reduced as Meghan had hallucinations from it. She would say to me, "mom look at that giant….. Oh never mind it was just another vision thing." She knew she saw things that weren't real, like post it notes all over the walls, or a giant lady bugs.

We put into our body things that we don't even realize and question. I would watch so many things going into her IV, and ask, "What's that?" It was a different answer each time, usually an anti-biotic, or an anti-fungal, or pain medication, or something for anxiety. All I knew is that Meghan's insides were toxic and full of all kinds of drugs; she had become a walking pharmacy.

The steroids made her emotional, as did the birth control pill. Her blood pressure was constantly high and this was from anxiety. Meghan was fed up, and she told her kidney specialist just exactly what she thought.

63

"I've had enough, my legs are weak, I hate the commode, I am emotional and I don't like pills." She blurted out in one short fast and very loud sentence. "Ugh, not the stupid tight cuff again," she cried out. This was so far from the Meghan who never complained.

"Let's take it when she is resting to get a more accurate reading" the kidney specialist suggested to Paula. He assured Meghan that he would make sure that all the nurses took her blood pressure when she was at rest so that they got a more accurate reading as they were considering adding blood pressure medication. Yay, another pill.

Chapter 7 – Mom on a Mission

Ten days have passed by since the *Code Blue* was called on Meghan. The fear and the anxiety have teamed up within me like a tag team in wrestling trying to take control. What if she was at home when the seizure happened? What if it happened when we were out for a walk? What if it happened in the car? Fear usually follows my "what if" times, and I decided that I did not want either of these as my friends. Rather than worry about what might or might not happen, I developed an action plan and began a detailed log of Meghan's medications. I would now keep track of her blood counts and also of her drug levels in her system. Onlookers would now see me with my purple binder accompanying me to every meeting, every test/scan, and every clinic or specialist visit. I insisted on printed copies of all her blood work and of all her medication charts. Call me crazy, I looked like the oldest student in a teaching hospital, but it was more than that for me; I was my daughter's advocate and fully loaded and armed I would be for every instance that would come our way. I also kept a log of her daily food and liquid intake and of her temperature and her blood pressure. All on one nicely planned out Excel spreadsheet I was able to see at a glance all of the key areas in Meghan's treatment and watch for signs of something going on. I would watch for fevers that accompanied a high white blood cell count, this would indicate signs of a possible infection; these things on their own may go unnoticed and I wasn't going to risk anything being missed again or misunderstood. For instance, today as an example, Sunday May 22, 2005. Meghan's red blood count or hemobloben (as she called it) was 89. Not too bad, but a bit low. If it went lower she would require a transfusion. Her platelets, which help blood clot, were somewhat low at 29; which indicated to me that she may need them also if they dropped farther as anything below a count of 25 is considered a very high risk for bleeds. Her blood pressure was 131/86. This was elevated for a 15 year old girl but not cause for alarm with all her

65

medications it had been a constant high level of pressure. Her temperature was 35.9. This was GREAT. I loved it when her temperature ranged between 35 and 37 (Celsius). White blood cell counts were measured a bit different. We got a total white count, and also a grans count. Meghan had a white count of 0.9, and a gran count of 0.3. Today she was what we called in the chemo world as neutropenic. Infection was now a big worry with counts low like this. So I would now definitely watch for fevers closely and hope for the white count to come up so that she would have an internal fighting system in place. But for now we gown up and wash up when we see her. I would leave my binder in the room with her when I am not able to be there and have left strict instructions with whoever is with her that they log everything. Log in her food intake, any new medications, and any procedures. Document, document, document; I wanted the names of doctors who come in and why. McMaster was a teaching hospital, and it was pretty much a guarantee that doctors were going to come in and out, residents from all areas of medicine. She was my baby girl and I knew she was terrified and for her to see that I was on top of things, well I hoped that this gave her some peace of mind.

Meghan was now only 48.4 kg (106 pounds). I just couldn't get used to the metric system; no matter how long I tried, how hard I study, I will always be old school, pounds and Fahrenheit are how I relate. Wow, 106 pounds, she should be a healthy weight of 130 pounds. I worried so much about this, but they, they being the doctors and nurses, told me that she would gain weight, especially while on steroids.

After morning rounds, the team decided that Meghan could go home today. Discharge day.

My mind drifted for a moment as I wondered *how many of these discharge days lay ahead*. Shaking my thoughts, I focused back onto the joy in my heart and was not going to think any further than this very moment. Discharge day! My mom would call this a "praise the Lord day."

Our morning started with bloodwork to see how her blood counts were. Results came back showing that platelets were low, and it was advised that she receive a platelet infusion before she left the hospital. Just our luck, none were available. Can you imagine a hospital with a blood bank within it had run out of platelets? An order was put into the Red Cross and the platelets arrived at about six o'clock that evening.

While we waited for the platelets to arrive, Anna came over with what looked like a fishing tackle box in her hands.

"I've been meaning to get this to you long ago, but the moment just seemed to never be right," she said as she smiled sweetly at Meghan. She opened up the box and inside was all different separated compartments of various beads. Most of them were small wooden round ones in all kinds of colours. There were also beads that had flowers on them and some were letters.

"Oh, the beads that everyone wears or hangs on poles" I blurted out.

"Yes, these are called bravery beads" she said as she handed both Meghan and I a tri folded paper that explained clearly what the whole program was about. "Whenever a child gets a finger poke, or a bandage change, or a treatment of chemo and many other things they get to pick a bead for that procedure and add it to their necklace."

Meghan looked closely at all the beads. "Cool" she said.

"Meghan I've kept track of everything you have been through so we have quite a few to pick out already, quite possibly more than one necklace worth." I understood in that moment why the other mom got choked up when she softly caressed the beads when we spoke in the waiting room not too long ago. I too was in tears at this moment. I understood what brave meant. These kids go through things not by choice but by necessity. The procedures and treatments are not pleasant but they do it to survive and there is nothing braver or more courageous than what these children endure day in and day out.

"What are the letter beads for?" Meghan asked.

"Well, some of the kids like to name their necklace. It can be their own name, or a pet name or family name, anything they like" Anna replied.

"Well the first one is going to be mine, I'm calling it Meghan, the next one, hmmm how about peanut because daddy calls me peanut," she giggled.

I looked at the handout that Anna gave me and what all the different beads meant. So many beads, so many treatments and tests. Purple is for bone marrow tests, *she's got a few of them* I thought. Green is for Chemo, *yep, quite a few of those also.* Pink ones are for surgery, heart beads are for echograms, and orange ones represent different scans and ultrasounds. Flowers are for tube insertions that could be either a feeding tube or a chest tube or even a catheter perhaps. With tear filled eyes I sniffled "there's even a special one for ICU" I quietly said. While Meghan continued to fill up her second strand named Peanut, the order of platelets had arrived.

Time to access the pic line, aka – The Picket Line, in they went, and we would soon be on our way. Platelets were a funny looking bag of fluid, you would think that they would resemble blood since they are a blood product, but they are the colour of caramel, or a double cream coffee.

Meghan said "I am going to call this stuff butterscotch, since it's sticky, and platelets make blood clot" I thought this was cute. I also thought and said out loud, "Maybe I could use a bag of scotch, minus the butter, yep, right in with an IV, just kidding."

The butterscotch was now in; we filled her prescriptions and were given a list of instructions to follow. Two very important issues were fluid intake and reconditioning. At barely over 100 pounds Meghan's leg muscles had atrophied so much it would take some hard work and dedication to strengthen them. So, we were to walk as much as possible and also try to climb some stairs; just a few steps up and down, not a whole flight. While Meghan and I got ready for our journey home Randy was busy at my house already and set up a bed in the living room for Meghan. This would enable her to spend her days on the main level and also rest there.

Meghan was afraid. She knew that once the platelets were infused she would be given the green light to go home. We were going home, to her own house, and I knew she was afraid. I hugged her, with tears in our eyes, we both thought of the *what ifs* for a moment. I kissed her soft cheek, and could taste the salt in her tears.

"Hey, your tears taste like butterscotch." We both laughed. "Home sweetie, we are going home."

When we arrived no words were needed to express what we felt Meghan's eyes, her smile and her tears said everything; Meghan was home, and home truly is where the heart is.

Randy and my mom were both there to greet us. Mom had cleaned the house top to bottom and a hand wash station was set up at the front door. It was a must for anyone to use before they could come in and have any contact with my baby girl. I wasn't going to risk any germs. We now had a television set up in the living room. Meghan eased herself into our navy blue couch that was trimmed with hardwood. I watched with warmth in my heart as she ran her hands across the soft deep pillowed cushions.

"Ah, this couch, I forgot how comfy and soft it was" she said with a sigh as she settled in and turned on an episode of Friends, her favorite show. "Wow, I even have a bed here if I want to nap, thanks Randy, thanks mom." I was so glad he had set up a bed there. Caitlin was so happy that her sister was home, nervous, but she seemed to handle things better than the rest of us. Caitlin has a sense of peace that dwelled in her constantly. My two girls were together again, under the same roof, and shared the same space. How precious this moment was. I took a deep breath, and began my first task as medicine mom. I had a lot of prescriptions to sort out. She was due for her first round of meds at nine. This evening's lovely cocktail would include cyclosporine – the famous skunk pill, Dexamethasone – aka dex the steroid, Ranitidine, - for the stomach acid, Amlodipine – for blood pressure, Magnesium, Tylenol, Nystatin, birth control pills, Septra – to prevent pneumonia, and a special mouth wash called Dr. Wilsons. I had a chart created for her medication and it was overwhelming. Mom came in from the kitchen and saw all the drugs laid out before me. She could see the tears pool in my eyes as she lay her hand on my shoulder and I felt the tension magically vanish.

It was bedtime for Meghan and Randy had noticed tears streaming down her cheeks.

"What's wrong sweetie?" he asked.

"The stairs" she replied, "I don't think I can do that many stairs and get up there to my room."

He hugged her and said "Awe sweetie, you aren't going to do them, we are, we are doing them together, you and me, and your mom will be right behind us," he reassured her.

"But what if," she started to say and before she could finish what she was about to say, as she hugged him sobbing he scooped her up in his arms and carried her up 13 stairs as if he was carrying a baby. He was, my baby. My baby was home and going to bed, her own bed for the first time in a month. My heart skipped so many beats and I had my own *what if* thoughts. I prayed, silently of course… "Oh God, please don't fall." Some things and some moments can't be put into words. This was one of them as I watched Randy carry her up the stairs.

The next couple of days were simply spent at home as I cooked and cared for my two beautiful girls. I would sometimes try to listen in on the sisterly conversation that went on, there was even the odd argument between sisters, but I cherished every moment.

Soon Meghan would be going to her dads for the weekend, and I wanted to simply enjoy my time right now as a somewhat normal mom. Whatever they wanted to eat, I made; oddly enough it seemed to be Alphagetti and grilled cheese. Snuggled together on the couch we watched episode after episode of Friends, a Friends marathon.

"Can I take these over to dad's house?" she asked.

"Sure, just don't forget them there" I replied. "Is there anything else you want packed Meghan? I'm getting your stuff ready, your dad will be here in about an hour." I asked

"I dunno, just make sure he knows how to do my medications" she said.

"No worries, I have the chart made up, and I will call Lanette to go over it," I assured her.

Gerry packed the car, helped Meghan into the front seat, and I handed him her medication bag with the chart I made up and off they went.

"Here I have a chart made up to make it easier, have Lanette call me when you get home, ok?"

'Cool, thanks," he replied and off they went.

Later that night I was startled by the phone. I picked up the receiver and fumbled as I nearly dropped it.

"Hello?" I answered.

"Meghan has a fever," I heard from the other end of the line "and we have called 3B and she is going to be admitted." She had only been home a few days before she went to her dad's for the weekend. I wanted to hit the wall with the receiver, I felt anger and fear in the pit of my stomach, and I thought to myself, *fuck not again.* Yes, I had a WTF moment. I was frozen with fear and in deep sadness, motionless in a moment of spinning anger and didn't even know what to rightly think or feel other than simply what the fuck! My heart took that leap again right into my throat. I am not sure I even answered him. I remembered that I simply hung up and tried to compose myself while the whole time I felt that sense of disbelief from what I had just heard. I knew Gerry and Lanette must be terrified also. We were all in this together and my heart felt their pain and upset also.

"Come on Caitlin we have to go, Meghan's in again" I seemed to mumble not wanting to hear my own words. Soon after we pulled into the underground parking, I punched the button with my parking pass and parked in the red zone. Caitlin and I made our way up to 3B. All of this started to become way too familiar for my liking, I didn't want it anymore, and God knew this was in my heart.

Fevers – one of the symptoms of HLH is fevers, I thought. I was so worried that the fevers might indicate that the HLH had reactivated. Thinking the worst was something I always did. No matter what the situation was, by nature I worried. I was having a hard time shaking those two unwanted friends called fear and anxiety; they seemed to follow me like shadows and were almost impossible to shake. I took after my dad in that aspect and with a deep breath I pulled into my heart a bit of my mom at that moment. "Let go and let God," I whispered. Mom would always say, so that is what I was going to do, or at least try to do.

71

Meghan showed all the same symptoms that she had when she first got admitted back in April. "Keep your worries in check" I would say to myself. I could feel my teeth grind as I clenched my jaw tight, so that Meghan would not sense my fear. I didn't want Caitlin to sense it either, but hiding things from my Caitlin was almost impossible, we are like two peas in a pod, so I knew she would feel what I felt even if I said nothing; it's just how we were. Kissing Meghan's forehead, I felt the heat of her fever against my lips. She looked so exhausted, I put on a movie for us, Bridget Jones Diary 2, and it wasn't long before Meghan nodded off into a deep sleep. Caitlin sat quietly and watched the movie with me, however, my focus was not really on the movie, I was in prayer mode; eyes opened, and heart pounding prayer mode. I prayed in my heart those silent prayers from the deepest place where tears dwell before they even emerge as tears. I prayed from this deep place within me that she get over this and get home. When my insides felt the calm that comes from such prayer it was then that I set out on my fact finding mission. I said to Caitlin, "watch the movie for a bit more, mommy has to find out some more silly medical stuff. Okay sweetie?"

She nodded. "yep momma."

I discovered that they put Meghan on three different antibiotics and antifungals.

"Can I have a print out of her blood counts?" I ask the nurse on duty. As I stood in the hallway outside her room and looked over her counts Dr. Meado approached me.

"It appears to us that the HLH has reactivated, this is our concern" he expressed in that special tone of his, and as silently and as slowly as he arrived, he departed just the same and left me with that terrifying thought. *Reactivated, God NO. It can't be.* Meghan had already past the deadline of her eight week protocol. What was initially supposed to be eight weeks had become longer because of setbacks! *Reactivated I thought to myself, this can't be, it just can't be,* I thought out loud. *Could our worst nightmare be repeating itself? Is it possible that it is about to happen all over again in her frail body right now?"* I wasn't going to accept this, not after so much already; two comas and a code blue. No I wasn't going to accept something called reactivated.

Gerry had left for a while and then returned to give me some relief as I needed to get Caitlin home. Meghan was settled and stable for now, so I kissed her softly on the forehead still able to feel the heat of her fever with the clamminess of her sweaty skin. I headed home and this night would be given over to God. I called my friends from church, gave them yet another prayer chain request and updated them on the situation. After making my phone calls, I logged onto the computer and sent out emails to all the prayer chains that Meghan was on and called my mom to give her an update.

"We need more prayer mom, and lots of it." I said to her while tears choked my every word. *Oh God how I need my dad right now* was my first thought.

I wish he were here to hug me, but he was now my angel to help me through all of this. Still, I missed him so much. His hug is what I needed so bad. I had to feel those hugs from within now, to dig into a memory of him as he held me tight as a little girl and to feel the strength of his arms around me. *A Father's hug* I thought and smiled.

Chapter 8 – Tests and Grades

As I slowly walked around the halls of 3B, the strangest of feelings overwhelmed me. I wondered if the nurses could see it in my eyes, the tears that built as my footsteps pounded the tiled floor in time with my heartbeat. It was June and other kids who aren't in this place were about to graduate from school, taking exams, passing tests, and moving forward in their precious lives. How did life bring us to this place? A question I continued to ask myself over and over and there truly was no answer that brought any sort of peace to my mind or calm to my heart. *My God can this all be real our new reality* I hated the thought. But as I wandered around the children's ward of McMaster, the reality truly hit hard because my own daughter was an occupant of a room. Almost three months ago we began this journey that brought us here; a journey that I wondered some days if it would ever end. Occasionally everything felt okay, that I had accepted this reality as our new temporary way of life, that instead of driving into work, I drove to the hospital. Most days however my insides would scream to wake up from this nightmare. I wanted to just unhook Meghan's IV, get her dressed and walk out; go home and pretend that everything was normal, that nothing was wrong and all this sickness would just disappear. Our reality was not so and all of that was a distant dream; a dream that I prayed would come true someday as it was my constant prayer and the prayer of so many. So I continued my walk around the halls with so many mixed emotions and anger built in me. I was mad that so many kids had to fight for life and it was just so unfair. My mind wandered back to what normal kids would do right now, in the middle of a weekday at school. It was so different here, kids took tests yes, but they were tests like bone marrow aspirations, blood cultures, lumbar punctures. They should instead have taken exams or year-end field trips and received report cards. A field trip for Meghan here wasn't a trip to the zoo; it was a porter escorted ride in a hospital bed downstairs for an x-ray, scan, surgery or even ICU. Some passed and some didn't. Banners were taped across some of the doors. *"Congratulations Michelle," "Way to go Kyle."* Will a banner of congratulations be placed on my daughter's door for a successfully passed test or a course completion; the course being a round of chemotherapy? Some of these children had successfully completed such programs; a program that if they passed and made the grade. Guess what? They got to continue to live.

Suddenly I would hear a bell ring and it would surge through my body. It should be the recess bell or the bell that indicating it was time to change class.   In here, however, that bell was a call for help; a code blue perhaps. My soul felt the eerie chill even as I thought about it now while I wrote this book. "Oh God, please help the children" was my constant prayer.

As I walked the halls and then ventured out to the 3F clinic and also towards ICU I held in my hand a special shirt for Meghan. So strange, when my daughter should send around her yearbook to her friends in school to be signed; that she decided to circulate a T-shirt for the nurses and doctors here to sign. Meghan insisted that I get the shirt signed, 'Mom go do it because I plan on going home tomorrow, and I can feel it."   I wasn't about to argue with her, and if she felt she was going to be discharged I trusted her intuition. So with a strange feeling I continued to walk and track down nurse, porter, doctor, and health aid. *It should be her high school year book that was signed and not this shirt* I kept thinking to myself. My heart was in turmoil, I knew Meghan was excited and couldn't wait to wear her signature shirt full of well wishes, but for me it was heart breaking as I sensed her trying to find a thread of normal in her life. Meghan would soon go home, not for summer break, but for a break to continue with her schooling of completing protocol 101 as I called it. So far she had passed her tests and collected a bravery bead for each one passed. Meghan admirably faced each day with courage and grace that no one will ever fully understand. Each day held promise and hope, if life would bring us to it, God would bring us through it.

So with tears in my eyes I continued my I walk around the ward and smiled to the moms that were busy taking care of their child.

I chatted with nurses that have become such an important part of Meghan's life.

"Please sign Meghan's shirt," I asked as I handed them her white rugby shirt with red sleeves and a colourful sharpie marker. I still had to acquire a few more signatures on this shirt so I made another round in 3B and headed over to the 3F clinic to see if anyone had returned from a break or started a shift. Meghan wanted all her favorite people to sign so that she had it to take with her when she left. I suppose in a way it would help her feel strong at home knowing that she had the support and love of so many of the nurses and doctors here.

I met with Dr. Nora outside of the clinic; she was on her way to ICU. I remembered her so well from that very first day.

"I pray for her always," she smiled as she wrote a special note in Arabic and handed me back the coloured permanent marker and the shirt.

"Well, it looks like I've got everyone on this shirt now that she wanted, time to head back to her room, and thank you again." We exchanged one last smile made my way back to her room.

Alleluia! Was all I could say this morning, yes prayers were answered. "Alleluia" and "Praise the Lord." My prayer last night was: "Dear God, just a little up, just a little raise in the counts, and then I will know. A little up please, a little up means no HLH, so please God, just a little up in Jesus's Name I pray, Amen" You see this was the indicator that would decide if Meghan was in or out, a rise in her counts. She felt in her heart yesterday that she was getting her walking papers, a discharge slip, so I merged my faith into hers and prayed like crazy last night.

Answered prayers indeed! As I came in to 3B it wasn't long before I discovered that the fevers had also come down, and Meghan's counts were on the rise.

"If her counts continue to rise," I was told by that special doctor that so silently appeared and disappeared all the time, "then she can go home" he said. I felt the smile seed of adoration for the Lord as it grew in my heart again.

If they rise I thought to myself. *Of course they will rise; God is in control of this.* My faith wouldn't have it any other way. I just loved it when I felt answered. What the doctors attributed to the good cocktail combination of antibiotics and antifungals, I attributed to prayer. Sure I appeared to listen intently with a look of gratitude across my face, but that grateful look that I wore was for the one who answered my prayer. Still I listened to their reasons behind it and when I had my moment I gave them my reason.

Before being discharged today Meghan had to have another round of her Chemotherapy – VP16, and then we would be able to go home. It would save us a trip to the clinic tomorrow by giving it to her tonight. I always got an eerie chill when I watched them administer chemo. A fluid so crystal clear yet so toxic that gently splashed around in the glass bottle carried by the nurse as she walked towards Meghan. As I sat in the chair beside her bed I looked up at the fat glass bottle. A nurse in a special blue gown with long matching blue latex gloves and full face shield reached up to hook it to her IV pole and connected it into the pic line. It looked so clear and so crisp. It looked more refreshing than spring water. I watched as the tiny air bubbles floated on the top of the transparent toxin. How can something that looked so harmless be so horrible? I knew it was doing a job, but it is also damaging other things at the same time. What was going to be the price paid for all of this?

"Meghan we have a lot more beads to collect" I said. "I am going to go and try to find Anna and see if we can get caught up, think of a couple more names okay and I will be back in a jiffy."

"Sure mom and I've thought of the names for the next two strands, lil brother and lil sister."

I thought back to when the doctors had the talk with Meghan about what to expect to happen to her with chemotherapy. I knew one price to pay was hair loss and the inability to have children. I just put these thoughts out of my mind and replaced it with a question to God.

"What can I do?" I asked from an obedient heart.

"Be who you are, and love her" was the answer I instantly felt in my heart. So that was it, I was to simply just be her mom and pamper her with love.

With the collected beads, she strung up two more strands while the chemo finished.

"I think I will wear these two home and she threw them around her neck as we packed the car and headed home.

We pulled into the driveway, made our way to the front door and a surprise awaited Meghan; two beautiful bouquets and a letter from her friend Mitch. Apparently he had been to the hospital earlier, but she had already been discharged, so he wanted to surprise her with them at the house. Mitch had become a dear friend to Meghan. I could see the excitement in her eyes; this was the perfect homecoming for her, flowers for a pretty girl.

'Do you think he likes me?" she asked with a grin.

"Um, hello, there are two bouquets, that would be a definite yes." Mitch was a tall handsome young guy, with light brown hair and a fairly muscular build. He was a clerk up at the grocery store around the corner from our home. I shopped there one day, a few weeks ago and I literally ran into him, poof smack, I bumped right into him as I likely wasn't watching where I was going as my mind was on picking up a few things to take to the hospital. I noticed his nametag. "Mitch," I read it out loud, and extended my hand.

'Hi I'm Meghan's mom," he smiled, and gave me a hug.

"How is she, can she have visitors, when is she coming home, how is she?" His concern and feelings for her were quite genuine.

"Yes she can have visitors, just go to 3B at McMaster and ask for her, they all know her there, but hopefully we will be home soon." So he must have arrived there just as we were being discharged.

We settled in, and Meghan went straight to the computer so that she could thank Mitch, "I hope he's on MSN," she said with excitement and eagerness. I thought to myself, *just a teenager with a crush,* and for that moment everything felt normal and I liked it.

One of the most devastating things that chemo would cause for a young girl or woman was hair loss we all knew this. Meghan's chemo treatments caused it to fall out slowly, so her hair continued to become thinner and thinner. We had hoped that she would not lose it all, but it appeared that this was not the case and her beautiful hair was going to vanish. Today was hair washing day, and this was when we usually witnessed a dramatic change. Randy was over to help me with it and we decided to wash it in the kitchen so Meghan could just sit and relax. Randy had propped up some cushions on her wheelchair so she was high enough to just lay her head back just as if she were in a salon.

Mom's sister, my Auntie Dora, had loaned us a portable wheelchair. It was cool; you could fold it up and fit it in the trunk of your car. My car was a small Ford Escort, so the space for storing things in the trunk wasn't that large. The wheels were small, not the kind of chair that she could push herself in, but rather one that we could easily wheel her around in if she got tired from walking. We decided to make use of it for her hair wash; it was perfect for placing in front of the sink in the kitchen Randy always helped me with these things, I got over emotional when I saw her hair thin and fall out. I just didn't have the words and I knew it broke her heart, she tried so hard to be brave but I knew that it was brutal for her. Meghan's hair, so long, so blonde and so beautiful and it was shedding daily. My God she was a beauty. Now she kept her hair in a braid so that it didn't get everywhere as it thinned. As Randy brushed out her hair, so much of it came out. We just looked at each other, neither of us expected so much to come out; it was so thin.

"Meghan if you want we can cut it now, or wait until we see Mario about your wig" he quietly said to her.

"Wait" she replied while her hands covered her face so we couldn't see her tears.

"That's OK" he answered, "we can put it back into a braid till then, it's just a couple of days."

It was early Tuesday morning, July 26th and today we journeyed into St. Catharines to meet with Mario. Mario runs Wigs for Kids, a program that supplied free wigs to children with cancer. Anna, her child life worker from McMaster, had put us in touch with him. Meghan was going to be measured for her very own natural hair wig. We arrived to find that no one was in the salon; Mario was kind enough to have set up a special appointment just for my baby. He knew that she would be sensitive to what was about to happen and completely cleared the salon for us and only us. Randy drove, as he usually did, and his daughter Courtney came along with us, as Meghan wanted her to help pick out something special and that looked real. We weren't quite sure what to expect, if wigs would be there, or if they would be ordered. All of this was just so unfair for a 15 year old girl to have to go through. Lanette met us there, as she and Gerry lived in St. Catharines.

Mario took measurements and made Meghan feel very calm. He suggested that he cut her hair now, but she was not ready for it. The wig would arrive in a few days, and we would come back for the final fitting. It was going to take three heads of natural donated hair to make the wig of her choice. Meghan decided on highlights and low lights mixed in with the blonde. The wig would be stunning and came from the love and generosity of those that give their own hair, so that she could have something special.

'This will be your hair, you can style it, wash it, and when you come here next, we will cut it the way you want" Mario assured her. It was sweet the way he made her feel so beautiful and special. Randy, Meghan and Courtney went to the truck to wait. Lanette and I stayed back to ask a few questions. Mario wanted to us understand that the more normal we treat her in the wig, the more normal she will feel. He knew from experience how devastated young girls feel when they have to shave the final bit of hair.

"It will be a difficult visit the next time" he added.

"It's great that Courtney came with her," Lanette said to me.

"I know, and hard for her I am sure as she watches all of this crap happening to her best friend that has become like a sister to her" I said.

"Ya, I imagine it is hard, but poor Meghan is the one it's all happening to, she is one tough cookie," and we shared one of those hugs in an embrace of tears, mom and stepmom crying over and loving the same child. Powerful.

August was fast approaching, and I had a 16th birthday to plan. Yep, on August 11, Meghan would be sweet 16. Gerry didn't want to plan a party because he felt that Meghan wouldn't want it.

"Oh yes we are having a party" I told him. There was no way I was not going to have this happen. I began my secret plans of a dinner at a local buffet restaurant, Tucker's Marketplace; Meghan loved this place and had no idea I was planning anything other than the dinner. I let her know that we could go to dinner, just a few of us, but to keep it simple and just a few friends and family. She made her list. Mitch was on the top of it, along with her best friend Heather and another friend Kaleigh. Family of course would also be there, which included Randy and his four girls, my Caitlin and Ian her brother who was Lanette and Gerry's son. What Meghan wasn't aware of was the secretly planned after dinner party that was at our church. I had made it an open invitation so I wasn't quite sure just how many people would actually be there. Courtney was so sweet and sent emails out to all of Meghan's friends on the computer. A few of my dear friends from church said they would look after food for us.

"Please don't do a lot, we are having dinner out first, and then coming here for cake, keep it simple, please." We later found out that simple was just not an option. We still had a few days to go, and a wig to fit, but it felt that everything for once was going as planned.

Mario called, the wig arrived and so we made it there that same day for the fitting. Lanette met us there for moral support. I was a nervous wreck, so Randy once again came to my aid and drove. Caitlin and Meghan chatted the whole way there; sometimes that little angel of mine knew just what to say and when. She had this gift of making Meghan feel relaxed and at ease. She chatted and chatted all the way there, but when we got there Caitlin didn't want to go in. It was ok, Lanette and I went in with Meghan and Randy stayed in the truck with Caitlin.

There were so many things that ran through my mind. I could only handle one at a time, so a lot of it was put on the back burner for my mind to deal with later. Sure, that is really what happened, NOT. I always go and retrieve things from the back of my mind and drive myself crazy while I continue to stew about them. I knew the birthday party was coming up fast. I also knew that there was going to be a re-assessment of Meghan's condition in late August. There was talk of the possibility, and a strong possibility for sure that she would need a bone marrow transplant, BMT. This thought scared me the most and I didn't want to even think of it, but yet I did. I would try as best as I could to push it aside and would pretend at times that I was totally in the conversation that was being had at any given moment much like the one now between Mario and Meghan about what to do with her hair. So back to the shelf went the jumble of thoughts and into the present I returned to focus.

"Mom, I don't want a shaved head," Meghan cried.

Mario immediately said, 'Oh we don't shave it, I will just give you a very short sexy haircut." Sexy was all she needed to hear, so she said "ok" with a bit of a smile. As he began to cut Meghan's hair shorter and shorter and even styled what little hair was left, Mario stopped and stared at her and commented "Meghan, may I say something?"

'Sure, whatever," she was so sad.

"Well when your hair does grow back in, you should really consider keeping it short; this style is hot on you." He was bang on, Lanette and I were stunned.

"OMG," Lanette said. I just looked at her. "Wow, Meghan, he is right, your hair that short looks amazing, and I am not kidding, it is so beautiful."

Meghan's eyes just stood out so big and blue. Her neck appeared so long and slender with strong striking collar bones. "Wow" I said again, "Meghan short hair is fantastic on you."

"You may not even want the wig," Mario said. "Can I get you a mirror?" he asked. In this part of the salon, separate from the rest, there were no mirrors, it was easier for the girls to transition slowly he said in our last visit.

Meghan agreed to the mirror and actually smiled, "It's not so bad" she said as she turned left to right admiring his sexy style he just gave her. "Now can I see the wig?" she asked. He put it on, and styled it. It was beautiful long and blonde, with chunky highlights like she asked.　She had her side bangs, and you couldn't even tell it was a wig.

"Pretty cool" I said, "now you have the choice of going short or long, and look stunning either way."

"I gotta go show Caitlin" as she quickly left the salon with a bit of a smile and a light in her eyes that I haven't seen in a long time.

Mario gave us a special stand to put the wig on when she wasn't wearing it so that it would keep its shape.　The hair in the wig was hand stitched and was very natural looking; you could not tell that it was a wig unless it was off her head.　"Now to wash it, I recommend these," he said as he handed us some salon quality shampoo and conditioner.　"These are the best ones for wigs, and will keep the hair soft."　The instructions were simple, wash it in the bath with shampoo, and then condition and brush it out; lay it on a towel to soak up some of the water and place it on its stand to dry.　She can then curl it if she likes, tie it back, do whatever she wants with it, it's her hair.　He smiled and handed me the stand and the box for it. Lanette and I made our way outside to join the others.

"Mom, Caitlin says it looks better than my old hair did before I was sick," Meghan shouted as Lanette and I walked towards Randy's truck.　I didn't say anything about God at that moment, but we all knew in our hearts that behind every cloud He does have a silver lining.　Meghan climbed into the back seat of Randy's truck with her sister and I sat up front with my honey.　I waved to Lanette as we left the parking lot for home.

"Wait, stop, I want to go in there and get a hat," Meghan screamed as we drove by a western store in St. Catharines.　"I want a new white hat to wear with my wig at my birthday dinner, please please mom," she pleaded.　I didn't even have time to even answer before Randy turned the truck around and headed to the store.

"Great idea Meghan, and I can look for new cowboy boots" Randy replied.

"Um, ya, 'cause yours have duct tape on them" she laughed.　I loved how the two of them would laugh and joke with each other.

Chapter 9 – Sweet Sixteen

Only a few days until her sweet 16. Gerry still had some concern; he felt that Meghan wouldn't want people to see her with her scars, with a wig and with a puffy face from the steroids. He wanted me to cancel the party, but I decided I wouldn't cancel. It felt normal to throw a sweet 16 party for my daughter, and we all knew that normal was something that was desperately needed. Most importantly I knew that Meghan would love it, however it turned out. Still I respected his thoughts and feelings, so I talked with Heather, Courtney, Mitch, and a few other friends, we all felt the same that Meghan would love a party and so the plans continued. Her sweet 16 was going to happen with the help of some wonderful people. Reservations were made at Tucker's Marketplace, but Meghan still had no idea that I had planned a big party at the church hall after dinner. No one let the cat out of the bag.

The big day had arrived, so I suppose I should start the day off where it started, the morning. I went out and picked up two gigantic bouquets of flowers; orange lilies for Meghan, and crazy colourful spring flowers for Caitlin. I also picked up 16 roses and took them over to the restaurant for a surprise at dinner. Heather and Kaleigh were in charge of decorating the hall. Ronni, one of my dearest friends, took charge of ordering all kinds of food for the guests at the church; it was her gift to us. Wow, amazing! Thank you my sweet friend.

Happiness was written all over Meghan's face. This was a fantastic idea and we haven't even got to the hall for her party yet. Food, food, and more food and a whole lot of laughter. Meghan, being a teenager, borrowed a sexy top from Heather. It was different shades of turquoise with white patches randomly scattered. Sleeveless, and to my surprise she openly revealed her scars and stretch marks, and even the bandage covering her pic line. She had no cares at all. It was her day and she was dressed to knock them off their feet; Mitch especially. We washed her wig and let it dry naturally. Her hair had the aroma of fresh rain and summer coconut lotion mixed together. She spritzed herself with her favorite perfume, Ralph. To top off the outfit was her new cowboy hat that she picked out at the western store. Meghan looked like a star. Her outfit was incredible and the blue brought out her gorgeous eyes. Stunning, simply stunning

The staff at Tuckers Marketplace had decorated the restaurant with balloons and ribbons for her birthday. The buffet could only be described as food heaven, so much to choose from and the desert table was amazing. Prime rib, pasta, salads, potatoes of every kind, soup, stir fry, and we could go up as many times as we liked.

"Mom, they even have Alphagetti," Meghan laughed as her plate looked like an artistic creation of food. "Oh, I am going to eat it all" she laughed as she walked beside Heather.

"Meegs" Heather screamed with excitement. "Did you check out the whip cream and chocolate mousse?" together they laughed. I was so happy to see and hear the laughter and conversation and it warmed my heart that everyone had an amazing time. My mind tried to wander through dinner as the anxiety would build inside about getting her to the church and if we could truly pull off the surprise. Being that I was a regular church goer, Meghan would think nothing of me saying "honey, before we head home, I have to swing by the church to pick up some mail left for me." So we then had a plan that Heather would have to pee so badly and she would insist that Meghan go in with her.

Success, we arrived at the church, Heather would have won an academy for her performance of a bladder about to burst. We went downstairs to the basement hall where the washrooms were, "Surprise" everyone yelled in unison. Surprise was an understatement. Wow, even I was shocked. The word had gotten around that there was a beautiful girl turning 16 and all who loved her and cared for her were invited to come. There was a constant stream of people coming in and out, bringing gifts, flowers, and especially hugs. My sister Pam and I had spent the weekend before scrapbooking two albums for Meghan's birthday. We created a page that people could sign.

The albums depicted her life up to this point and included her most recent life changing events that involved the HLH.

A young man approached me from the far side of the room. I wasn't sure who he was, but I had an idea.

"Hi, I am Darryl." I shook his hand and admired the beautiful bouquet of yellow roses he had for Meghan. He was one of Meghan's close friends through Facebook.

I smiled back, "Hello, thank you so much Darryl for coming" and then felt a tap on the shoulder from the other side.

"Hey, Ed, hi, thanks for coming," it was my next door neighbor and his daughter Kyla.

"Aye, she's looking good" he said in his Irish accent. It became somewhat of an open house party. I saw so many loving faces that have supported us on this journey. We took pictures, shared hugs, cried a little, well okay, cried a lot. Gerry came over and thanked me.

"You were right, I was just scared, but you were right, this was a good thing to do," he said as he hugged me.

"We are all in this together, as a family," I reminded him. "Check out the scrap books, and remember to sign them."

Meghan had wandered over to the two of us. "Hello dear dad" she said, "I'm 16 now can I ....," and before she could finish her sentence her grandpa spoke up and said, "She wants the keys to the car Gerald, get used to it" and they both laughed. I didn't have much time to talk to his parents at the restaurant, but knew that family from Gerald's side would soon arrive.

"It's a lovely party, very lovely" his mom spoke up. "Gerald stand with Meghan and your dad so I can take a picture" she commanded. Mrs. Rush loved to take pictures. A few close friends of mine sat at table and chatted, Ronni and Karen. The overwhelming show of support had me in tears. My cup runneth over!

While we planned and celebrated a sweet sixteen, the team of doctors at McMaster were busy also as they planned and searched. Their plan was to go ahead with the BMT (bone marrow transplant) because it would likely be the only way to eradicate the HLH from her body. Lumbar punctures and bone marrow tests showed that HLH cells were present but inactive. These inactive cells needed to be whipped out and from what little I understood these messed up cells were still coming out of the bone marrow and could reactivate at any time. Currently, they weren't in that destructive mode, but they were messed up. The only way to fix the problem was to wipe out the hard drive, so to speak and get rid of all of it.

I was so frightened for what was just around the corner. Now that several matches were found, all we needed was for someone to say yes. My faith told me the best match would be found. I thought of it as a search and rescue mission. A new perspective sometimes made it easier to get through all the stuff. I knew that when I put things to Meghan in a simpler term it helped ease her mind also. I suppose she did it also by giving her meds nicknames like butterscotch and skunk pills. Only God knew for sure what went on in her pretty little frightened mind, and I prayed constantly that He eased it first, and then help the rest of us who needed it in this journey.

An email arrived September 22nd, a blessing I should say, someone said YES. The date was set for admission to Sick Kids in Toronto for October 16, 2005 and transplant would take place on October 27th.

Meghan received a perfect match from an unknown male donor that came from overseas, somewhere in Europe. He was also apparently middle aged we were told. How do you ever find the words to thank someone for that? There just weren't the words to say how I felt, how we all felt for someone who stepped up to the plate like this to save her life by giving her the gift of his marrow. I was at a complete loss for words and the poetic side of me took over. Poetry was something I wrote often, inspired by God. So, here it was, everything that transpired that day while I worked at my desk in my home office downstairs:

"Someone Said Yes.
I'll never forget that moment it all caught me by surprise,
As I read that special email tears flowed freely from my eyes.

I called out to my daughter "Sweetie, I need to talk to you."
She hummed and hawed a typical teen, "Oh mom, do you have to."
"Please come here it's real important I need to talk to you right now."
"Ok, Ok, I'm coming sheesh relax mom don't have a cow."

I looked into her pretty blue eyes sit here I've something to say.
"Um, ok, mom you're freaking me out why you acting this way?"
As I looked at her with tears my words were; someone said yes.
Our prayers were heard and answered Sweetie - someone said yes.

We held each other; we cried a lot, overwhelmed with emotions inside.
Gratitude, happiness, love, joy, all we felt we could no longer hide.
"Do you think it will hurt him I don't want him to feel any pain.
When he gives me his, marrow to give me my life back again."

"Yes it will hurt a bit I but I thank God for what he is going to do.
It's the most incredible act of love and he's doing it just for you."
My friend you are our silent hero, who you are would be a guess.
You'll be treasured and loved always thank you, for saying yes."

It was September 27th 2005, on this day we went into Toronto for our meeting with the BMT team. Two head doctors were there to represent the BMT unit. My mind wondered from the meeting as I watched for signs to know this was the right path.   We were given a tour of the BMT unit and I was so impressed. Each room had its own private bathroom and bathtub, not just a shower, but a tub.

Dr. Assaga spoke to Meghan; he was delicate in his wording. "Meghan it saddens me to say that you will lose all your beautiful hair." To his surprise Meghan broke out in laughter.   He looked at his colleague and said, "Well I haven't had that response before."

Meghan turned to me and quietly said, "He doesn't know does he? He can't tell."

"I guess he can't," I replied.

Meghan then turned to him and said, "this hair, I am gonna lose all this hair?"

"Yes, I am afraid so."

She chuckled and said, "Oh that's ok, 'cause it's a wig," and continued to giggle. I knew how much it meant to her that a doctor who should know a wig, didn't. It made her feel that much more herself.

During our pre-operative consultation, we were all given a lot of instructions and rules that had to be followed at Sick Kids Hospital. We were also given a list of things that needed to take place before she attended in October for the actual transplant. We needed to make a trip to the dentist, have a port put in; which is a day surgery in itself. Also, Meghan was to get a Pulmonary Function test, and a Depo birth control needle to ensure that there would be no bleeding at all during transplant and afterwards. When we closed up the meeting, Dr. Assaga asked if we had any questions.

I did, of course; I asked about her donor match. "What was her match out of 6?" I asked.

"Oh, she didn't get a match out of 6, she got a 10." I was confused, "I thought they could only test and match 6 rejecter matches." (I had done my homework on BMT matches).

"Yes, that was the normal, and acceptable match, however, we can check for 10, and she got a 10 out of 10 match from a male European donor." Then and there I had all that I needed to confirm in my heart that this was definitely the right step to take next. As frightened as we all were to think of what Meghan would encounter in just a few weeks away, it was what had to be done. This was Meghan's only chance for a cure.

I said a prayer of thanks, quietly. "Lord I prayed to you before asking you to find us a match. Lord, you brought to us perfection, a 10 out of 10 match. We are blessed. I was so grateful for a match being found, but then to find out You, Lord in your perfect love, answered my prayer perfectly, Thank you Jesus," and I then quietly said "amen."

"And my people will be filled with the things I give them!" says the *Lord – Jeremiah 31:14*

Chapter 10 – Grace

Well the weekend had arrived, a new beginning that terrified and excited me at the same time. It was the weekend that Meghan would be admitted to Sick Kids Hospital in Toronto for her BMT.

Both Meghan and Caitlin were at their dad's, and I would meet them at Sick Kids on Sunday with Randy.

Today, Saturday October 15th, 2005 - I feel so much anxiety, confusion, fear, worry, and I feel very very alone. I know that I am truly not alone as I have Jesus, but deep inside there is such a fear in me with this bone marrow transplant now actually about to happen. In just a couple of days, Meghan would be hit with a countdown of days of Chemotherapy and other drugs to completely wipe out her entire operating system, so to speak, and then we pray pray pray that it grafts and her new marrow grows.

I went to the cemetery where my dad rests, Memorial Gardens. It's just up the road from me, and I desperately needed my dad today. Being alone all day, I felt that this was the place for me to go. Dad left this world suddenly from a heart attack a couple of years ago. He and I were best friends; we would meet for lunch and just talk and talk. Dad and I shared a special relationship, he confided in me and I in him. We understood each other spiritually, and would talk about something that we called "the knowing." Oh how I miss those conversations. Talking about things that no one else would ever understand. Sharing our sense of knowing things, and how it often freaked us out. I remember dad once calling me to come over. He had a premonition about a car accident involving my brother. He was so frightened because he "knew" it would happen. I watched the tears build in my dad's eyes as he talked, and then gently said. ""Remember dad, sometimes the knowing is accurate, but not as severe as our mind makes it. Dad, I feel that things will be OK, because if we both felt the same "knowing," then it would be a real bad thing, but since I don't feel it, then things will be OK." Dad felt better about the accident he knew was about to happen, but still was worried. We then got a call from my brother, he had slid off the road, but was fine. The car was damaged a fair bit, but he was OK. I don't think anyone else in my family knew that dad and I had this connection. So here I am, at my dad's resting place, with the weight of the world on my shoulders, and I couldn't get that sense of "knowing" from him.

I cried and I cried. "Dad, oh how I need you right now, I am so afraid of this whole journey, and I don't know how much more I can take. I am only just a mom, who is trying so hard to hold things together and I think I am about to burst wide open and totally lose it." I cried for hours as I sat on the grass. I just didn't want to leave, because here there were no phones, no computers, not anything except spiritual peace and quiet. "Help me dad, from where you are, I know you can help me. I know I can't fall into your arms and get one of those great big awesome hugs, but I know you can help me because you are in Heaven. Dad, please ask God to let you help me." I didn't know if dad needed permission to ask the Lord, but I didn't see any harm in asking him to ask.

It was time to get up and collect myself and conquer what lay ahead. As I was leaving, I turned to say one last goodbye and the bench beside where I was standing caught my eye. On the bench was scripture.

." .Peace I leave with you, let not your heart be troubled the things of this world, nor let it be afraid." John 14:27   Need I say any more.... "

Sunday morning and it was church for me; no other place I would rather be than with my church family as they always gave me so much love, strength and support. Randy and I got ready and headed out for the 10 a.m. service. Today was a baptism of three babies. How perfect! We were all going to re-affirm our baptismal vows also. This service was exactly what I needed to strengthen me for Meghan's admission to Sick Kids.

The drive into Toronto later that afternoon was not one that I will ever forget. I was anxious to see both Meghan and Caitlin and at the same time terrified about the upcoming transplant. I had all the confidence in the world about the hospital, the rooms, the doctors and nurses.   It was the fact that I think I overeducated myself about the whole BMT and knew how life threatening of a surgery that it was going to be. Children are pretty much taken to the brink of death and brought back again. *Brought back again*, that was the thought I needed to hang on to and trust.

We arrived outside of the hospital and waited near a large statue of a colourful moose. I saw Caitlin as she ran towards me. I was so glad to see her it seemed like it had been forever. For a little girl, she gave the biggest hugs.   I like to think my dad had something to do with that. She told me how she played on the elevators going up and down.

"Oh momma, dad got in trouble 'cause he was taking pictures inside the hospital" she giggled. Sick Kids Hospital was quite spectacular; as this was why Gerry was taking pictures I'm sure.   I remembered the first visit and that it was almost fun to be there in the lobby.   There were all sorts of shops where you could buy any type of gift for a child from clothing to books and toys.   There were also many restaurants and a large open cafeteria with different food vendors inside. The colours were spectacular; bright and beautiful and the hospital possessed an atmosphere that would make a child smile. Meghan was quiet, which I expected and her heart was as nervous as mine and likely more so. We didn't say much, but made our way up to the eighth floor to check in. She was in a room that was decorated in pink.   Randy was great with Meghan, as he always was, he brought to this whole day a sense of relaxation and peace but I knew how deeply worried he was also. Check in was a surprise. The nurse simply had us put Meghan's things into her room, and said. "Well we just have to take some blood work, and then that's it for tonight, we won't be doing anything until the morning, so go out, have some fun, and be back by 8:30 p.m."

We all looked at each other with surprise, smiled and agreed. "Ok, let's go eat" said Gerry. Hand in hand I walked with Randy as we headed downtown Toronto by foot, since Sick Kid's Hospital was so close to everything, it was a nice walk and the weather was perfect, not too cold on this October evening.

Meghan picked the place, Hard Rock Café. We entered and were escorted to our table. So here we were Meghan, Caitlin, Randy, Gerry and I seated at our table and I realized that this would be Meghan's last meal at a restaurant for a very long time and it choked me up. Perhaps it was the whole emotion of the day that made me over sensitive but still I got choked up none the less.

The manager came over to welcome us and said "If there is anything I can do, let me know." She left and walked over towards the bar area. Well, my mind began to stir, so I got up and walked over to her.

Meghan asked, "Mom, what are you doing?"

She knew I was on a mission and the woman did ask. I approached her, "Excuse me, you asked if there was anything that you could do."

"Yes," she said with a smile.

"Well, I have a little story to tell you" I began. "That beautiful girl over there, my daughter Meghan, is going into Sick Kids Hospital tonight, after our dinner here, and she is going to have a bone marrow transplant." My eyes filled with tears, as did Catherine's, the manager. I continued, "Well, Meghan picked your restaurant to have her last meal in," I said, not realizing how scary that sounded. "What I mean is that she can't have food outside of home cooked food or special food after her transplant for over a year, so I just wanted you to know that tonight is a very special night for her and for all of us."

In the back of my mind I thought, *what if we never again get to have a night out together, what if she doesn't pull through this whole BMT thing.* As quick as the thoughts came, I wiped a tear, and pushed them away again.

"Leave the evening to me" Catherine said, "And thank you for sharing this with us."

Gerry and Randy each ordered a beer and I knew that this was a hard evening to share as a dad and stepdad. We ordered burgers, fries, chicken fingers, and nachos, I think someone had fish and chips also. Catherine then came over to our table with a gift for Meghan; she gave her a teddy bear with a Hard Rock Café t-shirt on it, and a Hard Rock Café Monopoly game. The entire wait staff and bartenders then climbed onto the bar, and began a song and dance dedicated to Meghan. I can't remember the song because silly me didn't write it in my journal and so therefore as I wrote this I was at a loss as to what the song was, gosh darn it. I do remember that they asked Meghan to go up onto the bar with them, and she said, "Um thanks but no thanks, just in case I fall, I can't risk it." Ya good plan I thought and knew that she was not going up there for anything; what a look of relief she had that I agreed she shouldn't go up.

"I'll go up" said Gerry. He was eager to join the performance.

"No you will not" said Meghan, "not a chance you are going up there dad, no way dad, sorry, you are not going." Well there was no winning that argument. When it was time to go, Randy and Gerry were all set to split the bill in half and to our surprise the entire evening was on the house. How wonderful was that? Meghan was touched and had tears in her eyes.

"Thanks mom," she said, "because you told them all of this, and they were able to show kindness and now we can show it to someone else someday." It was in those types of statements that came from her heart that continually revealed the most beautiful soul I have encountered, I felt blessed. Even in the moments that were supposed to be for her, like this special dinner, she thought beyond all of it, captured the kindness of others in her heart and emanated it to the world that we all have the opportunity each and every moment to show kindness and do good. Meghan was blossoming through this whole journey; she now saw life from a whole new perspective. Now, she was thrust into a life experience that caused hair loss, weight gain from steroids, stretch marks and scars all over her body. What mattered most to her now was life and kindness that people showed and her being able to show it back to others. We are all meant to learn something from everything we go through in life and then we are supposed to pass that on as we go. Her heart inspired me. Meghan was now a teacher to show us what grace looked like. It shone through her even in the toughest moments.

We made our way back to the hospital and got Meghan all settled in. Oh how I didn't want to leave her there on her first night alone.

"She will be fine," the nurses said, "nothing would happen until the morning, so try to go home and rest because the next few days would be very stressful and full of a lot of tests and procedures."

So, we got her computer hooked up so that she could talk through MSN messenger. I felt so grateful for modern technology and that because of it Meghan would be able to communicate with Heather, with Courtney, and with all of us. I got all her things put away, and dilly dallied a little so that I could be with her just a little longer. Eventually the time came when we had to say our goodnights. Meghan and I couldn't look each other in the eye it was too painful. I held on to her for as long as I could without looking like a desperate mom about to crack.

"Time to go sweetie" Randy said as he gently touched my shoulder. I held it in all the way home and didn't want to cry in front of Caitlin but I ached so badly for my baby girl.

All I could think about was that Meghan was alone in that big city with the weight of the world on her shoulders. I wanted to crawl up beside her in bed and hold her like I did when she was a baby. I wanted to breathe in the scent of her all night long. I wanted time to freeze in the moment of our love. Unlike when we first found out about her HLH and how I hated time and wanted to fast forward it. For I knew what was ahead now; I knew the dangers of the chemo. I prayed. "Oh God, give her peace and strength, please let her feel my love even when I am not beside her. Please bestow upon her calm and understanding to know that I am with her."

"So don't worry, because I am with you. Don't be afraid, because I am your God. I will make you strong and will help you; I will support you with my right hand that saves you." Isaiah 41:10

Chapter 11 – Circus Room

We had now begun our countdown days. Actually it was an 11 day countdown, yesterday being day 11; the admission day. But when I did my countdown, it began the day she started with that horrible chemotherapy again. Oh, how I hate the thought of all of this. I waited at home for Gerry to arrive so that we could travel in together. It was a silent awkward drive in, but I was grateful for the company. The fear of facing the big city of Toronto myself overwhelmed me. Gerry and I had worked out a schedule, as one parent had to be in the hospital or at Ronald McDonald House at all times so that Meghan always had one parent present. It was a Sick Kids rule. Gerry was only able to stay until about noon, it was my first day with Meghan alone and it was going to be an interesting one at that.

Meghan's treatments began late in the day. I just let the doctors stick to their schedule, which was timed to the minute, and I would do my job; which was to be the best mom possible. The list of her drugs for this 10 day round of torture would be lovely chemotherapy cocktails such as Busulfan and Methotrexate. Other drugs such as that skunk pill again – Cyclosporine, Cyclophosphamide, Cotrimoxazole, Acyclovir, Ondansetron, and Phenytoin were also introduced again. These next 10 days were to be timed right to the minute. If anything got in the way, then the whole procedure could risk being cancelled. So at this hospital I was a silent mom, I didn't question or interrupt, I let go and let God. I still wrote, but not as diligently as I did at McMaster.

My daughter was now officially a Sick Kid's kid. Special things happen here, and today was a very special day. We were invited, along with about 20 other patients and parents to attend a private concert put on by a famous Canadian group. I think I was more excited than Meghan was. We went to the concert, somewhere on the eighth floor and Meghan was able to meet, greet and get autographs. Shortly after Randy arrived with my mom and Caitlin and we were all played a game of Monopoly with her new game from Hard Rock Café in the visitors lounge. This lounge was where families could gather before the kids became neutropenic. It sure felt good to see everyone and to have that sense of family around. I knew it meant a lot to Meghan as she was so worried; even though she wasn't showing it.

So far there had been no adverse reactions to the Busulfan, her first strong chemotherapy. The doses were high and I remembered when we came in for our consultation, a couple of months back, that there was this little boy who passed us in a wheelchair in the hallway during our tour. His skin was so grey and almost transparent. That poor sweet boy. I remembered thinking that he looked like death itself, and it frightened me that day just as it did on this day. Was Meghan going to have that same look, would she even make it out of this whole ordeal? *Oh Lord pull her through this*, was my only thought and prayer.

Tonight was my first night at Ronald McDonald House. The hospital insisted that a security guard walk me to the house as it can be risky at night in some areas of town. Once inside, I made my way to the room that would be shared by all of us while we went through this with Meghan. The whole theme of the room was a circus. The ceiling was painted like a big top tent, red and yellow. It somewhat freaked me out and made my head spin when I laid in bed, but it took my mind off of things for sure. I had with me my laptop so I was able to talk to Meghan on MSN. The wonders and blessings of technology, boy was I grateful.

October 20th countdown day seven of the 11 day cycle. I arrived at the hospital fairly early this morning from Ronald McDonald House, made my way to the glass elevators and up to the eighth floor. When I entered her room, I noticed a strange necklace around her neck. I can't explain why but this pendant creeped me out, I didn't like how it made me feel at all. Meghan knew this and she said to me "I can tell by the look on your face that you don't like this" she stated.

100

"What is it, and where did it come from?" and "no I don't like it and it has to come off now." It was one of those moments where my faith would give me intuitiveness and it simply had to go.

Things had become so fast paced and scary. Tests were constantly being done. They drew blood all the time, and sent Meghan for scans of God knows what. Since Meghan's counts were still okay she was able to leave the room for her procedures but once they moved her to isolation, in a few days, then everything would be done in her room in complete sterilization. Today we got news that her kidneys were functioning at only 50%, however they were being monitored closely and carefully and her medication would be adjusted to ease and assist the situation. Meghan was also taken for a chest x-ray earlier in the day. Soon after I arrived the doctors came into her room in a frenzy.

"We found a shadow, we believe to be a tumor in the lungs" the doctor informed me. "It's a round shadow, and it doesn't look good so we have booked an urgent CT scan" he added.

"But, it's time for chemo" I said not even realizing how odd that sounded. Dinner time, chemo time. Chemotherapy had become commonplace in this world we were now in.

"We are stopping all treatments until we assess this shadow. If it is what we believe it to be, then the transplant will not take place." Within minutes she was rushed by a porter and escorted into radiology for her scan. What transpired in the moments that followed was best summed up in Meghan's own words in an essay she wrote for English months later.

Miracle at Sick Kids - by Meghan Rush

I walked into the room where the CT scan was to be done. I felt so small compared to the giant scanner. I can somewhat imagine how a photo feels being put through a scanner or copy machine. They would soon strap me to the bed no wider than my body, and I would slide back and forth through the scanner which resembled a monster size sprinkle donut.

The room had the smell of hospital clean. It also had a slight odor of rubber, probably because of the latex gloves that you would find by the box full in almost every corner.

The nurses and the doctors were all waiting for me. "How are you feeling Meghan?" they asked. Quietly I would just say "fine," despite my fears of being hurt again. It wasn't that long ago that I had already had one of these scans done. It hurt. They couldn't use my central line, which is a temporary main access line to an artery, called a Hickman. If they used the Hickman, it may have damaged the line. I had to have a needle, and so they gave me a new IV, for the scan only, in my hand. The vein collapsed and went into a spasm. It hurt so much. The nurse had to come and hold the IV against my hand tight to keep it from spasm and possibly doing damage. I had a bruise the size of the entire back of my hand when it was done.

Both my mom and I were scared this time. But relieved that they were going to use the Hickman and just put the contrast solution through it slower as to not damage the line. That was a relief. My mom tried to calm me down and read to me. She found a goofy pop-up book and used a funny voice to read me the story. It was lame, but funny, she did relax me. I think we were both relaxed.

She then put on this heavy lead apron. It was to protect her from being exposed to any radiation. It sure didn't look like a cooking apron. She looked like a blueberry. "Good Heavens" she said, this thing is heavy. She then went to the corner that the technician directed her to, sat on the edge of her seat, clutching onto her cross in prayer. My mom prays a lot.

The doctors began to hook up the IV contrast, and pump it into me. They would then position me in various poses, mostly with my arms over my head. I would have probably looked like a frozen ballerina doing a spin, straight legs and arms over head.

The bed then moved through the donut. Over a loud speaker you would hear. "Breath in, hold, ok, breath normal." This would happen over and over as they took each picture. I remember thinking to myself, please let there be nothing wrong, please.

All of a sudden a sense of calmness came over me. I heard a voice, which I thought was my moms slowly repeating. "Relax Meghan, just relax." My feet and legs were being rubbed at the same time that I heard the voice. So I just assumed it was my mom. My feet felt so warm, the touch was gentle and delicate and had such a calming effect.

As I passed through the donut several times, you feel like the machine speaks to you, but it comes from the room behind the big glass wall over the loud speaker. The voice over the speaker was not like the one I heard telling me to relax.

My fears and thoughts of what they might have found on the scan were now replaced with a feeling of calm and safety.

The scan took less than an hour. Mom helped me get back into the wheelchair. I was too weak from the earlier chemotherapy treatment to walk the whole distance back to my room on 8B. We passed Dr. Assaga on the way back to my room. He was on his way to view my results.

When we got back to my room I talked to my mom about the scan and how she helped me relax. "Mom, I really enjoyed you rubbing my feet and legs while telling me to relax, it really helped"

"What do you mean Meghan, I was in the corner far from reach in the chair praying, didn't you hear me praying? Meghan, I didn't touch you, honestly honey, I couldn't even reach you, and it wasn't me."

Actually I remember saying to my mom. "Um mom, by the look on your face I can tell that you didn't touch me or talk did you." It was then she told me of how she prayed so hard and how she remembered looking at my feet and how pink they looked.

We both realized that God was with us and that I was touched by angels or God Himself. We cried and hugged. We were still waiting for Dr. Assaga, he arrived in about half an hour. His hands were clasped and he said with a smile on his face, "great news, it's just a pocket of pus."

My mom was still smiling, and had tears in her eyes. I began to cry also. It was the greatest feeling. My mom said "See how fast God works, He turned a tumor into a pocket of puss." She smiled and said again, "amen to that and thank you God.

I know that I have been touched and blessed. By angels, or by God, either way it is a miracle and it was given for me to share with my mom and everyone else. I smiled and said to my mom, "I love you mom."

Her essay; wow beautiful and so vivid. For me, it was a miracle and in more ways than one. I had my own journal entry for that day but chose to only share with you Meghan's essay because its beauty and innocence to this day touches my soul. For your information, the shadow the doctors saw lay directly where the pendant was that Meghan wore that day. I did follow God's instruction and tossed it out.

I had to call my church friends, ministers, and family, absolutely everyone and tell them all about this miracle. AMEN for it all. How fantastic that God can turn a tumor into a pocket of pus in the matter of a few moments.

I should have marked today down on the calendar. Today was a moment in the history of this whole crazy, terrifying journey. Today was the last day that Meghan would receive chemotherapy. We have reached the end of the treatment before transplant. I arrived just shortly after 9am, made my way through the lobby and into the cafeteria. I bought a croissant to bring Meghan, she loved them and she would just enjoy the sweet butter flavor of a warmed up croissant with extra butter on it. I picture her as she would peel it apart to savor each bite. She would dangle it over her mouth and let it land gently on her tongue. It would simply melt in her mouth. So I got two thinking I would enjoy one also. In a few days she would not be allowed anything from a cafeteria, or a bakery, or a deli. The diet would be *low bacteria*.

I went through the checkout. "Will that be everything?" the young girl at the cash said.

"Yes," I replied, "Just the two croissants, thank you, and extra butter please." I made my way toward the elevator and I let out a heavy sigh. I was sure that everyone could hear me as it was one of those Ahhhhhhhh moments. I was so excited to see my baby girl. Excited, boy I never thought that having a round of chemotherapy would bring excitement, but this one did, it was her last chemo treatment ever. Even though this would be her last dose for life, she still had not received the horrific side effects that would arrive any day now. Meghan would have mouth sores, and possibly more than that, her hair, all of her hair, and her fingernails, and her toe nails, eye lashes, eye brows, everything that regrows was about to completely fall out. *Can't think of that today* I thought to myself as I got off the elevator onto the eighth floor. Today we would celebrate with croissants the last chemotherapy treatment to ever enter her precious body.

I entered her room. "Mommy" she greeted me with a smile. Oh, how I loved it when she called me mommy. "What's in the bag?" Meghan asked.

"Today my dear, is a good day, it is the last day of chemotherapy. No more poison will ever enter that beautiful body of yours again" I reminded her. "Croissants, warm with butter," I added with a smile, as I pulled both of them out of the warm paper bag, the aroma was wonderful. "

"Are they both for me?" she added.

"Of course." I smiled and handed them to her on the neatly folded napkins that were also tucked inside the bag.

Shortly after, the nurse arrived with her last chemo cocktail and hooked it up into Meghan's IV pole. While being hooked up the latest results arrived from her kidney function test. The previous test was a concern as it showed the kidneys quite a bit below normal function range, 50%, which caused extreme alarm. However, this one now revealed a functionality of 94%. A+ on this test, pretty impressive.

"How is my sister?" Meghan asked while she picked apart the last bit of her croissant and seemed to just stare at it, her question and sweet voice brought my mind back to the present.

'She is ok" I replied, not sure where this conversation was about to lead.

"Mom, I worry about Caitlin, she is my only sister, I don't want her to get sick like me, I worry about her being alone." Truth of the matter is I worried about Caitlin also. I worried that she might one day end up with the same HLH, but the doctors assured us that it was not the hereditary type that in fact was induced by a virus.

"Well, it's funny that you ask this today because I have planned a movie night with Caitlin for tonight, we are going to see Dreamer, just the two of us" I told her.

"Oh mom, that is so cool, she will love it 'cause you know she is a horse freak" Meghan said excitedly. "I wish I could go," I heard her mumble quietly.

"One day we will all go to the movies together, and when you are out of this place I have a surprise for you at home that will allow us movie night right in the living room whenever we want it."

She smiled, "Can you bring in some DVDs for me to watch on my laptop?" she asked.

"Absolutely" I replied, "I will gather some tonight so I have them when I come in tomorrow." I kissed her on the cheek "I should get going, your dad just messaged me, he is in the family lounge outside waiting to come in."

"Ok, love you, hug Caitlin for me, have fun at the movie, and go on MSN later, okay?"

"For sure sweetie, have fun with your dad, love you lots," and I closed the door gently behind me and made my way out into the lounge.

'She is all yours and it's a good day," I let him know as I shared the results with him. 'Oh, she is having her last chemo ever, so you may want to get her a little something to surprise her. I brought her a croissant and the little monkey ate mine also, I didn't

106

have the heart to tell her that one was hers and one was mine so I am gonna grab a sandwich to go." We continued to walk and talk at the same time. "Oh, maybe you can grab her some magazines or stuff to draw in, she loves to colour."

"Ok, I will hit the gift shop quickly, let me ride down with you and walk you out." We shared the elevator down to the main floor, after grabbing a sandwich from the cafeteria I headed out to the front where Randy waited to give me a ride home and Gerald went in the other direction towards the gift shop.

Movie night with Caitlin tonight, I was so excited to just spend this time with my sweet little thing. Caitlin had been so amazing through all of this. No one should have to watch their sister go through what she has witnessed Meghan go through. I cry as I think about how brave she was, and how left out and alone she must have felt a great deal of the time. Tonight was her night with me at the movies and we were going to eat junk, relax, and have an absolute perfect night.

"Oh Caitlin," I called for her as I opened the front door.

"Just upstairs doing my homework momma" she shouted down. Oh how I love it when she called me that, she doesn't do it all the time, just now and again but it was just so darn cute.

"Ok, well put it aside, we are going to the movies, I think there is a movie called Dreamer or something like that."

She came running down the stairs, "For reals?" she said. "Who else is going?" "No one, just you and I, and don't worry about eating either because tonight we are having hot dogs and popcorn, and whatever else you want. It's all about you tonight." She leaped at me, hugged me and didn't say a word.

Off we went, just the two of us to watch Dreamer, a movie about a little girl and her love for a horse. Caitlin had wanted to see this movie so very much, and I could tell by how she watched it so intensely that she had nothing on her mind other than the movie that played for her. In a quiet whisper she then leaned into me and said, "Momma, can I get some gummy bears? Meghan loves gummy bears."

I smiled. "For sure, I will go get some and maybe a bag of red nibs also." "Yum," she replied. It warmed my heart that even on her special night she thought of her sister. Meghan absolutely loved gummy bears and it somehow made us both feel that she was with us.

Tomorrow was transplant day and it would be an early trip in. Even though it was Gerry's shift, I would not be anywhere else but with Meghan on this day. So both her dad and I would be by her bedside through the transplant. A friend from church, Saint Claire, was going to drive me in; he had driven me a few times before. God knew the crazy fears I had to travel by train or subway; so amazingly, He worked His plan so that a fellow parishioner who happened to just drive by Sick Kids every day on a job for the next while, would be able to drive me in. How awesome was that?

"You know there is an old man, who many mistake as a homeless person, who sits outside of Sick Kids Hospital on a bench every day," Saint Claire began his story to me. "This man goes by the name of Father Murphy, he is an old retired priest, he sits outside of the hospital and prays every single day for the doctors, nurses, and all the patients of the hospital. He just sits and prays for hours and hours." Saint Claire continued to tell me all about this man on our journey in. I looked for this perched Father Murphy on a bench as we approached the hospital entrance, but I suppose it was too early. If I had a chance I would try to find him later on today.

"I don't see him anywhere" I said.

"Well, I am told that he often wears an old brown coat" Saint Claire replied, "perhaps you may see him later or another day." I pictured in my mind a man that looked somewhat like a monk.

Apparently, Father Murphy had been praying there for many years, and most didn't even know that he was a priest. I thought to myself. *Imagine that, a man for years and years sits on a bench outside of this world renowned hospital and prays each and every single day for the entire hospital.* I was stunned.

"Kinda makes you wonder just why this hospital has world class status and is known for the talent of the doctors and nurses, yet no one knew about the old retired priest that prays for hours on end" I said to Saint Claire.

"Yep, there is more to the miracles that happen in here than one realizes." I kept this warm thought in my mind, a comfort to now know of this holy man and how he felt it was his mission to pray for this hospital.

"Lord," I silently prayed, "please somehow bless this man and let him feel the gratitude in my heart and soul for his constant and vigilant prayer." I was very touched to know about this, on this particular day, the day of her transplant. I turned to my friend, "It's funny sometimes how God works things, to have you tell me about this man today, on the transplant day; well it has eased my mind, because I know the power of prayer, and that is what will pull her through this surgery." Wow, talk about a blanket of Heaven right over this place.

Saint Claire was able to find a spot briefly and dropped me off at the front doors. Again I looked around to see if I could spot an old man in a brown coat on a bench, but he was unseen. Knowing that he was there was enough. I grabbed a quick muffin and tea in the cafeteria and headed up to the eighth floor. Meghan was still fast asleep when I arrived. I knew that a lot would need to happen today to prepare her for the move to her isolation room, so I wanted to make sure I was here really early.

I had my camera with me today, I wanted to take pictures of this new beginning, memories of a day that I wasn't sure would even happen until that stranger said yes. Today was a day I feared only just a couple of months ago, with hopes that we would never have to be here, that Meghan would never have to go through any more procedures, yet we had arrived here to this very day. What was initially only supposed to take eight weeks has now been seven months, and here we are at a beginning again. I wasn't even sure exactly what a bone marrow transplant was or how it occurred. But here we were, transplant day, new marrow and a new day.

I quietly leaned over Meghan, and whispered "Good morning my baby." She woke with a sleepy head, turned to me, and gave me an oh so cheeky grin, and then nodded off for a while longer.

During the morning rounds, the nurse on duty had mentioned that the donor's marrow was now being extracted in the hospital just around the corner. I couldn't believe it, a complete stranger, within walking distance, was harvesting his own bone marrow so that my daughter could live. "Can you tell me anything about him?" I asked her eagerly.

"I do know that it is definitely a man, he is middle aged, and I believe from overseas."

"Wow," was all I could think or say. "He came all this way, for Meghan." I said to her in a tone that quivered with emotion. The awesomeness of this whole thing was bigger than anything I imagined. "Can I at least give him a letter?" as I felt the need to thank him.

"Yes, we have a form, you can write the letter, we have to read it to ensure that no names are exchanged, and if you want to meet, you can, but it will have be a year from now."

"I need to write to him," I replied. "He will get it before he leaves won't he?" I asked.

"Yes, he will get it today if you can get the letter to me shortly" was her answer.

"Wonderful, please get the form to me, and I will do it now."

When Meghan woke, I had finished my letter to the donor and with it was the poem – Someone Said Yes. "What were you doing?" she asked me as she squirmed in her bed just as she did as a baby.

"I was writing a letter to the donor, and giving him the poem also" I replied.

"What?!! We can write to him? Do you know who he is?" she said as she sat up quickly.

"Yes and no." I replied. "Yes we can write to him, but no I don't know who he is just that he is in the hospital across the road, and that he is a middle aged man from overseas." We both cried feeling nothing but the precious gift of love.

"Well, it's time for that special scrub down bath I have told you about Meghan," nurse Michelle said as she entered Meghan's room wearing Tweety bird scrubs and a stethoscope around her neck. They called it a stats bath; it is given to transplant patients before they head into their isolation rooms. Patients were disinfected from head to toe with a thorough wash with a special soap and were then dried by the nurse who was completely gowned and gloved. I was previously given instructions to have her clothing washed in hot water with bleach, and dried, then put directly into new unused clear plastic bags and sealed. This bag of clothing would then come to the hospital sterilized and would go directly into the room with Meghan. While the nurse bathed my baby, I went and finished the letter to our special friend and grabbed her bag of clothing.

As Meghan walked down the hallway, alone and quite a distance ahead of me towards her new room, I followed with my camera and her bag of clothing. The sun shone through the window at the end of the hallway and it framed Meghan as she walked with a heavenly glow of light that cast a mystical shadow down the hallway behind her. She looked like an angel draped in a sheet. *Maybe she is* I thought.

We were shown this room once before during our consultation appointment and I never forgot how clean and sanitized this whole floor was kept. There were several rooms; I think possibly six or more. One full wall in each room was an air purification wall. The air circulated hundreds or possibly thousands of times per minute, I can't remember exactly, and was filtered. We would be guaranteed that there were no germs of any kind in those rooms. There was a glass wall at the front of each room with a sliding glass door that led into what was called the ante-room. It somewhat felt that we observed Meghan as if she were in an aquarium and we were in an observation room. Here we would enter, wash up, gown up, glove up, and if we wanted mask up. There was one long ante-room in front of two isolation rooms. Anything other than paper must be wiped down with sterilizing wipes before it entered her room. No stuffed animals, no food, and no contact. Computers must be sterilized, as must the cords and anything else that came into the room. Nothing could touch the floor. Games must be sterilized if they had plastic pieces. If you touched your face or hair while you are in the room, leave immediately, go out and wash again, and re-glove; then you could re-enter. No nail polish or artificial nails were permitted in isolation. Eyeglasses must be wiped down. Gowns and gloves were mandatory;

a face mask was recommended but not mandatory. Do not touch anything. We were to leave slippers in the anteroom and they must be put on; no street shoes in the isolation room. Keep purses and bags outside in the anteroom as they are not allowed in the isolation room. Meghan was not allowed to put her feet onto the floor. If she needed the commode we had to put towels down first and then she could use the commode. If you had a cold, or cold sore, or anything at all, you are forbidden to even come into the area and should not even come to the hospital.

So, we had our list of rules and there were also rules posted in each anteroom so there was no room for error. When you were ready and sterilized from head to toe you simply pushed the button and the glass door slid open and allowed you to enter and be with your child. Meghan had a neighbor in the room beside, a girl the same age as her, Kelli. We were introduced to Rick and Leanne, Kelli's parents in the anteroom. Kelli had only been in there a couple of days and so far everything went well for her. She received stem cells from her brother, which was very similar to bone marrow.

At about one o'clock in the afternoon Meghan became fully settled in LAF isolation room #4. Again, I can't tell you how incredible these rooms were; no wonder Sick Kids was one of the best hospitals in the world and luckily for us it is only an hour away. Barb, her nurse for today, a young woman who couldn't be much older than 25, came in with three bags of what I thought was blood. I went out into the ante-room where she was in prep mode for the transplant of the marrow. It was all wrapped in sterilized towels.

"Is that the marrow, for some reason I didn't expect it to be red?"

"This is it" she replied with a smile. "Meghan will be getting 1.5 liters of marrow. It is slightly darker than blood with a different consistency and richness." I went over to get a closer look. I was being a bit sneaky as I read the labels, hoping to find a bit of information about the donor. Barb knew what I was up to. "You won't find anything on the labels" she said with a smile. "All parents have such a curiosity, understandably so, but we don't even know his identity."

"His," I said, thinking again of a kind man from overseas who is saving my daughter's life. I closed my eyes and said a quick heartfelt prayer.

When we hear of a surgery such as a bone marrow transplant, we think exactly that, a surgery; at least I thought it was a surgical procedure. I didn't even ask how it was performed when we had our initial consultation a while back.

"Is the doctor going to be here soon to perform the transplant?" I inquired.

"No, I will be doing it" said Barb. "I simply hook the marrow up to her IV central line, just as we would do if we were to give her blood or chemotherapy. The doctor is available if something goes wrong, but the actual procedure is quite simple."

The marrow would simply enter her body and then like magic, the blood would separate and the marrow would travel right to the bone where it was needed and then we would wait for grafting to begin. I was fascinated that all the parts of the marrow, the reds, the platelets, everything in those three IV bags would actually have the ability to go where they needed to be once inside her veins. It was like they had the ability to think, so completely mind blowing to me. There would be several things for us to watch for; fevers, GVHD (graft vs. host disease) and VOD (veno occlusive disease). Fevers were due to the blood counts being completely wiped down to nothing and the possibility of infections and disease entering her system. With Meghan being 16, and the risk of onset of her period, they have added two birth control pills a day as well as the needle Depo Provera. Menstrual bleeding when all her counts including platelets were so low and going to go right to zero, was not an option. It simply could not happen and could be life threatening.

Gerry and I were both in the room with Meghan while her marrow was being set up. We were excited and frightened at the same time. I brought in my camera and completely sterilized it so that we could capture this day forever. A new beginning, our turning point that we had longed for and waited for was finally here. She would no longer ever need chemotherapy, and slowly one by one the drugs that

114

were in her system would start to be reduced as she began to normalize day after day.

This was the day that they call day 1, and from this moment on we will count the days. When we reach day 100, we were told that it would be a monumental day and that things would start to improve from that point on. I wasn't quite sure what they meant by improve and I didn't want to ask in front of Meghan, but 100 days seemed like a very long way away.

"What are we going to be in for?" I whispered silently to myself as I watched the marrow slowly make its way down her IV line. Suddenly I knew what I had to do and it was pray. So I said out loud, "Gerry, Meghan, I need to pray over this marrow before it enters your body" Meghan just smiled, as did her dad. Well Gerry may have thought it goofy, but he knew what I was like in regards to my faith, so I just did what I needed to do. "Lord, thank you, thank you for the blessing of the man who gave his marrow, this marrow, so that our Meghan can live. Lord as it travels along this IV line, purify it, keep it clean and perfect to enter her body to sustain her and Lord let the transplant work. This marrow is a gift we shall never forget and as it saves her life we will always give thanks, in Jesus's name we pray, Amen." And as I finished my prayer I watched it slowly enter her body.

"The whole procedure will take about three hours," Barb added. Gerry stayed for the transplant and for the first night he would have his shift so he headed over to Ronald McDonald house to get himself settled in.

"See you in a couple of hours" he said as he brushed my shoulder in comfort.

"Absolutely," I answered.

"Bye daddy I love you," Meghan shouted at him.

"Love you too peanut, see you in a bit," he responded. Caitlin was going to spend the weekend with her dad and his family so I had to get home shortly to be with her before she was picked up by her dad tomorrow. Nothing much else would happen here we were told, as it's the first couple of days, so I said he should have time with Caitlin as she needed it. It would give me some great time with

Meghan over the next few days also as well as some time to talk with the nurse on duty. I knew that Meghan would lose all of her hair, all of it, on every part of her body. She had not experienced that before as her hair had thinned and was cut extremely short for her wig, but she still managed to keep some and her eyebrows and eyelashes; this time however it was going to be different. She was given such large doses of chemotherapy during the countdown and the effects of that would soon appear. Also, Meghan was also told that she would never be able to have children after the transplant, that her reproductive system would be permanently adversely affected. Meghan and I didn't talk too much about her not being able to have children, at 16 not having children didn't seem as drastic to her as losing her hair was. I said my goodnights to the nurses at the station, made my way out of 8F and headed to the elevators for the first floor. Gerry and Randy were waiting in the lobby for me. "See you in the morning" we both said to each other as Gerry made his way back up to the eighth floor.

"How did it go?" Randy asked.

"Did you know that the nurse did the transplant? Odd I never thought it was such a simple procedure."

"Really? I had no idea" he answered.

We held hands and walked down to the underground where he had parked.

"Oh I am so glad that this day is over, now we just wait. They call it day 1 and we have to get to day 100 before we can feel secure and safe," I repeated to him what I was told earlier. "Can we go to the drive thru at Timmies and get a tea please?" I asked. "Then I am going to go straight home to Caitlin. Mom is there with her now but I have some work to catch up on so I won't be staying over, okay?"

"Not a problem, I am here for whatever you need," he assured me as he took my hand and kissed it while we still held on to each other for the drive home.

"Hey Caitlin, I'm home" I shouted, "I'm going to pop in a frozen pizza, okay?"

"Sure mom, nannie got me McDonald's earlier, yum" she shouted from the basement.

"Hey mom, thanks again for staying with her, I don't know what I would do without you," as I hugged my mom close I could smell french fries. "So you had fries too did you?" I laughed.

"Well of course, I couldn't resist" she replied. "How did it go today? I was praying so hard" she told me.

"Well it is actually a simple thing to transplant, much like a blood transfusion" I told her, "and the nurse was the one that did it."

"Really?" she replied as curious as I was about the whole procedure and as surprised also.

"Do you want some pizza? It's almost done." I asked as we could smell that fresh baked goodness. I breathed it in deeply as I opened the oven door.

"Oh heavens no, I had a chicken McBurger," as she called it, "I can't eat another bite, and I have to head home to do some more of Meghan's special laundry" she informed me in a tone that was both sad and proud at the same time. It must break her heart to not be able to hold her granddaughter close but I knew she did in her heart and prayers, closer than we could imagine. Mom headed home shortly after that and I went upstairs with some crispy double cheese pizza hot from the oven.

"Pizza is done if you want some, cheeky monkey. I'm taking my laptop upstairs for a bit. Can you pack your bag for your dads so it is ready for when he picks you up after school tomorrow? Remember you are spending the weekend with him." I shouted down to Caitlin as I made my way upstairs.

"No thanks mom, I still have some cheeseburger and fries" she sweetly shouted back.

"Hey where's my hug?" I asked "Come up here missy I need a hug."

"Okay momma, coming up." I continued to head upstairs with my journal and laptop, signed in to MSN to chat with my baby, ping, a message from Meghan my heart skipped a beat, so thankful for technology and being able to communicate with my baby. We chatted about silly things, it was small talk but nevertheless it was special. It was hard to sign off MSN when all I wanted to do was to continue to talk to my daughter. But I knew I needed time to rest, pray, check emails, take a bath, and possibly just a moment of peace amongst all the craziness.

I got up early, showered, headed to moms to pick up Meghan's clean bag of sterilized clothing and to drop Caitlin off as mom would take her to school today. Saint Claire would pick me up at 6:30 am at mom's house.

When we arrived this morning I noticed an old man as he sat on a bench wearing a brown coat. *Father Murphy,* I thought to myself as I went inside, I smiled at him, waved, and he nodded to me as I went inside. I didn't say anything to him, respecting his privacy to his mission and prayer. I was in the mood for a warm croissant, so I stopped at the cafeteria and ate it on my way to 8F. It was now day two; I entered the ante-room, went through my routine of washing and gowning and then entered Meghan's isolation room. I tried to contain my emotions; I thought something was terribly wrong. I knew I was only in the room for a brief moment, but one glance at Meghan and I was terrified. Meghan was alone, on her computer, and she just looked up when the only excuse I could come up with fast and blurted out was "Oh crap, I need to pee, be back in a second sweetie." I needed to escape before my expression caused her to be afraid. I found Barb who was still on day shift. "What's wrong with Meghan?" I asked in a tone that left me utterly breathless as if I had just run a flight of stairs. Actually my heart raced and I felt like I had just run a marathon.

"Nothing," she replied, "she is doing remarkably well and there have not been any fevers at all so far."

"Why is she the colour of a lobster?" I asked with a shaky voice, worried that something went terribly wrong. She was terribly pink, like she was burning up or badly sun burnt.

"Oh, that is completely normal for her skin to be that colour, she was given such rich blood/marrow, that her red count now is extremely high, no need to be alarmed, the colour will fade to her beautiful skin again, and the count will lower, it is completely normal."

Meghan honestly was the colour of a lobster. As I entered her room, I blew her a kiss and made sure that my fingertips never touched my lips, it was the simple soft motion and the only way I

118

could kiss her, which she caught on her cheek as she would turn it to me.

"My skin is itchy" she said as she fidgeted and rubbed her bald little head. "Look at my pillow mommy," as tears rolled down her cheek, hair had rapidly begun to fall out.

"I know sweetie, I know." I couldn't cuddle her or hold her; I just grabbed a tissue to dry her tears. "It will grow back and even more beautiful than ever." I promised with my heart breaking yet again for all the pain and suffering she has had to endure.

She sniffled, and then said to me as she held out her arms, "check this out mom, pink," as she pressed her finger onto her forearm and lifted it off. "Pink makes the boys wink" and she laughed "well that's what Nana B would say." Nana B (Gerry's grandmother), used to say it to the girls all the time when they were so little. She would dress them in pink frills, ruffles, and sweet hand knit sweaters. "Pink makes the boys wink," she would say as she smiled and played with her great granddaughters.

I met Gerry in the family lounge just before he was to go in to see Meghan. We were now on Day 4 of the 100 day countdown and I needed to catch him up on a couple of things. It was also Halloween, and the hospital was a wonderland of costumes. Nurses switch up their scrubs for costumes such as; butterflies, fairies, witches, pumpkins, angels, and so much more. The kids that were in isolation, however, couldn't have candy. Instead they brought Meghan a treat bag full of colouring books and crayons and we all got to play bingo over the intercom system. All the kids won, that's just the way it was around here. I let Meghan chat on the computer, and colour, and excused myself to go have a lunch and meet with her dad. I specifically needed to talk to him about her hair loss and that it was drastic. Gerry and I were getting along very well these days and I liked it. Our only focus was our daughter. I greeted him with a hug and a few tears.

"She is doing well today, no fevers yet, but her hair," and I started to cry. "Gerry she is completely hairless." I cried and he just hugged me.

"It will all be fine, it grows back, well on most people but not me," he said as his eyes rolled upwards to indicate his balding head. He made me laugh, this balding ex-husband of mine, and I knew he would make Meghan laugh as she needed it also. We went down to the room together, washed up, gowned up and went in to see our baby.

"Hey dad you have more hair than I do now," Meghan laughed.

"Ya, but I am still old and ugly, but you on the other hand are cuter than ever. Too bad I couldn't look that good bald."

She grinned, and I took that as my cue to blow her another kiss. "Catch this one," I said and she turned her cheek so that my softly blown kiss would magically land on her sweet little cheek. "Love you," I said.

"Love you more," Meghan replied, "Hug Caitlin for me and tell her to go on MSN, okay?"

"Will do, and I will catch you on the computer later on, muah," as I blew her one last kiss. Oh how I wished I could just wrap my arms around her. It was so hard to not be able to touch my child and let her feel my love. I pushed the button for the door to slide open, entered the ante-room, threw out my gloves and put the worn gown into the laundry bin, removed my slippers and put on my running shoes, grabbed my purse and headed to the lounge. I kept my coat and backpack in the lounge locker so that I wouldn't clutter up the anteroom with too much stuff. Gerry and I shared a locker and we could also keep snacks and things here to cut down on the cost of always going to the cafeteria. I then made my way to Ronald McDonald house to get my things and head home to see my Caitlin.

Randy met me at RMH, and all I could do was hold on to him and hug him and cry.

"Get me out of this crazy circus room," I said, "Its making me feel like I am spinning out of control more than I actually am."

All I could think of was how badly I wanted to be home and get Caitlin ready to go trick or treating. Randy dropped me off just before it became dark. I was excited to take Caitlin trick or treating. She was going out as Dorothy from the Wizard of Oz. I had made her a dress out of blue and white gingham fabric. The dress looked more like a skirt with an apron front on it. However it was easier to make it like this rather than use an actual pattern. She wore a heavy white sweater underneath. She looked so cute with her hair in braids and her rosy cheeks.

"Look mom, grandma let me wear lipstick." Mrs. Rush and I smiled at each other. Grandma was over at our house to help Caitlin get ready.

As soon as we arrived she handed Caitlin her shoes "here you go Miss Dorothy, all sparkly and ready for you to click your heels." Grandma Rush had so sweetly made these wonderful ruby slippers which were covered with red glitter.

"Whoa," Caitlin said with wide eyes and a cheeky grin "thanks Grandma these are the best ruby slippers."

"You're welcome" as she kissed Caitlin on the forehead, "just don't click your heels inside the house or you will have red glitter everywhere and I'm sure your mom won't want to have to clean it up."

"Okay grandma, thanks see you soon up at your house, don't let Jake eat my candy." Jake was grandma and grandpa's dog, an Airedale Terrier who had more energy than one could imagine. Caitlin considered Jake to be her dog; she loved that dog and called him Jakey Boy. Grandma and Grandpa drove away.

"See you in about an hour," I shouted as I waved to them from the front door. Caitlin slipped on her ruby slippers, and grabbed the basket with Toto in it. Caitlin had a look of sadness on her face.

"Do I have to wait for an hour to go trick or treating?" she asked.

"Heck no, since I can't be in two places at once then we will have to resort to plan B," I said to her as I put out a big bowl of candy on the front porch with a help yourself sign.

"Come on, let's go, I have an extra bag in my pocket for you also" she smiled and then we headed out.

"Is it ok that you just put the candy in a bowl like that, what if they take it all?" Caitlin asked in a concerned tone.

"Well, when it's gone its gone, I hope they aren't greedy and that they don't take the whole bowl, but we can't control what others do now can we?" We talked, skipped and ran from house to house. Well she ran, I just walked with a couple other moms and she met up with her friends from school.

It was a great night, one that Caitlin deserved and that I so badly needed. My mind, however, would wander back to my bald headed baby who lay in a hospital bed. When I say bald headed, I mean it in the sweetest of ways. It reminded me of when she in fact was a baby. She had that same new baby scent, I don't know why or what caused it, maybe it's just like a rebirth of everything in her system, but it smelled just as wonderful as when she was a new baby. Oh how I longed to touch her and hold her, my 16 year old sweet baby. My mind would wander to Meghan, and then back to all these healthy kids who ran from house to house and screamed *trick or treat;* my world was split in half, I might have been physically with Caitlin and tried my hardest to not think of Meghan, but how could I not, I wouldn't be the mother I was if I couldn't think of her. Meghan had her dad with her, and I knew that their plan was to watch scary movies and have a fun night together; still all of this was so heartbreaking. *Day Five.* I thought, *tomorrow was only day five, this was going to be a long journey.* I put the thought out of my mind and came back to the present.

"Caitlin, did you get any Kit Kats yet?" I hollered as I felt the need for chocolate. Exhausted and with two full bags of candy we made our way home. Dorothy, oops, Caitlin dumped her bags out all over the floor and began to sort things into piles.

"Hold on, not so fast, grab your bag, we have to head to Grandmas, and to Nannies."

"Whoa, more candy," and she scurried out the door left a trail of red glitter behind.

"Do they get candy at the hospital?" she asked as we drove over to see grandma, grandpa, and Jake.

"Most of the kids, but not your sister, not for a little while yet."

"Oh, that's sad," she said as she gazed out the window. We arrived at grandmas to a very happy pup that waited in the front room

122

for her. "Jakey boy!" Caitlin squealed as he licked her rose coloured cheeks. She collected her candy from grandma and grandpa and we were off again.

"Okay now off to nannies, one last stop then home, okay Miss Dorothy?"

"This is the best Halloween, and a lot of candy for sure momma" with a smile she reached out and touched my hand.

Mom loved to decorate, whether it be Halloween, Easter, or Christmas, heck even Thanksgiving. She decorated and then decorated even more. On the front lawn of her house were these wooden cutout characters that my dad had made, Casper the friendly ghost was my favourite. There were also several pumpkins made of wood and painted with all sorts of faces on them, some cute and some scary. The front lawn was an ornamental Halloween wonderland.

'Look at you, what a pretty Dorothy, oh and the slippers, my goodness Caitlin what a great costume."

"Look Nannie, I even have Toto in a basket," as she showed mom her little dog inside the basket.

"Well I have a special treat bag for you" she said to Caitlin as she handed her a jumbo size chocolate bar.

"How are you holding up?" She softly whispered to me.

"I could use another Kit Kat" and smiled only a half-smile as mom handed me a bar and it tasted like heaven. I hugged my mom and said "She needed this night to be so special, thanks for the extra treats." Looking at her ruby slippers I thought *there's no place like home*, as I held back tears.

I pulled into the driveway and together Caitlin and I walked up the front steps, there were only a few candies left n the bowl.

"Cool," she said, and walked passed it into the hallway. Caitlin took off her shoes, and proceeded to dump the rest of her candy onto the floor. She started sorting her candy, one pile for chips, one for gum, and one for chocolate bars. 'Meghan is gonna need candy mom" Caitlin blurted out as she continued the sorting process. In that moment she began a special pile for her sister. I was touched, deeply touched, and I again witnessed that even in her moments that were special to her, Caitlin always thought of her sister and put her sister's needs first. I knew that in my heart as she went from house to house that she too had her sister in the back of her mind. My eyes filled with tears. Tears of a mom blessed with two amazing daughters.

"I am going to fill the bath because you Miss Dorothy, need to wash the makeup off your face and soak your feet.

"Okay mom, lots of bubbles okay? Want some chips?" she replied.

I made this bath extra special, lit a candle. "Enjoy your bubbles; I will be stretched out on my bed so holler if you need anything. Oh, and I grabbed some chips."

"Thanks momma, take whatever you want." Caitlin was chin deep in bubbles and candle light and she loved it.

Chapter 13 – Cherished Hug

We cried together today. I sat with her for hours in her room and offered the best comfort I could for my baby. She knew she was put on more drugs, which included Morphine for pain management. I came closer to her bedside, as close as I could without touching her.

"Hug me mommy," she cried in agony. She didn't have to ask me twice, I knew it was something they didn't encourage, the contact, but my baby desperately needed a hug from her mom, and it was the medicine that only I could provide to help heal her broken heart. I hugged her, a long tender hug, and kissed her sweet bald head. I knew I broke the rules, but the hug is what she needed most, to feel safe in her mom's arms. It was a hug that I will cherish forever, her velvet skin against my lips as I gently kissed her forehead. The smell of her was intoxicating just like the smell of a newborn to its mother. We watched TV, and then Meghan spent some time on her computer.

"I am going to head out now before it's too late, ok sweetie?" I said to her.

"No problemo momma," she replied. "Just be sure to go on MSN when you get to Ronald McDonald House so we can chat, I need to know you are there."

"Absolutely," I said as I kissed her forehead again and headed out. The only thing I had on my mind at that moment was how wonderful it felt to hug and kiss my child. Both Meghan and I needed that reconnect. I arrived at Ronald McDonald house and journaled first before tackling MSN and work.

"Wednesday November 2nd - Day 6.... It was so hard not to cry in her room today. Her hair is completely coming out now. I don't even know what to write tonight. I've emailed so many to pray for Meghan. I just hate seeing her so sick. She has morphine now, is on so many drugs. I need to focus on all the miracles so far and trust God to get her through this. I sure wish

125

I wasn't alone. Time to tuck in and be with God. Nite nite. Oh, Touched by an Angel is on, gonna watch.

Thursday Nov. 3rd – Day 7 - Today Meghan had several fevers, 38.5, - 39.8.c that's 101 – 103.5F, roughly. She had an ultrasound this morning. The results showed no change from the one a few days ago, which is good because the liver has not enlarged anymore. She had a CT scan and Dr. P came to get me with results. Everything looked fine. The posterior pocket of fluid is actually smaller. The front pocket is the same. Kidneys and liver fine, liver still VOD, but responding to the medication. They are increasing one of the meds to help the liver function. The methotrexate has been stopped as it would be very harmful on her liver if she was to continue it. During the CT scan I was praying a lot again and have asked many to pray and keep praying. There is a lot of talks in amongst the parents today about the power of prayer. Leanne has been praying for Meghan, - keep strong baby girl.

I met with some of the other parents in the family lounge tonight for a bit. Sometimes it's good to have some grown up time, and talk about the positives going on with everyone. Leighann and I were both heading back to McDonald House, and it felt so good to talk and walk a bit with another mom. She is praying for Meghan just as I am for Kelli.   Her daughter Kelli is doing real good. I know Meghan looks to her for inspiration, knowing that she will pull through her tough times too. We all hang on to a common thread through all of this, each and every one of us hangs on to hope, and to faith, and to the power of prayer.   I have added all the kids to my prayer list and Meghan is added to theirs. We have become the BMT family, bone marrow transplant family.

I sometimes feel so very alone in all of this. Gerry has Lanette, she is our alternative person. We had to select a third person that would be allowed in Meghan's room, and Lanette being her step mom was the obvious choice. I still feel very alone. I am here alone with my thoughts, and I am alone at Ronald McDonald House alone at night. I just want my baby home, and to have everything back to what should be normal. I don't want to live in the hospital world any longer. "Oh God help me," I silently prayed as Leanne and I walked to RMH."

Friday morning, and I was glad Friday had arrived. I loved the cool morning walks from RMH though, they would give me time to pray as I pounded the pavement, step by step making my way down the busy street and into the hospital.

"Good morning peanut," I greeted Meghan as she was already up and sat at her computer deep in conversation with her peeps on MSN.

"Meh," was her grunt greeting for me.

"Are you okay?" I asked.

"Probably not mom, I am in the hospital, and um I am bald, and look like a freak I am sure, and I feel crappy today" was her answer.

"Well your attitude is a typical teenager at least," I said. "Sorry you are feeling like crap." We didn't have much to say, but she knew I felt bad.

"Sorry mom," she said.

"Meghan you never ever have to be sorry or say sorry to me, not for any of this, okay?" I reminded her in a soft voice.

"Your dad is coming soon, probably near lunchtime" I reminded her.

"Mom, he likes to wander, he doesn't stay in here much, but that's just dad," she mumbled.

"It's hard for him to see you like this sweetie, but he is here, and if you want him to stay in the room with you he will, I will talk to him."

127

I met Gerry at around lunchtime in the family lounge at the locker where we kept our coats and backpack and whatnot. "She is in a bit of a funky mood."

"Oh, why is that" he asked.

"Gee let me think, she is bald from head to toe, has no friends to hang out with, can't eat what she wants, is terrified of what is going on, and feels ugly at 16," as the words came out I sounded the same as Meghan did to me just moments ago.

"Sorry I asked" he sarcastically replied.

"No I am the one who is sorry, I just am grateful you are here, and please stay with her a while, she mentioned to me that you wander."

"Ok, I will stay in the room longer, but sometimes she is on the computer with her friends and I just sit there, so I go for a walk and talk with parents or doctors," he said as he let out a heavy sigh.

"I know it's hard to see her, but even if she acts like she doesn't want you there, trust me she does, she hates to be alone." I gave him a friendly hug, and headed to the elevators.

Freedom, I felt guilty, but I felt liberated. Randy was waiting out front of the hospital for me. The ride home was welcomed yet I was exhausted and moody.

"Hi honey, how is she doing?" Randy asked. I felt the tears build up, pool and then roll down my cheeks.

"She is holding on, and being brave, but I know she hates it all, and so do I" I replied. "Can we just not talk about it all for a bit, let me get myself composed and later we can talk, I am just exhausted from the past couple of days?"

"Yes sweetie," was his only reply. I seemed to hear it a lot and didn't know if it was just his way of brushing things off or if he just felt as lost as I did and had no words.

"Let's just get home," is all I said, "I just want to be home with Caitlin."

I wasn't home for very long when the phone rang. "Hello?" I answered.

"Hi, Ang, its me." I recognized it to be Gerry, and immediately I replied even before he could finish saying me.

"What's wrong, what happened?"

Gerry began to tell me "I was in the cafeteria because they were going to give Meghan a bath, so I left her room."

"And!" I demanded.

"Well I heard them calling code blue for the 8th floor, I just dropped everything and ran, I knew it was Meghan," his voice shook with every word like an earthquake. "I just knew it was her that they called it for, I ran and literally dropped my food and everything, I was so scared."

"Gerry, please" I screamed on the phone expecting the worst and before I could finish my cry he reassured me that Meghan was okay and that everything was fine. "What happened? She was fine when I left, well as fine as she could be what the hell happened" I inquired as we continued to talk.

"She blacked out and it was apparently because of her blood pressure being too low."

"I want to know more, tell me everything." Gerry filled me in on most of the details and this time I felt his worry. I could picture him as he frantically ran up to the eighth floor. He didn't even take the elevator because he couldn't wait. I imagined him as he heard the code blue announced for the 8th floor in Meghan's wing and the panic that must have hit him to drop everything and run. When he got to her room, he told me that he could barely see her as she came too; there were so many doctors and nurses in her room. Just outside was Rick and Leanne, and they were able to give Gerry comfort and support that he needed.

"All I could think of," he said to me, "was knowing how frightened she would be and she would need to see my face, so I ran all the way up to her room."

"I am glad you were there for her" I said to him, "she needs you too you know, this little girl of ours needs her daddy."

"When she looked at me and our eyes met I smiled at her and waved and she knew it would be okay and then I fell apart with Rick and Leanne" he informed me as I could still hear the tremble in his voice.

"I am glad they were there for you, they must have been terrified also," I said as I tried my best to comfort him.

"They have never experienced a code blue and they were so frightened, they didn't know if you had left yet and Leanne was so scared you would come here to some bad news."

"It's all okay now, right?" I was feeling that nothing truly was okay.

"Yes, she is okay, it was a fainting spell that lasted about 30 seconds, but she is fine."   He continued to fill me in on what the doctors had planned on doing now. Meghan was given Potassium and was put on a heart monitor. She needed to increase her fluid intake also and I believe a bolus of IV fluids was ordered for her. It's a tricky situation, because with the VOD the fluid intake has to be monitored and limited and with the low blood pressure she needs fluids to keep her stable. Thank God she was in the best place right now with everything going on. I was happy that Rick and Leanne were there for Gerry. Meghan felt the strength of her father as their eyes met in the crowd and her dad felt the strength of two wonderful friends. We will all get through this one day at a time.

"God will strengthen you with his own great power so that you will not give up when troubles come. " Colossians 1:11-12"

Sunday November 6 – Day 10
".... Talked to Brook at 8:30 this morning – Meghan still has her fevers and her B.P. went to 80/44 during the night.

She was given a bolus and it came up to 110/70, which is good.   They need her to get rid of fluid – The liver counts are coming down also, which is good. Brook assured me and said they see this sorta stuff all the time and some get it worse than others.   Meghan is just going through a very rough patch. Today is day 10 – when engrafting can start. A sign of it is having the white cells come up. Her count today was 0.4. It has been 0.1 for days so maybe it's a turning point & things will get better from now on. I spoke to Gerry . He was asking how I felt because he knew that I have been around Zoe, Randy's daughter, who has been sick. Gerry said we have to take all precautions and that he can stay at the hospital, I just have to let him know. He is going to talk to Meghan's nurse, Brook, and I will also. I just feel so terrible not being there to see Meghan, but I don't want to run the risk of her getting exposed to anything. Maybe this time he is right. I know I am feeling lousy now, and also did last night. A bit lightheaded and upset stomach. I will talk to Brook later and let Gerry know what I plan on doing. Maybe it's God's will I stay home and away from the hospital. Being so upset about not going to the hospital, and knowing that Meghan was still in a very bad state, I just broke down. Randy took my face into his hands and said "This could be the turning point, maybe she will go to the bottom to rise to the top." I felt like God himself was giving me these words. Maybe this man was brought into my life at this time for the sole purpose of helping me with all of this.   --- a time and purpose for everything under heaven. Ecclesiastes

I spent some time with Caitlin today up at 5 Star ranch. Its pouring rain outside, and I am sitting in my car as she tacks up the pony for her ride. The amount of rain pouring down feels like heaven is crying with me. Somehow I don't feel so alone and frightened. I need to let go of a lot of things. One thing, for sure, is the anger that sometimes builds up because I often feel so alone in all of this. It's a good thing that Gerry offered to spend time with Meghan while I am a bit under the weather. I need to let go a bit with some of my issues.

It's just so hard. I have been raising my girls alone since they were 8 and 4. Every moment of my life has been to have them in my loving care and make sure they were safe. Now I am in this situation that I can't control or fix. How do I really let go of it? Boy do I need to spend some time in prayer. I think I need a trip up to the cemetery to spend time alone with dad. Even though I can't physically be with him, his spirit is with me always.

Tonight I spent in prayer, and cuddle time with Caitlin. I feel a sense of relax over me and I know this feeling. It is answered prayers/prayers being sent to heaven. Thank you God, thank you friends, thank you family, thank you strangers. To all who have prayed, who are praying, I thank you. Always and forever.

Brook was still the nurse on duty covering Meghan. I was so relieved to speak with her this morning. "Great news," she said, "Meghan has had an excellent night. No fevers for 24 hours, and her blood pressure has remained constant at 126/70. The GVHD rash looks good, we are happy with the rash." How odd does that sound, that they are "happy" with the rash.

What it means is that engrafting is taking place. They look for signs that the body is trying to reject the marrow, because that actually means its accepting it or at least attempting to. Being that it is a slight GVHD rash, it shows them that her body is not rejecting the transplant thus far, and that counts are starting to come up. Her stomach girth (measurement) has also gone down by 1.5 cm. It seems so odd to speak this medical language. When in my life would I use the word girth either spoken or written. Odd.

I believe in answered prayers, and I believe we have hit the turning point. Joy in my heart has replaced the fear from only just a day ago. My prayer today. Dear Sweet Jesus. Let the healing continue. Touch her, cleanse her and heal her from head to toe. Please the Lord in Jesus name I pray, AMEN.

Step down; well it's actually a step up. It's the point when you are moved out of extreme isolation, back into a room where

132

there isn't a glass wall separating you from the rest of the world. It should be a time of excitement, yet Meghan was terrified. She became withdrawn, and wouldn't talk to anyone. It's almost like she lost all hope and have given up. "Whats bothering you," I asked her. "Just a lot of things momma, what if I faint again," in a tone of quiet fear she spoke the words softly. "You are still getting the best care ever, it's because you are getting stronger and better that they are moving you, it's a good thing." I held her hand all day, just like when she was a little girl heading off to school and didn't want to break away from me, she held my hand tightly back, all day long we stayed connected. She wanted me to stay in her room with her tonight, and it broke my heart to have to be strong. "You will be fine Meghan; they encourage you to be on your own." I will be just up the street at Ronald McDonald House, we can chat, and I can stay until 10pm. I knew that I could stay if I decided to, there was a place for me to lay beside her, but I knew that she needed to know she would be OK. Oh God let her be OK, was my prayer as I headed off to the circus room at McDonald house. "Meghan, I will leave my cell phone on all night, and leave it beside me, so you can text me, or call me any time at all, OK." This made her feel a little better.

November 10, 2006 - God hear my prayers, Please , Please give Meghan a good night's rest. Send angels to bring her peace. Please in your Son's name I pray that she have sweet heavenly dreams, and peace and calm in her heart. Hear her prayers Lord Jesus, let her sleep restfully, in Jesus' name I pray, AMEN

Friday November 11, 2006 - Day 15- Remembrance Day

Right now it's 11:11 on the 11th, what a time to journal. Today Meghan was still very very emotional. Not wanting to get up and crying a lot. Two days of this was too much. She needed to get it out and others saw it too. A psychiatrist came to talk with her – It was good, she cried and got some things off her chest. The doctor was very impressed with Meghan's strength and how she and I were so close. She was apparently very impressed by me and my relationship with Meghan and that we pray.

Meghan was in a deep place of despair, neither the psychiatrist nor I had any idea of just what was bothering her until she finally let it out.

"Mom, in the isolation room they don't have any mirrors" her voice was shaky. "I am afraid to look into a mirror." Simultaneously the tears built up in both the doctor's eyes and mine. I reached for her hand. "Meghan when you are ready we will face the mirror together, I won't let you face this alone I promise." She squeezed my hand and I brought it to my lips. "I promise my sweets, never alone" and kissed her hand.

"It's amazing to witness such love and support between mother and daughter. Meghan you are a very lucky girl to have a mom who cares so much and loves you so much." Tears pooled in her eyes and I was touched. "I will leave the two of you alone to talk and Meghan please know that I am here for you also." She gently touched Meghan's shoulder and left the room.

"Can we do it now mom, can you help me with a bath and then stay with me while I look in the mirror?"

"If you feel you are ready, yes I can and will, I promise I won't leave you".

I filled the bath for Meghan while she remained in her room. We were able to add a packet of oatmeal bath to the water to keep her skin feeling soft. When I went back to her bedroom area I saw her sitting on the edge of the bed, her head was down and her feet were swinging back and forth like a pendulum. For a moment my mind went back to that very first day in McMaster where she had that very same fearful look while she stared at her feet, back and forth, back and forth. My mind seemed to swing as much as her feet did.

"It's all ready and I will draw the curtain so that you can't see the mirror until you are ready okay?"

"Okay, thanks mom." She gathered her robe and new pajamas to put on after her bath, slipped on her slippers and shuffled her way into the bathroom. As I helped her into the tub I made sure that she could not get a glimpse of the mirror and had a sheet taped over it in case she changed her mind.

"Mom this feels nice to just soak in a tub, thank you so much for always being here for me."

"It's the only place for me, by your side always. I told you I am not leaving you alone in this."

"My skin looks so weird with no hair mom, it's strange to see it, but it feels soft. I know I am looking at myself, but until I actually look in a mirror at the whole me it's just not the same thing, know what I mean?"

"I do honey."

"Okay, I think I am ready to get out", and with a deep sigh she continued "Let's get this over with."

I stood in front of her with a towel stretched open for her to climb into. Her back was still to the mirror and we were moments closer to her confronting a fear that had paralyzed her for days. With her back to me I held open her robe and she gently put her arms in. Wrapping my arms around her also I whispered. "Just let me know when you are ready and I will step out of your way."

"No mom, just turn around with me, don't let me go, okay?" We both had tears and slowly we turned around together. I quickly pulled the taped sheet off the mirror. Meghan's legs gave way and she just sank into my arms and sobbed.

"Oh my God mom, oh my God" and she wept and wept.

I didn't have words because there weren't any. Nothing could bring comfort in this moment she needed to just feel what she had to feel.

November 12, 2006 – Day 16 - Today was very emotional and very incredible. Meghan still cried a lot, but it was good for her. She ate well also. Her counts are great and she is healing very well. Tonight was pasta night also. Randy met me in the family lounge at about 3:30 - Meghan wasn't ready to see anyone yet, so she didn't come out into the lounge to see him. I know this saddened him, but I also knew his heart and he would understand.

My church youth group, namely Kate, a wonderful young woman, have put together a "Pasta Night" fundraiser dinner for Meghan's needs. We left for our night of fun and fundraising. It was so much fun, and incredibly supportive of everyone who was involved. The church was full, and overfull. There was a silent auction to help raise money. My family was there, and also Uncle Vincent. People lined up to be seated for their pasta dinner. Jamie and Stacey also came, and I was shocked when Jamie handed me some money. What an incredible friend to help me so much, he is very special. We couldn't stay too long, but I did thank everyone for all they were doing, and that their love and support, and their continued prayers are never forgotten. I will keep them all in my heart and prayers always through this journey.

We got back to the hospital at about 8pm. I called Meghan twice while we were on our way, and she was so teary eyed. I just hate being away from her, I am so torn at times as to what to think, say or do. Randy and I both went back to Ronald McDonald house, and I think I just collapsed in his arms and fell asleep. "

While I was back at the hospital today, my family had all pulled together to give my home an extreme home makeover. You see, we were given a list of things that needed to be done in my home from Sick Kid's Hospital in order for Meghan to be released. I think of it as a hug for my home. I cry just thinking of it; newly painted rooms, a new bed for Meghan, the ducts cleaned, carpets steamed, floors washed, laundry done, dishwasher installed, my car detailed, special filters on the furnace, all stuffed toys and bedding in her room

136

removed, windows cleaned. The list was endless, and it was all being taken care of by some amazing people who I loved dearly. God bless them all.

My shift at the hospital was done. It's 1:00 pm, and Gerry was here to take over. I was heading home to spend time with Caitlin. We scheduled some horseback time up at 5-star ranch with Becky, Ronni's sister. We arrived to a very cold barn, snow had fallen and the roads were a bit slippery and it would not be getting any better. I parked where I could easily pull out when we had to leave. Caitlin tacked up her horse and I sat on the bleachers with a few other moms. One of the moms asked if Caitlin had any brothers or sisters. I took a deep breath and then a bit of the story came out.

"Yes she does, an older sister, who is in Sick Kids hospital right now, but hopefully coming home soon." The guilt I felt as I told them of Meghan ate me up while I sat and sipped some hot chocolate. I felt that my place wasn't at a barn and that I should be at the hospital; then I watched Caitlin ride, and it was all put into perspective. She needed me as much as Meghan did and this time was precious to her. "Her father is there with her now, so that I could spend some time with Caitlin," I replied. I then got into the whole explanation of how we took turns, and how it allowed us to both have time with our own families. Through tear filled eyes and crackling voices I could hear the understanding in these women. They could feel my pain, my turmoil and my strength, because at that moment, the only place I needed to be was right where I was – sitting in a freezing cold riding arena, sipping hot chocolate and watching Caitlin have just a few hours of pure enjoyment with her horse. After her riding lesson, we took a little drive, and had her favorite McDonalds for dinner. It was a quiet night at home, in my own bed, with Caitlin cuddling me. The house was almost ready, just a few more things to do, and some dusting and vacuuming.

Meghan had a day pass with her dad today. I suppose it was a way of slowly getting her back out and about before her actual discharge day happens. I was so surprised when I saw them pull up into the driveway.

"Just out for a drive with our girl", Gerry said to me as he rolled down the window. "Oh, and we also need another warmer coat for her to go home with, the weather is much colder now than when she was admitted" he added.

"Oh, good plan, thanks for thinking of that", I answered. "Hang on I will get her some better shoes also". I added.

"Thanks Ang, she looks good, eh?, She's off of all her IV medications now too". We both smiled at each other, "yes she does, and looks like she will be home soon".

Meghan reached her hand out to me as she cried. "Mom, I can't come in, because I'm not home yet." I understood, she wanted to be home and not have to go back to the hospital before she came in. Meghan knew that she would have a new surprise room decorated for her by her Aunt Karen. It was so hard to see her as she sat in his car and not having her come home. I just wanted to put my arms around her and never let her go. I did understand that she didn't want to have to come in the house and leave, so I just let her make the decision to stay put in the car. Her discharge day would come very soon and that moment would be so wonderful for her. I let her decide how she wanted her visit right now to be and all she wanted to do was drive by and see her home and then spend time with her dad as they drove about, so that is what they did, we chatted by the car for a bit and then they headed back to the hospital.

Would this day ever arrive? I had hoped and prayed for it for so long and now the day was finally here, discharge day. We have had discharge days before but this one was different Meghan was coming home today with a new beginning.

I stayed home to meet with the nurse who came to the house and go over all the medications with her that Meghan had to take. Gerry would bring Meghan home from the hospital. Meghan would require an IV bolus for hydration for a little while each evening. While I talked with the nurse my insides felt as if they were about to burst; all I could think of was Meghan coming home any moment.

"I'm sorry if I am not all together here," I said to her.

"Understandable, and no need to apologize, I will come back this evening to hook up her IV" she replied. Soon after she left

138

Meghan and Gerry arrived. It was mid-morning when Gerry pulled into the driveway and Meghan was home at last. My heart raced with joy and I wanted to run over to her, but I let her take that first step. She stepped out of the light green Ford Focus wagon, with help from her Dad and her smile said it all. She had on her favorite pajama pants, pink shades in a plaid pattern. She also wore her black fleece lined black hooded jacket with a new pink hat. *Pretty in pink* I thought. Meghan spent the day just relaxing; we were home, the three of us, our family and it all felt amazing. We watched movies, cooked and ate as a family.

"Look Mom, they have the same bead program at Sick Kids" she said as she took a strand of beads off her neck and handed it to me.

"Can you put these with my other ones? It's not as pretty and I didn't collect all of them, I just wanted to come home."

"Oh, I didn't know they had the bravery bead program there also." I replied as I took the strand from her and went to hang it on the tall lamp with the other strands. "Wow, Meghan you realize that you have five beaded necklaces now," the lump in my throat just sat there as it absorbed tears and choked me with so much emotion I was overwhelmed.

Nannie came over and watched Meghan while I took Caitlin for another horseback riding lesson. I knew mom wanted some time alone with Meghan to spoil her rotten and pamper her; after all it had been many weeks since she had been able to see her sweet granddaughter. Nannie and Meghan were so cute to watch together.

Five Star Ranch was only minutes away from our home and I knew that Meghan would be fine with mom. Also, these lessons and this riding time was important to Caitlin. Today she rode a horse called Faith. How cool was that?

It's a very strange feeling to get the local newspaper and to find that on the front cover is a picture of your daughter and her story. It sent chills through me to have read this article and to have it sink in deeper into my soul that the words, the events, the treatments, the suffering, the hope, the everything; it was all about my daughter, and it was all very real. The article spoke of hope, of the love and generosity that so many have shown through this journey. I suppose the best way would to simply put in here the whole article, and have it hit your heart, just as it hit mine.

"December 2, 2005   *Teen battles rare disease*

What began as flu symptoms for 16-year-old Meghan Rush in March turned out to be a life-threatening illness called Hemophagocytic Lymphohistiocytosis or HLH.

As a result, the past eight months have turned the Rush family's life upside down. A bit of cheer, especially at this time of year, is hoped to help in more ways than one. This Saturday, December 3, a fundraising dance is being held in Meghan's honor. Meghan's illness is a 13-syllable word that describes a rare blood disorder. The exact cause of HLH is unknown but it's believed that infection fighting cells called histiocytes, which are supposed to travel through the body destroying foreign material and infections, go haywire overproducing and causing damage to bone marrow, the lymph nodes, liver, spleen and brain.

As a result, the M.M. Robinson student has faced a barrage of treatments, including 40 blood transfusions, countless steroids and medications, more than 25 rounds of chemotherapy, two stays in the intensive care unit, a lumbar puncture and finally, and bone marrow transplant on Oct. 27.

"We've all been run ragged throughout all of this," said her mom, Angela.
Especially Meghan. The teenager can't go to the mall or movie theatre because public places could wreak havoc on her weakened immune system. Instead, Meghan's friends come to her home. However, it means she can't even attend this Saturday's benefit being organized in her honor.

"The outpouring of support we've received is wonderful," said Meghan's dad, Gerry. Gerry's coworker put together this

Saturday's fundraising and morale-boosting party. It's her way of "paying it forward."

The picture of Meghan in the paper, with her pink angora hat, was heartbreaking. She wore her bravery beads and held her teddy bear that she named Saint, which was given to her by my friend from church Saint Claire. Her face was all puffed out and pudgy from the steroids. When her friends would see this, they would be shocked; she did not look like the Meghan that they would have remembered.

I woke up not even wanting to think of or consider going to a dance. I didn't want to leave Meghan home, but I needed to make an appearance at least. So many people were supposed to be there to show their support. All of Randy's family, my family and friends, and friends of friends, probably some complete strangers, and it was for Meghan, to help with the cost of so many things, and to give Meghan a special gift. I told Meghan that all this is for her that she is to do whatever she wants with the money. We truly didn't need any of it, and the whole idea was incredible, but what touched me more was the way everyone pulled together, the way a perfect stranger showed up at my door with a small TV because he thought that she might need one in her bedroom.

She wasn't just my Meghan anymore, she had become everyone's Meghan, and I decided that I would continue to let the paper know of her progress through this very personal journey.

The dance was a huge success. So many friends and family offered support. There was a long table full of prizes that were being put up for a silent auction. Everything from gift certificates to stores and restaurants to jewelry and even some furniture were up for auction.

Mair, a co-worker of Gerry's, was in charge of this event and the love and support she had shown both Gerry and myself was incredible. We danced and I watched as so many had a wonderful time.

We were now on Day 45 of the 100 day count. It was quite cold on this 45th day, a Monday morning, December 12, 2005. Gerry was on his way over to pick up Meghan and take her to her clinic appointment at McMaster; she went twice a week for blood counts, and urine tests. When my phone rang mid-morning, my heart jumped into my throat.

Gerry's cell phone, oh God, no not again, I thought. *This can't be good if he is calling me, he never does, and they should have been back by now.* I picked up the receiver,

"Hi Ang, her urine test showed blood in the urine and she is also retaining too much fluid, so they are admitting her for a couple of days. Dr. Meado said it was fine tuning that they were doing. Her kidney functions appear normal, no albumin," he continued to talk as I cut in.

"So the liver is Okay?" I asked, "No VOD recurring?"

"I was told that her last pee was good, they are measuring it and fluid is coming off nicely." He replied.

I went back to the hospital and I walked into her room in 3B with a heavy weight within my heart. I felt the nurses look at me and I felt like I was going to break down. We had just come home from Sick Kids in Toronto, and now we were back here at McMaster.

"This is all normal" Sonia said to me, "When a kid comes back from transplant there are always a few things to sort out and deal with. She will be fine; it's just "fine tuning" as Dr. Meado said. I could tell by the look on Meghan's face that she was terrified.

She did not want to be here, "things are going to go crazy ass bad again" she said with a tremble in her voice.

"No they won't" I assured her. "You are getting some meds to help get rid of the fluids, and they are going to watch your blood in the urine and your counts are down a bit, but it will get better, it's all good." Deep down my spirit was praying, "Oh God, please let everything be okay."

"Mommy, I know you never do, but can you?" she pleaded

"Yes" I said, "Yes, I will stay here tonight with you." I knew that Caitlin would understand, she could have a sleepover with Nannie. I just knew that I had to stay, I too was worried deep inside to leave her here with the fear that I could see in her eyes.

"Oh thank you mommy, thank you." We hugged long and hard. We woke up fairly early, Meghan was so relieved to know I was there the whole night, and mine was the face she saw first thing in the morning. "Mom, the scariest thing about hospitals is that it's always a different face, and no one tells me anything, and I feel so lost and scared. I don't know what is going on" she said to me.

"Whenever you are afraid just pray Meghan, pray pray and pray; that's what I do" I reminded her. And of course pray was what I did last night. "Please God, just a little up; just a little up was my prayer. Please dear God, just a little up."

"Wednesday December 14, 2005 - Praise God, her counts have gone up. I prayed and prayed, God just a little up. Please just a little up to let me know that marrow is still growing. Her whites went from 3.1 to 3.5. Great little up, thanks God."

Being that it's about 10 days before Christmas, there were a lot of things going on at McMaster for the kids. There were some sport celebrities who came in and had goodies for the kids. Sears had brought some stuffed toys; the OPP also had gifts for the children. Meghan was doing her best to enjoy it all but she was after all in the hospital and not home where she belonged and longed to be. However she did love getting gifts. What girl didn't like gifts? Especially stuffed animals. The Hamilton Bulldogs hockey team, came in and gave the kids stuffed bulldog toys; very cute and kind.

Today we were now at the halfway point, day 50, December 15th, 2005, and we were discharged to go home today. I couldn't believe it, 10 days until Christmas and I would have my daughters both with me. I had so much to still get ready for this Christmas at home. I had a few ideas about gifts, and the food would be incredible, so I was glad to have a weekend to get some of the shopping done and the planning. Caitlin and Meghan would go to their dads together this weekend and then I would have them home Sunday night, and then clinic day on Monday.

It's Christmas Eve and it's a quiet time at home with just my mom over. It has turned out to be a very emotional night, not just because of the obvious, that it was Christmas and we are home celebrating, but sadness, frustration and upset have all come to surface with Meghan. I knew that one day everything she had been through would eventually come out it was just way too much on her gentle soul and tonight was the night. I had very few words to sooth her frustrated broken and fearful heart, what exactly can be said with all that she felt. She had thoughts of back to when it was a normal life for her, when she could wear pretty clothes and not worry about her stretch marks. She thought back to when she had long hair and could wear it up or down and put on a party dress and go out. "Remember the winter formal mom, when Courtney and I went and got our hair done and went in the limo? No use putting me in a dress now, or even think about having a date. I'm hideous mom, just hideous. I'm fed up, it's not fair."

I didn't know what to say, tears just flowed. I opened my mouth to try to let something out and I was speechless. I had no words of comfort for my baby.

Nannie stepped in, "no more talk of this stuff, we have presents to open, and a lot to be thankful for." Meghan dare not say anything to Nannie, because it's not often that mom speaks up like that.

"Ya Meghan cry another day, tonight we get presents and its Jesus' birthday too, so maybe cake tomorrow," Caitlin added as she cuddled up to her sister. "You open the first gift okay?" Caitlin said so sweetly and I felt some of the sadness lift.

We had a very yummy dinner, a small turkey for four, stuffing, carrots, mashed potatoes, and apple pie for desert, and chocolate, lots of chocolate.

After dinner, Reverend Sue came over to give us a little home Christmas Eve service and communion. First she stopped in the front hallway and used the hand sanitizer in the wash station that we had set up. Anyone who came in had to do the same and I was strict about it for sure. It wasn't the same as going to church, but with her weakened immune system, Meghan still could not venture out. My head was in a million places. I had a fiancé, who seemed to be drifting away from me. Randy was home with his girls and I missed how this Christmas was supposed to have been. Meghan missed how things use to be with her friends. I knew her friends loved her and it was their fear and sadness of having to watch Meghan this way that sometimes kept them away. Still, it was hard to explain to Meghan that her friends were likely scared and not sure how to act around her with her illness. I didn't want Meghan to feel any more different than she already did.

"Meghan, everyone acts the way they do and we can't change it, we can only change what we can and how we act" I tried to explain to her.

"Oh I get it, like that Serenity Prayer that I have posted on my computer desk. Cool, I get it now." The wonderful Serenity Prayer, she loved it, and now it was God's way of helping her understand behavior. .

My mind wandered also to thoughts about dad and how much I missed him. He was always the center of our Christmas and would be the one to hand out gifts, carve the turkey, and say grace. Mom must have felt his loss so deep they were so incredible together and I knew she wished he were here with us this Christmas Eve, but I felt his strength from heaven above. I took a deep breath; it was our Christmas Eve here at home, just the four of us. Tomorrow, both of the girls would go to their dad's for the next five days, so when the clock would strike 10:00 a.m. tomorrow morning, Christmas Day, I would be left alone. I have felt that knot every year for the past eight years; it was how we did things on Christmas Day. It was our normal arrangement. This was a mixed up feeling I had for sure, in a strange way I welcomed that knot because it represented normal, and at the same time I did not look forward to it at all, "Have courage and be strong" I told myself.

It was Christmas morning, Happy Birthday Jesus, and thank you God for my many blessings. Oh what a mess my eyes were this morning. I didn't even attempt to dry the tears because they just kept flowing like a river. My girls were still with me and to see the joy on their faces as they opened their gifts was something I needed so badly. I gave Meghan a camera as her main gift as she wanted to start scrapbooking and take pictures. Caitlin's gifts had a theme, they were all about horses. The pile of gifts seemed to just multiply. I know I

145

may have gone overboard, but it was an absolute blast to spoil them just a little.

Gerry would arrive at about 11 now which would give me an extra hour with my sweet girls. They were all packed and ready to go, we had our gift opening and now the house looked like a disaster, and that dreaded moment had arrived, I was alone.   This year was different, there were times that I didn't even know if we would have Meghan here for Christmas and we still had a long way to go as we were only at day 61. So much could still go wrong up until day 100.

"Don't let her be around anyone sick" were my last words to him.   Gerry just looked at me, I'm not even sure what the look meant, but I got the message. Of course he wouldn't let anyone that was sick be around her and I felt foolish for even having said it right after the words rolled off my tongue. Yes, I knew he would take care of her, but deep down the worry didn't subside in, me after all I was her mom.

I left the mess for a while, went upstairs and filled the bath. The girls had given me some new bubble bath, as they knew how addicted to bubble baths I was. So I filled the tub with the lavender scented bubbles and watched as they multiplied under the running water. The fragrance made me think of spring, and I soaked away my sadness if only for a short while. I cried a lot and prayed even more. Praying in the tub was something I did often, odd, maybe, but it was the most private place that I could pray. I could just let everything go, and give Him all my fears and worries, my thoughts and feelings.

So I began, "Lord, help me," seemed to be what came out first, and then I cried. "I don't think I can do this, I am so scared every day, Lord please hold me and help me." I missed my girls so much my heart ached, so I just soaked and cried for what seemed hours. I even remembered letting some water out so that I could add more hot and refresh the soak.

Chapter 14 – Timing

A new year and a new beginning, in more ways than one. Meghan had a fresh start with new bone marrow and a new life. Her strength had improved a great deal and she was finally able to get upstairs to her room at night. She had been sleeping on the bed that we had set up in the living room, but knew it would only be temporary until she was able to get upstairs on her own and now that time had arrived. Each and every day we would work on the stairs a bit at a time, so that her strength would build up and enable her to climb them to bed at night.

January 5, 2006   Day 72 - Boy you would think that I never worked or had a job because I never seem to write about it, or even think about it, but I do. I work as an advertising sales rep for a wonderful company. My boss has been amazing, and having a satellite office I have been able to call my laptop my office, and take it wherever I go. I worked from Sick Kids, Ronald McDonald House, and McMaster, even a coffee shop, or a friend's home. I really need to spend some time focusing on work, and get back on track. So, today I decided to accept an offer from a friend of my sister's. Her name is Jane, and she is my new cleaning lady. I feel real embarrassed having a cleaning lady, but I decided that the most important thing is a clean house for Meghan. I can't devote the time to it, so I have hired her. House work and I don't get along that well, I do what needs to be done, but have never liked it. I thank you Jesus, for the blessing of a cleaning lady. Boy does that sound like an odd prayer.

January 24, 2006, Day 92 - Today we had the 3 month follow up at Sick Kids. Gerry drove all of us in, well Randy, Meghan, and myself. Meghan was very nervous, but I feel she had a good visit.   A lot of positive came from it.   We are decreasing the Ovral (birth control pill) down to one a day, and also her Norvasc (blood pressure pills), they will go down to 10 mg. In three months she could be off everything.

Meghan had a PFT (pulmonary function test), and also a CT scan of the chest. I prayed again during the CT scan. It was the same room that Jesus touched her in before. I felt his presence again. We go back again in 3 months on April 26th, 2006. Well it's late and time for bed. More tomorrow, goodnight.

January 27, 2006,   Day 95 - Anna called and let me know that Meghan had won, or should I say was chosen, for the "Help a Child Smile" trip to Florida.

There are 2 foundations – this one and the Make a Wish Foundation. In order for her to apply to Make a Wish, she has to be selected for this one first. So, we are going to Florida. Not sure when, it could be months from now, but we have been selected to go.

January 30, 2006, Day 99 - Today at clinic was a very different and difficult day. Counts were great. Platelets 123, Reds 82, and whites 11.1

The liver function had improved with coming off the pill (Ovral) – the ultrasounds were good, no changes. Everything looks good.   Yet I am so strained from a piece of news. Nodules on the right lung, is it fungus, is it a histio cluster, or nothing. A biopsy in about a week will tell us.

Dear God, hear the deep cry of my heart even in the silent moments, Lord please keep healing Meghan, Please no HLH. --- amen

Does it ever end. Oh Meghan, I love you, hang in sweetie never give up always believe. Why do I go to the worst case scenario and live in it in my mind? Its most likely fungal or *nothing, but I fear the worst and wish I could shake it. There are no other signs, everything looks good, yet I am afraid.*

Dear Lord—

Help me to be strong when I feel so lifeless – put wind in my sails of my sinking ship and set us all on our healing journey. "

We passed Day 100, the day that was supposed the turning point to let us know that the marrow has grafted and was now in full growth mode. What a relief to hit that turning point and yet there were still issues, Meghan was with her dad over the weekend and he would take her to clinic on Monday morning. She had a cough, and both Caitlin and I have a flu bug, so I am a bit worried. I had hoped that when we hit this point in the journey that smooth sailing would develop, but it didn't seem to be the case. Why did it feel like it was one nightmare after the next. I worried about Meghan every waking moment.

I got a call from Gerry, Meghan was being admitted as she apparently has pneumonia. *Does it ever end,* was what went through my mind. *Seriously, when does all this hell end for my poor sweet girl?* Part of me wasn't surprised, it was best that she was in hospital if she was fighting something hard. I can only imagine how she felt she has had more than a lifetime's share of hospital admissions, tests, and everything. She just wanted to be like every other teenage girl, this was too much for anyone. I was so grateful for computers and technology because when I couldn't be there physically, I could hook up to the internet and voila, instant communication. Meghan and I chatted via MSN, and I felt closer in some strange way even though I couldn't physically be there to help her, I could at least stay on top of things through the wonders of MSN.

Tuesday Feb 7, Day 107 - Today mom stayed with Meghan all day and she is staying tonight also. The ward says NO NO to anyone who has a cold sore or virus, so I pretty much am staying away. Meghan's counts are a bit down, but that would be because they take it from the line and not a finger poke. I worry about the HLH since Dr. Meado said the cluster could be that. Oh, I think I forgot to mention that they found a cluster in her lung, and were going to biopsy it. Well, I sorta wish he never even said that. Why is it that I try to diagnose her myself – I take on so much worry.

I am taking some time to get my head on straight. I've been searching and praying first that the HLH not be there and maybe this is God answering those prayers. That they are finding out about any infections and fungals. The CT scan will show us if anything has changed. Maybe they are looking more at the fluid pneumonia now than anything else.

Ronni is picking up my mom tomorrow morning. Hopefully she can come back later in the week. I am scared to go up there, frightened to hear bad news.

I wish my dad was here to give me a hug and hold me. I feel so alone in all of this. I wish he was here for mom also, I know she could surely use one of his famous hugs.

I pray, Dear Jesus, Please be with my babies. Have angels watch over them. Please Jesus touch Meghan and heal her. Use the doctors and medicine, use the nurses, give them loving hands, healing wisdom and tenderness of heart. Jesus please hear the prayers of so many to heal my Meghan, your child. I so badly need you. Love and Amen, I ask all in Christ's name, love Angela, your daughter.

Well my cold sore turned into a full blown cold virus and now Caitlin was also coughing. Why, why why, when Meghan was about to

150

have surgery why did I have to get sick? I can't even be there, but it allowed others to be with her.

Meghan's surgery was scheduled for somewhere between 8 and 10 p.m. They were to take the cluster from the lung to see what exactly it was. Meghan would be admitted into ICU after the surgery for a couple of days, just as precaution. I wasn't sure if there were things that I wasn't being told, but then they couldn't keep things from me as I was her mom; yet my mind created scenarios all the time. What if quite often was followed by some crazy notion that my mind would create. I was trapped in this constant turmoil of fear and anxiety and I needed out. It was all just precaution they all assured me. I just hated not being there and having to hear things second hand. How was a mom supposed to relax when her child was going in for surgery, and she couldn't even be in the hospital? It tore me up inside, and then I would see my little Caitlin trying hard to fight a cold, trying to be brave and coughing so hard. I needed to shift focus, leave Meghan in the hands of the Lord and all those tending to her and take care of myself and Caitlin. I was worried about Caitlin's cold because I would think back to when Meghan first got sick and we were told that it was just a cold virus.

"Okay, relax," I say to myself. "Focus on getting Caitlin and yourself on the mend, this is just a cold and will take a few days to clear." I took a drive to the drug store just around the corner and picked up what I needed to get us through this, some Tylenol, lozenges, and cough medication for missy Caitlin. When I got home I put another call into the hospital and asked to speak to Meghan's nurse, she assured me that Meghan was only going into ICU as a precaution; there was nothing that they were keeping from me. "Relax," I told myself, "let go and let God." I needed to trust Gerry and Lanette that they would continue to be there just as they have been.

Shortly after I got off the phone with the nurse Gerry called, "She's going to be okay" he assured me, "ICU is just for precaution." His call was timed perfect; I needed that reassurance from him. I closed my eyes while I listened to him and gave it all to God.

Friday Feb 10,   Day 110 - Meghan had her surgery at about 11pm. All went well. She has a chest tube in and is in quite a bit of pain. Gerry stayed all night and all day Saturday – Lanette was staying over Saturday night. Gerry called me at about 8 am on Saturday, he said they had taken enough of the cluster to do about 50 biopsies.

Saturday Feb 11, Day 111 - I got to talk to Meghan quite a bit. She is in a lot of pain, very sore. She is feverish on and off and is barfing from the coughing. I believe Meghan got some reds today, and all her counts look excellent, it's just a process of getting to the bottom of it all now.

My family was wonderful, as were my friends, especially Ronni. She had her own set of medical complications, yet she always managed to help me out. I don't know what I would ever have done without her support. She was a Godsend for sure. Ronni had been there to offer drives, lend support to my mom, and to single handedly pretty much be the driving force behind Meghan's 16th birthday party. The list just goes on and on as to how much this woman continually gave. I am grateful.

My sister Pam, Meghan's Godmother, also helped so much. Pam has two young boys of her own, Graeme and Ethan, but managed to have them looked after by her husband Brian or her mother in law, or even my mom, and then would come to the hospital to help my baby. I don't even know how to thank all the wonderful people in my life, how they have given so freely of their time, and energy and have sacrificed to come to help.

Thursday February 16, Day 116 - Today was a day of answered prayers. As many days are in this whole journey. My faith has been strengthened, tested, and then strengthened even more. The Dr. came in and told me that one of the pathology reports came back that it is NOT HLH – Praise God.

Miracle after miracle, answered prayer after answered prayer. Meghan looks great and is fever free. All other reports are not showing anything serious at all, it may be something they call Boop Pnemonia, but she isn't showing all the signs. Then the strangest thing happened, with a gentleness in her eyes, Dr. Hatlee said "If I can't diagnose it, it's Okay" I felt like God was so alive in my heart He is healing my baby again and I am going to tell the world."

I remembered the moment so clearly when Dr. Hatlee said she wasn't concerned if she couldn't diagnose the pneumonia. Now don't take that the wrong way, what it showed to me was that sometimes things can't be explained. With over 50 biopsies performed they weren't able to diagnose the specific type pneumonia. It simply was healed. Dr. Hatlee knew that it was more important that Meghan be healed and that she was able to go home. Dr. Hatlee recognized that it wasn't her place to keep a well child in the hospital for the mere reason of having pride get in the way that she wanted a confirmed diagnosis. Dr. Hatlee was one of the best doctors on staff, and it warmed my heart that she knew that to get Meghan home where she could truly continue to heal was what needed to happen next. Meghan was fever free, there was no pneumonia that they could confirm and her counts were good. Today we were going home.

Meghan's bed was set up in the living room, and was elevated a bit on the low end so that it would help drain anything out of her lungs that remained, just a slight elevation. Caitlin was going to stay at her dad's house in St. Catharines. I felt like a new mom who has just brought her baby home for the first time. I couldn't seem to relax, and I guess I wouldn't until this whole journey was done. I set up a mattress on the living room floor right beside her bed as I didn't want to sleep upstairs; it was too far away and now that Meghan was home I did not want to leave her side. I couldn't be with her during her surgery, so I wasn't about to go anywhere now. As I set up the mattress from Caitlin's single bed on the floor beside Meghan I saw that smile on her face that I just adore.

"What are you doing mommy?" she said with a grin that was complete love.

"Well having a sleepover with you; like I am camping out, is that okay?" I asked.

"Duh, ya, of course" she was so adorable that it made my heart melt. I tucked her in, tucked myself in, said our prayers and had our girly chat. In between our mother daughter moments Meghan would sneak a peek at her computer.

Meghan's eyes filled with tears and she began to sob. "What's wrong sweetie?" I asked.

Some of Meghan's friends were having a girl's night and because of their concern for Meghan's health she was not invited. She simply wanted to be a normal teenage girl and hang out at a sleepover with the girls and not with her mom.

"Well we are having a girlie night too" I said as I tried to make it fun, "and besides, the best girl is right here with me and I am the lucky one." I could only imagine how very alone Meghan must have felt. Some of her friends stopped coming around and the only contact she seemed to have was through MSN. I didn't have the words to help with the sadness that kept multiplying within her. I just constantly prayed that things would change, that normal would return, yet it seemed so far away. *Would it ever return* I thought.

"Oh, please mom," she replied but she stopped crying, if only for a moment.

Morning came, and I was greeted with "Mom, you snore" yes, apparently I snore, and quite loudly I might add.

There was a positive change, school. Meghan had been approved to be home schooled. It was a must with her recovery from Sick Kids that she could not attend school until September at the earliest so she would continue her education with grade 10 Math and English right here at home. I felt that this was fantastic as it would help her feel somewhat normal. She would have school tests, the best kind. She may not be in a physical school, but the program and the homework would be the equivalent to what her friends have taken or would take, so she now had something in common with them again.

Her math teacher was about to arrive, and when I opened the door, I was in complete shock. "Ms. Bell, Mrs. Anderson? Do you remember me?" I asked. I was in a state of complete disbelief. Then we both laughed. Mrs. Anderson was my PE teacher, and my math teacher when I was at the very same high school that Meghan attended. Talk about a small world and talk about feeling old.

"Oh my goodness, Angela" she replied, "I would never forget those brown eyes." It made me feel that the boundaries the Lord stretched to bring people into this journey were incredible. This wonderful teacher, whom I remembered very well, was now retired and did some supply teaching on the side. Elsbeth is what I called her now. Elsbeth would now teach my child and I was very blessed. She and Meghan hit it off right away and I knew Meghan now had a new friend, teacher and confidant. I knew they would share a lot. A new part of Meghan's journey had opened up, home schooling, Meghan was excited.

Meghan was off most of her medications and her recovery had come along quite nicely. She still coughed a bit and seemed to have developed a gag reflex when she ate. When I think back to when she was just a toddler, she had the same problem, gagging. If something upset her and she cried over it she would then gag and well we all know what happened next. So this is what I dealt with now. How do I get her to calm down enough so that she would be able to keep food down? She was almost afraid to eat in case she would gag and bring it back up. I would bring it up at our next clinic appointment.

We arrived early enough to be first in the finger poke clinic lab, and then we made our way up to the 3F clinic.

Monday March 20, Day 150 - Great clinic visit for Meghan, probably the best one she has had. We are down to 50mg of Cyclosporine in the morning, and then the penicillin and that's it.

We got to the car and the gag thing started again. I scolded her all the way home, and felt guilty, but I don't understand what is going on. I wish she could snap out of this

155

coughing and gagging thing. She didn't even react to her great counts and the clinic visit, she just keeps thinking of her gag reflex, it's the only thing on her mind that she is afraid to eat and then throw up. Randy talked with her a lot tonight, and I am grateful for that. Sometimes I have to be hard, and it breaks my heart, but I am still her mom, and she needs to eat to stay strong. Maybe I am too hard on her, I don't know, I am just afraid of her going back in the hospital. She is doing so well, but needs to eat to keep strong and maintain her recovery process.

A few weeks have gone by and every day has been one battle after the next as I have dealt with my baby who I truly believe has developed an eating disorder. Why wouldn't anyone listen to me when I expressed my concern over her lack of eating? She never felt hungry, she wouldn't push herself and her motivation has just bottomed out. I wish I knew what to do, wish I knew how to motivate her; even mom has tried everything. She even insisted that I try some tough love and sit with her and make sure she eats. Oh God how I felt completely helpless not having any clue at all of how to deal with this new phase of this journey. Was it a new phase or were we now embarking on a complete different ordeal? Meghan didn't understand it, nor did she even seem to have the desire to try to understand and conquer this one.

I spoke with Gina at clinic; I even asked if they could put her back on steroids. Imagine that, I requested that my child go on a drug just so that she eats. Oh Lord, help us all.

I decided to just have a heart to heart with Meghan, to let her know the dangers ahead if she didn't try a little harder to get some food into her and not just a few bites either. I put it to her plain and simple that she had to take hold of this or it could mean the end. She promised me she would try. I told her that it's not me she had to deal with now, it was God. I have let her know that I have put her one on one with the Lord. He had pulled her through this far and she was to deal with Him with regards to her eating habits. I didn't like to feel angry and frustrated.

156

"Meghan," I said, "You have come so far, and been through so much. This part of it is just as important. You may not be on drugs, or in a hospital, but if you don't start to eat better, you will get admitted again and have a tube shoved in your nose all the way to your stomach to feed you."

I knew that she didn't like my firmness, but like mom said, time for some tough love. Literally, my days had been filled with monitoring her eating habits, and having our daily battles. She could be so sassy at times and she has used her situation to try to push me, to make me feel guilty for being hard on her. One person she couldn't seem to push around was Caitlin. She has tried, but Caitlin put her in her place a few times.

I can recall one in particular when she said to her sister, "Meghan, if you want a drink, get in your chair, or better still, get up and walk to the fridge and get it yourself." I wish I had the courage that Caitlin did at times. Well my frustration must have been heard through prayer and fallen into the hands of some special because friends and family have stepped forward and offered to help in her rehabilitation. Mair had set up an eating schedule for Meghan based on what she can keep down and what will help her to gain strength. As a champion fitness person and boxer, this woman was perfect to help with this. It was amazing to not have to fight and push her all on my own. She was now in the hands of one very capable lady and I knew we would soon see results. Unless you are thrown into the position of dealing with someone who has eating issues you would have a hard time understanding how draining and scary it was. On occasion I would find a half-eaten sandwich rolled up in paper towel and thrown/buried in the garbage. When I spoke with Randy and Caitlin about my findings, Caitlin giggled a bit and said "well at least she got up off her lazy butt and threw it out herself." That's one way to look at it I suppose, Caitlin always found the positive in everything. She is just that way.

"Well, I am going to confront her on this hiding food, and throwing it away as its not acceptable in this house," I told them both. Yet, when I went to scold her I felt a calm come over me as I looked into her beautiful blue eyes. She saw the wrapped sandwich in my hand and knew it was wrong. I could not say anything other than "sweetie, next time, just call me to let me know that you finished half, half is a perfect start." I thanked her for making the effort, and I was proud of her. We hugged and cried and hugged some more. Our connection was still very strong.

Tomorrow was clinic day, and we were now into mid-April with some pretty nice weather, perfect temperature to get little missy outside to walk. I have quite a few questions to bring up at clinic about Florida, that trip that Meghan was chosen for, and also if there is anything else that could be done about Meghan's eating. It has only slightly improved, she has her ups and downs with it all, but she was trying. Meghan had now become a wonderful young woman who had endured more than anyone I had ever known. She had been poked, prodded, biopsied, has had weekly lumber punctures, weekly blood tests, ICU admissions, and a couple of code blues, but she never complained and never got angry. She has grown each day within this journey. The love and gentleness that she had before have since become predominant and taken over and she now had compassion, faith, hope, and a tender spirit that most have not even witnessed from her. All of her new character traits were bright and beautiful and I don't even think that Meghan herself knew just how truly radiant she had become. Her looks have been attacked by medications; her body is completely covered in stretch marks that are massive. The Lord has worked on her daily, from the inside out, and she has become a very incredible young lady. Meghan had developed a compassion for the *"not so pretty"* people now. It's sad how people, young people, and even adults, are quite judgmental and we don't even know it. I myself was guilty of it and from Meghan's example I will never shy away again from someone with scars, or balding, or that simply might be a little different. Didn't Jesus say it best himself to take the plank out of our own eye before trying to pick splinters out of another's eye? As I lay cozy in my bed, alone and in the quiet of my home, children asleep, I decide to turn on CTS, (our local Christian television station) and see who was on tonight. My entry begins…

Tuesday April 19, 2006   Day 181 - Its 11:11 pm.   The last couple of weeks have been insanely stressing.   Meghan is doing well with her counts, but her eating and exercise are still not that good.   The girls spent the weekend, Easter weekend, at their dads.   I spent it with Randy.   He and I had words, and almost split up.   I didn't like it, but I am putting it aside, can't focus on his problems, I have enough to deal with here.

At this very moment I am listening and watching an amazing preacher. His words tonight for us to ponder are "In the marrow of your bones, is where your blood is revitalized" So, how odd he would refer to bone marrow for the cleansing of the blood I took some time to read over some of my journal tonight.   It's not been easy.   Today I lost it with Meghan.   Mom calls it tough love – and its necessary.   She needs to know the importance of eating. She and I have had so many talks.   I know she is so close to me, sometimes too close if that makes sense.   I talked with Anna, she is going to help with getting her stronger, and be a mentor and spend time with her.   Perfect timing, God, thank YOU.

Wednesday April 20, 2006 Day 182 -   Today is clinic day, counts are great.   Whites are 9.2, Reds are 121, and Platelets are 344.   Awesome.

The line isn't working.   We are probably going to have it removed next week.   Gina talked with Meghan about Florida. We got an email from Gina that Meghan isn't to go for another 6 months at least.   I replied completely agreeing with her.   There was no way that Meghan could possibly be able to go to Florida in the heat of July in 3 months.   Not a chance.

Tonight Meghan had some friends over.   Jesse and Courtney came to see her.   She was so nervous that she threw up just before they got here.   I didn't give her any flack over it. She is just a bundle of nerves with seeing friends that she hasn't seen for a long time.   She has so many fears that run around

159

rampant in her mind. She is so close to me. She holds my hand always, and wants me near her. It will be good for her to break away for a bit and see some friends, even if how we are is so nice, sweet and so loving, she needs her own time. Tomorrow Heather is coming over and they are going out to eat. I know Meghan is nervous, but maybe eating with a friend in a different setting will be OK. I let her know that she can bring whatever she can't finish home. Not to make it about eating out, but rather being out with a friend. The eating doesn't have to be a big deal tonight."

Meghan looked beautiful tonight for her girl's night out. A bunch of friends were meeting at Kelsey's for dinner to celebrate Heather's birthday. Meghan's hair had come in very short and sweet and she rarely wore the wig. Her eyes were bright and beautiful. Her eyelashes had grown in so long and dark, you would definitely call them baby doll lashes. With a coat of mascara and some eyeliner, oh my gosh, she was absolutely stunning.

"Wow, you look amazing, look at your crazy long lashes" I said to her as she came down from her room ready to go out. I knew she was nervous and we got into the car and I dropped her off.

"Meghan, you take control of what you want to do, what you want to eat, and just have fun. If you are too nervous to eat, then don't and I am completely okay with that, alright?"

I wanted her to know that tonight was about just being in the company of her friends from high school and to have an evening out.

"Do I look okay, really?" she asked.

"Are you kidding me? Just wait til they see you, man you have the best eyes going." I walked her inside and she met up with Heather.

"Meegs" Heather squealed, "OMG, you look amazing, holy crap look at your eyes." *She called her Meegs just like she used to, Meghan must love that* I thought.

"Ya I think I deserve long lashes after all the times mine fell out and these ones are real" she replied. "I'm heading out now,

Meghan; call me when you need a ride home, okay?" I waved and left the girls to be girls.

I had a talk with Heather on MSN about their evening out. Meghan had fun but "she doesn't eat much Ang." Heather asked, "is she okay?" I explained the whole situation to her and told her how being off the steroids caused her to not feel hunger and when she eats she feels like throwing up. Together, Heather and I, made a plan to go out for lunch just the three of us and then to go walk the labyrinth. The labyrinth was a beautiful peaceful place to meditatively walk. It's a large circular path, mapped out as a labyrinth pattern. Anyhow, you follow the path and it takes about 20 minutes to complete. The beauty of it for Meghan was that there were four benches just a few steps away from each section and she could easily sit down if she got tired. Heather came over and we headed out for lunch to our favorite place that we call the little restaurant; grilled cheese was ordered, with fries. Meghan ate maybe half a sandwich, and a few fries, but this time she actually kept it down. I think partly because I somewhat just ignored her and talked to Heather. I know she wants to be completely better, but something isn't right it's not like her to be like this, she has always loved to eat. Patience was what I had to hang on to now, patience. I continued to find food thrown away and wrapped up in paper towels. She would eat half of something and then hide the rest away to avoid any type of confrontation from either her sister or myself. I knew that she had been doing this at her dad's also and made them aware of it so they could look for hidden food which could be rotting somewhere hidden. What do I do? How does anyone handle this? She had gone through so much, I learned how to cope with most of it but I had no clue as to how to deal with this; likely because I wasn't supposed to. It's wasn't anything I could control, so I decided I was not going to even cause the arguments about it anymore. The doctors would decide.

Friday April 23, 2006, Day 184 - The surgeon's office called. The Hickman line comes out on Tuesday, yay. One more step to normal. No more line coming out of her chest. This

161

makes her feel so worried all the time, what if it gets tugged, or caught, or people see it. Oh she must feel like dancing inside that this thing will no longer be a part of her. Just another blessing and a step to normal.

Meghan is so happy she will feel so much more relief and freedom. Heather and Jen came over at lunch. Meghan was in good spirits and scrapbooked all day. Karen came at about 4, what a busy day and perfect timing too – Meghan needed friends to come over. Saturday - We went to Brampton to pick up Anna. Anna's little brother had a BMT when Meghan did and we really connected with her and her family. She spent the day here and we made jewelry. They had so much fun. Meghan also worked on her scrapbook. It's great to see her focused on something and enjoying it."

It was a great day of making bracelets and scrapbooking. Anna was so sweet, and a very beautiful girl. When I looked at her I was reminded of Snow White, in her beauty and her gentleness. Anna was good for Meghan and I knew their friendship would be a lifelong one. God blessed Meghan with this new friend for sure.   It's through the tough times that we truly see and find the friends that are forever. It seemed that as Meghan went through change, so too did her friends, some drifted away and new ones came into her life. It was all part of a plan and only faith got you through.

Chapter 15 – A Struggling Mom

Goodbye Hickman.   Yes, the central line was coming out today.   Mair went into the operating room with Meghan.   I am not sure how it even ended up this way, but Meghan and Mair have bonded nicely, and it was something they both wanted to experience together.   Dr. Meado came to see Meghan and also assisted the surgeon.   The surgery was one huge step, Meghan would be able feel normal again and to freely come and go and not have a fear of being looked at strangely.   She could shower and bathe without fear of getting it wet.   The skin would finally heal from where the bandages were constantly placed.   I waited for as long as I could and then Mair gowned up to go be with Meghan.   I was not sure if she could stay in for the procedure, but at least until she went under.   My heart felt conflicted as part of me wanted to be the one in there since I couldn't be there when she had her lung biopsy, and part of me felt relief.   I believed it was happening just as it should.

Surgery wasn't long, and I was able to see Meghan in recovery. I washed up and was led into the recovery area by one of the nurses. "She will be tender and groggy, so far no fevers, or reaction of any sort. Oh and Meghan actually asked if she could keep her line," the nurse mentioned as I walked towards my daughter. "She isn't allowed the one that we removed, however I have given her an unopened packaged one. It will make for an interesting page in her scrapbook."

"Eww, really?" I replied, "She wants to scrapbook about the line? Okay." I thought out loud.

Dr. Meado met up with me after surgery. "That's quite a remarkable little lady" he said to me.   "She asked me to please pray for her and to make sure that she didn't die."   He looked at me, reached out and took my hand. "I let her know as I held her hand like I am holding yours now that I would not let her die and that she would wake up just fine, and free from so many worries."

"Thank you, for loving my daughter" I said to him.

I waited beside Meghan, she faded in and out for a bit, but then I saw that smile and heard the one word that melted my heart "Mommy." I loved being a mom. Caitlin and Meghan, my family, my world, my everything.

As a mom or a dad however, some days don't go smooth at all, and I knew that every mom or dad has had those days when they would completely lose it. Days when the kids are not listening, the fighting and arguments are endless to the point where it builds and builds and builds. Well my day had arrived, it was one of those days when Meghan and Caitlin both pushed me beyond my limit and here is what I wrote.

"Wednesday & Thursday April 28, 29, Days 189 and 190 -Mom was a volcano. Yep I erupted. Completely exploded with my girls & I am ashamed of it. I went to see Dr. Tony and talked with him about a lot of things. When I told him that I erupted, he laughed. "Is that what you call it, I call it parenting." He said to me and then let me know that it was perfectly normal, and OK to get upset and discipline a child that was sick and going through so much. I will always be her parent, and should never feel bad for having lost my cool. He wants to see me regularly, and we are keeping a close watch on my blood pressure. I tend to take after my dad with that. I was prescribed something for my blood pressure, just a small dose to manage things. He laughed again, "erupted eh! I will have to remember that one."

When I got home, I spoke to the girls and told them that I can't let things get to that point again. "Let's make a fresh start" was my suggestion, and we did. The girls hugged it out and we all hugged it out. It wasn't going to be easy, but we would work through the difficulties and try to understand and respect each other better. I could have written a whole chapter on the fighting and the arguing that had transpired but after the advice from Dr. Tony I decided to just relax. I will keep our private fights and arguments out of this part

164

of the story. It was an emotional time and we are just as normal as every family.

Meghan always seemed so very tired, much more than normal. I was in the upstairs washroom when I heard the shuffling of feet across the hardwood in the hallway just outside the washroom. It didn't sound like footsteps but more like the sound of sandpaper buffing against wood. I heard a soft "mom" through the bathroom door. It was Meghan, she had to use the washroom and couldn't wait, so she decided to just come in and sit at the edge of the tub. All of a sudden she started to slide down like a wet limp noodle in a pot, she fainted. Thankfully I was there to catch her.

She was so frightened, and cried. "Mommy am I having a code blue here at home?" I assured her that it wasn't a code blue and that it was probably because of a number of things; it could be that she needed to drink more, or that she got up to fast, or that she was over anxious, or a combination of things. We cuddled, and I slept with her in her bed. As I held onto her I thought about how this poor child who had gone through so much that she related being lightheaded or fainting as a code blue. Her new normal left her in a constant state of fear of what may come next. The reality of what must constantly invade Meghan's mind and the fears she daily had to live with became so evident in that single statement, *mommy am I having a code blue at home?* I held her and calmed her and cherished this moment, I was a mom!

With Meghan now asleep I quietly made my way to Caitlin's room, she had fallen off her bike earlier. "How's your knee sweetie?" I asked as I stroked her cheek. "Oh goodness you even managed to scrape your chin too" I said as I sat on her bed with her.

"It all hurts momma," she said in a somewhat annoyed tone and pulled away from me.

"I'm going to get some new band aids and cream and change them for you and then I will lay here and cuddle you, is that okay?" Caitlin turned and faced me and waited for me to re-dress her wounds. I loved that she was very dramatic about everything, and she had every right to be.

"They are really bad cuts and stuff aren't they, momma?" She asked and insisted in the same tone.

"Oh they certainly are, and you are so brave" I replied as I gently placed a new band aid on her knee and kissed it softly.

"Did you use the magic cream from Grandma?" She asked.

"Yes, I did. The Germolene cream is on and doing its job." Being a mom is the best thing that has happened to my life. When I was taking care of my children, I was fully alive.

Today was Mother's Day. Both of my girls would come to church with me. It was going to be the first time for Meghan in over a year and I can't think of a better Mother's Day than to have both of them with me in my place of worship. My church is my family.

When we arrived, Bill and John helped to lift Meghan in her chair up the stairs into the church. Meghan didn't want to use the wheelchair access so we had started to fumble our way about it at the bottom of the stairs. I was going to help her walk up them, and then sit her in a pew and have her wait for me to get her chair. As soon as it was noticed that we had arrived my friends came to our aid. Meghan was carried like a princess in a chariot up the stairs and gently placed down so that I could wheel her in myself. I couldn't even remember any of the service; my heart kept going to the fact that both of my girls were by my side in His house on this precious Sunday called Mother's Day.

Time seemed to go by so fast. It was now June and soon Caitlin and my mom would be taking a special trip to Calgary. Mom was taking her granddaughter away for a fantastic birthday. The two of them were going to visit some of mom's family out west and have some time on a ranch with horses. Caitlin so desperately needed this. She has had to endure so much through this journey so having this amazing vacation with Nannie is a blessing beyond words. Thanks Mom.

"June 12, 2006 - Well here we are in June, seven months after transplants. I haven't written or journaled in several days, actually a few weeks.

166

Sometimes ya just need time away to get things straight, oddly enough they didn't straighten. It has been a tough go of things with Meghan emotionally. We started going to the gym. I spoke with them privately, explained her situations, and the manager there was amazing. She completely sanitizes the bike before Meghan uses it, and makes sure that no one is around when we are in doing some exercise. She also doesn't leave Meghan's side. Her experience is extensive, and she assures me that she won't let anything happen to my baby. We are aiming to maintain a weight of 118 - 120. After a short workout, a refreshing bottle of ice water, we headed home. It was time for a bit of lunch. I hope all goes well with the eating. My mind never seems to stop with the worry. It's a constant whir inside my head.

Lost Lost Lost Lost a word that fits me well these days. Randy wants to move to the country, I don't think I do anymore. I can't feel any more isolated. I know in my heart that we won't be together, but then something happens and I see the parts in him that I fell in love with. Are we meant to be? only God knows, well actually I do, but I just can't deal with facing that right now."

Having gone through what seemed to be the hardest times of this journey, I thought by now things would have returned to normal. I was so convinced that Meghan had developed an eating disorder. I've thought this before, and could not shake it; it would continue to come back at me over and over again. I would see her try, but knew that it was something beyond what she could do on her own. Meghan needed help and between the dietician and the clinic I sure hoped that they would get her back on track. Her weight dropped more and more each week, and it was now noticed at clinic, finally they took a handle on it and were not going to let it go. I was not going crazy, and now others could see what I had been talking about for a few months.

We recently had an appointment that included the works; bloodwork, weight, height, a CT scan, and ultrasound; since we were now six months post-transplant, it was something that was always done. During the consult part of our follow up assessment, when the weight was addressed and we were now all able and willing to talk about it.

"Can you put her back on steroids?" I pleaded with all of them yet again. An odd question, and it wasn't the first time I had asked it, but I knew that they would make her eat again.

"No" was the answer I got, and the answer I expected. "You just have to be patient, her desire to eat will come back, and she will enjoy eating once again" I was told.

"I am scared, I think she has an eating disorder now," was my reply. "She hides half eaten food in napkins and throws them out. I have found this on more than one occasion" I desperately informed them in a tone that begged for help.

When I confronted Meghan about it, she was so upset, and said she just doesn't feel hungry and feels like throwing up.

"Mom, I just don't feel like I am myself, I just don't enjoy food, and I don't feel like moving to the country, my hip hurts, my body feels weak." I tried to explain that she feels weak because she needs to eat, and that it's a cycle she will have to work on.

"Meghan, if you walk more then you will strengthen your legs and if you drink more you will hydrate your body and nourish your skin. Sweetie you need to fuel yourself." We cried together, and promised to work together. I assured her that we would not move to the country any time soon and that her home was exactly where it would be for quite some time. Ronni has promised to encourage Meghan to exercise and to take it slow. Right now I was too close to this situation; the fear of her having an eating disorder scared me. I didn't know what to do other than pray and trust that everything would be fine. One day at a time and today Meghan's best friend Heather was coming over. We were going to have a baking morning, all kinds of cookies, and then take a walk to the Labyrinth; our special place where we could walk, pray, and even sit on a bench to take a rest. I found peace there and there is where I knew Meghan would gain the leg strength that she so desperately needed. In the back of my mind was the thought of high school. She would head back in only a little while, roughly a month or so. *How will she manage the stairs, if she can't even walk a block, how will she manage anything at school?* I pondered my own thoughts to let go of her, to let my teenage baby go back to school scared me to death. This was a fear I could not show nor could I give in to it. I needed Meghan to know that I was confident in her abilities and that she would be back to her normal self. Normal, what was that? It seemed like a lifetime ago and long forgotten of what that actually was.

"Thursday, June 28 / 06 - Meghan is gone to her dad's and Caitlin leaves tomorrow morning with Nannie for Calgary. Two weeks without my girls is always hard. This time will be especially hard as Meghan has a biopsy coming up. Yes, her latest routine CT scan done this past Monday showed 3 nodules on her liver. Nodules, what are they, could it the HLH has come back, or possibly scar tissue. When Dr. Meado called me I was so upset. I pray it's something simple. God please let it only be a nothing.   I was praying for a nothing, I want a nothing, nothing nothing.   I didn't know what nothing was, but it was what I prayed for, nothing. No HLH, no disease of any kind, no infection, nothing God please nothing.

My poor baby has been through enough. I just want her well and strong to live a normal happy life. She is trying God and begs you for things to go away. Please hear her prayers and our cries. Please take this away, and please bless us all with good health and happiness. Forgive me Lord for all in me that you know, for when I have been angry and hard on her, I am so sorry Lord, forgive me.

Sometimes I wonder and wonder why are things still going on, how come this journey isn't over. God will it ever end. Meghan starts school and she needs to get this back in her life.

169

Oh please let it only be something simple that requires nothing. Oh please a nothing. I can't bear the thought of Meghan having to go through anything more.

Lord why do I worry so much? Why is it so hard for me to let go and let God? How do I get back to that place in me of complete peace and confidence that all will be OK? God walk with me, and hold me, hold Meghan, hold Caitlin Oh, Lord hold my girls. Give Meghan peace, strength and understanding and show her your awesomeness. Answer our prayers and let everything be OK with this new biopsy. I love you Jesus, love you so much.

Dear Heavenly Father, and Dad

As I write this letter it is also my prayer. Please hear me, feel me, touch me with tenderness and reassuring.

I feel like things are starting again with a new test for something on Meghan's liver. It scares me so much and I can't seem to let go of my fear. Dad, today I wished you could just hold me, hold Meghan. She needs to be held and to cry. She has been so brave and I have been unsupportive because I have been afraid. I need help from you Jesus. Take from me my worries so that I can be the best for Meghan. Teach us Jesus how to be, how to live and how to follow as we should. I need the strength to continue and endure this journey, Please refresh me in your spirit, love and bring to us miracles and blessings.

In Jesus name I pray, Amen"

Chapter 16 – Round Two

Some friends jump ship in a storm and some throw you a life preserver and rescue you. Truthfully if I were 16 I don't know if I could handle any of this, and I felt for all of these kids.

"Mom why have some of my friends vanished?" she asked in a voice so slow and low I sensed her pain in every word.

My response to Meghan in all her sadness was "well Meghan, God doesn't remove someone from your life unless someone else is meant to be there." How true it was. We had some pretty amazing young women and men who'd have stepped up to shown Meghan the fact she had some wonderful friends. Jaclyn, Kate, Heather, Katie, Karen, Nicole, Cori, Chris, Darryl, Matthew, Mitch, Courtney, Chris (aka Little Man) and many more. The most important thing is that Meghan never forgot any of them. Little man was the sweetest guy I have ever met, and Meghan's first boyfriend. Oddly enough I went to school with his parents, Pam and Jeff. Chris was no longer Meghan's boyfriend, they ended that relationship long before she got sick, but he had and always will be her dear sweet best friend. The two of them shared an unbreakable bond. Chris always popped in and checked up on her. They shared time baking cookies and decorating ginger bread men. There aren't many guys that would give up a night and come over to decorate cookies; but this guy was the best, a young love that became a wonderful friendship that Meghan cherished.

"Mom, I'm a freak, look at my stretch marks, I have no hair, I can't do anything, I don't look like me, I have no friends, I can't take it mom, I can't take any more" as the tears streamed down her cheeks.

Her hair and body issues resurfaced again. I knelt in front of her to comfort her. "Gina told me at clinic not that long ago that you would qualify for plastic surgery to help with the scars if you wanted to" as I pointed to her stretch marks.

"I don't want to fix them mom, they are telling my story, they are a part of me now, and feel them" she commanded me in a gentle

171

tone as she revealed her bare stomach.   I ran my hand over the stretch marks on her stomach, and her arms. Her body was covered with them, and I was afraid that they would be sensitive and tender.

"Do they hurt?" I asked.

"No, not at all, they feel like silk." True enough they were soft and silky, I was shocked, they caused no pain and to feel them it was soft like feathers on her skin.   I took a closer look at the position of the stretch marks that were on her upper chest, it looked like an angel was behind her and the wings of the angel cradled her.

 "Angles wings are holding you" I said to her, and pointed it out to her.

"Mom, these scars are mine, I have earned every single one, and I am not going to cover them up any longer. If my friends come over, they can see me for how I truly am, there is more to me than the pretty face and perfect body that I once had."

Wow, my daughter had forever changed, transformed from the inside out. I was proud of whom she had become but, sad and torn that it had to take such suffering to have it flourish.

"Monday July 24, 2006 - Today was supposed to be a clinic day for Meghan. We go every Friday, but I didn't feel like it, and Meghan didn't either. Her counts have been good, she is exercising more, and I thought we would just take a break. Almost three weeks ago Meghan had her liver biopsy and we haven't heard anything, so no news is good news.   I emailed Gina, said we would be in next week. Meghan so badly needed a break from all of this crap that has consumed her this past year. It felt good, normal, and we were excited that it was a complete week with no hospital visit at all. Amen to that.

The phone rings at about 2 PM today. Its Gerry. He is asking if I read my email. "What email." So he begins to read it to me. It was from Gina at clinic and it was not good.

The doctor has the results from the liver biopsy, they are concerned and want to see all of us, with Meghan, as soon as

172

possible. I read the email over and over, pretty much freaking out. I avoided Meghan for a bit, until I knew I could find the right words, with God's help of course, to tell her we had to go to clinic to face something. I called Randy right away to make sure he was going to take us. We pretty much went through the rest of the day with what was planned.

Tuesday July 25/2006 - The doctor wanted all of us in clinic by 8AM. We gathered for the meeting. Meghan beside me, and we held hands. He began to explain his findings. "Along with her weight loss and the recent biopsy done on the liver, when you put together what pathology was found, the weight loss confirms it." Wondering what would come next out of his mouth. "She has a rare lymphoma anaplastic large cell lymphoma ALCL, it's very rare." He said. "In fact, she is the second case we have seen here at McMaster."

"Are these two diseases linked" I asked. Basically they didn't know. So much emotion happened in the meeting. Meghan was frozen. I know she didn't understand a lot of the words. She whispered to me at one point, "do I have cancer?" "Yes sweetie, lymphoma is a type of cancer."

Devastation is an understatement. She was ready to go back to school, was trying to get stronger, and she was, but the weight just kept coming off. So much was said, so much not even heard . . ."

It wasn't too long ago that we were given our first diagnosis, HLH. It sometimes felt like yesterday, and then in only a moment it would feel like a lifetime ago. As we walked into that meeting today was nothing like the walk into our first meeting back in April of 2005. This meeting was a storm. I felt like I walked right into the eye of a twister. I didn't know what was going to happen, but I knew we were all about to be thrown around. My heart felt like it was being sucked out of my body and attacked. I held Meghan's hand tightly and tried

173

to fight the tears. They choked me, these tears caused pain. They stung my heart and soul, and I held them in, I had to, this was a moment where a mother or father could not show fear or tears. I couldn't show Meghan my upset. Deep within I just said two simple words. "Oh, God."

Meghan didn't understand the word lymphoma, but when it was confirmed to her sweet innocent mind that lymphoma was cancer, she broke down and my journal continued like this:

." . . Gina held onto Meghan at one point, kneeling in front of her wheel chair and holding her legs as they sat face to face. Both crying. "I don't want to die" Meghan cried. I just kept holding her hand tight, holding in tears as I didn't want to lose it in front of her. Gina said, "I'm not letting you go. We will fight, we will beat this thing, I know this sucks Meghan, and it isn't fair, but I am not letting go of you." "My fucking hair, I am going to lose my fucking hair again." I didn't care at that point that she swore out loud, she had every right to, and quite honestly my thoughts too were "How, the fuck can this happen"

How on earth was it possible for a person to have a bone marrow transplant, and to have that much chemotherapy, and then to get cancer? I didn't understand it and would ask questions when my mind was a little clearer. I sat there with Gerry, Lanette, Randy and our Meghan while a nightmare unfolded before our eyes. I screamed inside but could not speak. This twister had taken hold; I was so angry, and angry at God. I couldn't understand any of it. I watched as Gina cried, she held onto my Meghan to give her comfort and strength. Gina took over and gave every ounce of strength within her to Meghan.

"Oh God, how, why, what the fuck?" was a repeated thought over and over. I tried to breathe but found it difficult to inhale, my only thoughts were about Meghan and I was worried about how devastated she felt.

174

I don't know if she can do it, if she has the strength to go through treatments I thought to myself, *she's been through so much already.* People talked, Gerry asked questions, Lanette struggled to hold her tears in just as I did. Randy had his hand on my back just as he had done so before. Today I didn't feel that cold hard concrete of the lamppost; today I felt a cold hardened cement heart inside me, and I did not like any of this.

"If we don't treat her, she will die" were the words that broke the storm within me. Those words that felt like a loud crack of thunder broke my hardened heart in half.

"Oh God." I finally spoke quietly only those two words.

Meghan went with her dad and Lanette. Gerry wanted her for the afternoon, and I was glad. I needed to process all of this. I had to talk to mom and Caitlin, and the rest of my family; Caitlin, my poor Caitlin. How was she going to handle this? How was mom going to handle this? We all thought the journey was almost over, that things were improving, and in just a few more months school would start, then life would be that much closer to normal.

I went to moms, as Caitlin was there with her and would tell them together. When I talked at moms, I just broke down, sobbed and mom thought it was because of another fight with Meghan about her eating, or not exercising.

"It will be okay, she will get better" mom tried to assure me.

"No, mom, it's not that" was all I could get out in my first breath was, "mom, its Meghan again," and then I broke down.

"Well what then, what is it?"

"Meghan now has cancer." The room was still. It felt concrete, a heavy concrete atmosphere that weighed all of us down. A concrete heart broken in half in a concrete world; this was unbearable.

"She has cancer now mom, how are we going to do this? How do you treat someone who has just had a bone marrow transplant with chemotherapy? I don't understand it."

The news shocked everyone. It felt like I was telling a story straight from Hollywood, one of those terribly sad tear jerker movies that I had watched over the years; but this was real and it was my Meghan. While I was at my mom's I made a few calls. I called my sister-in-law Leighann; she must have called my brother Todd immediately as he was over at my mom's in about a half an hour. He came through the front door, in uniform, (Todd was a prison guard), we cried, hugged and I let it out. I cried and cried. I sobbed like a baby.

"Todd, don't stop hugging me, please." He hugged me harder and knew that I needed it so badly. Seeing my brother for the first time ever in his uniform gave me strength. He must have just left work and come straight over to moms. His hug was strong, and I am sure that Dad was somehow with us at that moment also.

A lot happened after that clinic visit. Gina got ready the appointments we were going to need to determine the plan of attack. The first test took place the next day, a chest x-ray. Wednesday would be the bone scan and injection and gallium injection. We would come back Friday for the gallium scan. The MRI was already done on the hip last Friday, but was not ready yet. It was set up even before we had this news.

When I got home I went over and talked to Ed next door. He had always been so good to me, a wonderful neighbor and wonderful man. His daughter Kyla watched my girls when they were little. Ed had always been there for me, ever since Gerry left and the passing of my dad. We talked, and I cried, he held me and hugged me, and for a brief moment it felt like he took the burden away.

Meghan's beads would continue to be handed to her with every test, scan, biopsy and round of chemo. I was losing faith and had many moments of just not giving a flying fuck about anything. I had felt that all my prayers were pointless and why on earth did she now have cancer when she had been through so much? Why did God let this happen? Yes, I was an angry mom and didn't even know how to feel any longer.

"Wednesday July 26 - I called mom at about 6:30 this morning. Meghan and I were at Randy's. I just couldn't face today alone and needed my mom with me. We were to be at McMaster for 8:00 am for the first round of tests. Bone scan,

176

and Bone Injection. Then we get a Gallium injections. I picked up my mom, poor Caitlin wasn't feeling well, and had thrown up. I had to leave her alone and it tore me apart. Mom and I headed to the hospital. We ended up in the basement in nuclear medicine. First was to get the IV put in so the first scan could be done. The Technician, Dave, was very good. I had an instant connection with him. The scan took about ½ an hour, then they inject something called Gallium and we are to come back on Friday. Dave was so spiritual, I was glad he would be doing the scan.

Friday July 28, 2006 -Meghan and I head in again. Caitlin is at Randy's. We ended up talking for the full 2 hours that the scan took. I opened up spiritually, and he "got it," commented and understood where I was coming from. I had been praying for someone to come into this journey that was spiritual also, and who would understand. He offered to do Reiki on Meghan, and I was thrilled. He is an answer to a prayer, no doubt about it.

Amen and I love you God"

I can remember how excited Meghan was when she got her central line taken out that she had in for Sick Kids; to be free of such an intrusion, and to get back to normal. Well today, her new line was scheduled to be put back in, what a way for a teenage girl to spend a Saturday, but it's when it was scheduled. This will be a port a cath, as they call it; it is under the skin so there are no external lines. It can then be accessed by the silicone bump that is under the skin. Not quite as intrusive and noticeable as a line hanging out, but still it's another operation just the same.

Caitlin was so worried. She was up and down with her emotions, and I wished I could help her. Anna from the hospital child life center recommended a group devoted to the siblings of cancer kids. So, she joined up the organization called Super Sibs, whose goal was to make her feel special, in any way shape or form dealing with this crap. Literally it was all crap, but how much crap was one person supposed to endure? It felt so unfair. I needed to spend time with just Caitlin; maybe a movie, or a weekend away.

I had a small window of opportunity to now be with Caitlin. When I got home, I said its movie night for just the two of us. Wow, did she ever smile, and it melted my heart. We went to see Pirates of the Caribbean, just the two of us. It was so much fun, we ate junk food, and for just a few hours, nothing else existed.

Part of me wondered what it would be like if we just took off; if Caitlin and I just vanished for a few days. But I knew we couldn't, even still, the thought was there and my world was not one that I wanted to live in. I would gladly trade places with a Pirate on the Caribbean right now.

I've kept the local paper up to speed with what was going on with Meghan; The Burlington Post has become part of our family, and it was our way of connecting to the community with what was going on with our Meghan. I use the word "*Our,*" because since all of this began, I have felt the need to tell her story. Her story needs to be told and Meghan herself asked me to tell it.

"Mom, people need to know, 'cause this can happen to anyone."

"Friday August 4, 2006 - As I was going to pick up some things for mom, I stopped at the sale table at shoppers. A woman handed me a large pink stuffed lizard and said "this would be perfect on Meghan's bed" - A little surprised she knew me, her name was Loretta. Her daughter goes to clinic, she and Meghan are close in age and will meet for sure. ...

Tonight I stayed at my mom's house. Perhaps we might see a movie or dinner, as it's just the two of us. Not sure, maybe just chill at home and relax. Ended up having chinese food and watching Simon Birch with mom. I asked mom a question, or started to, - "Should anything happen that Meghan, well . . . She said "yes," and then I just dropped the question, not even wanting to say the word, and here not even wanting to write it.

But it is there, it's the deepest fear in my world. I thought the "C" word was the worst, but the "D" word is far more frightening. I am going to believe that she will make it through this. Dad surely doesn't want her to join him, not yet.

Saturday August 5, - Since it is midnight or just past, I guess it is Saturday. I talked to Mary and she is looking forward to having us come tomorrow. It's the second annual BMT family reunion party. I am glad that Ronni is coming with me. I just couldn't go alone. I am sure people will ask questions about why Randy isn't there and why I didn't go up north. I just don't want to even talk with him right now, or with anyone for that matter, he needed to go up north to his trailer, and I had no desire to go.

God why all of this, what do you want from us? I just don't get it. I really hate all of this and my life; I just want joy and happiness, not hardship and sorrow. To be quite honest, I am having a hard time seeing any love in any of this. My two girls and I want you to take it all away. Please. I don't want to be angry and bitter. I need your help, so please hear my cry of my heart. Get her through this and make her well.

The BBQ at Mary's BMT family gathering #2 - Ronni and I got there about 2:30, and were the first ones there. What a beautiful home they have. Tarz and Mary are so nice. I made some gift bags for all of the kids, full of treats, and fun stuff. It was a big hit. I loved seeing my girls and having Ronni there for support helped so much."

There were times in the day when things just stood out so clearly, and I learned some new things. Mary was a nurse; I had no idea. She helped change the dressing on Meghan's port, as her surgery wasn't that long ago. She had some tender areas on her that needed to be covered up also with bandage, in case she decided to go into the pool. Yes, there was a pool, and a hot tub within the pool.

An oasis backyard and I felt so blessed to be spending the time there. We wore plastic leis, and the yard was quite tropic in its décor; our own little Hawaiian type getaway. Ronni and I found a couple of lounge chairs, poolside, and sat to enjoy the sun. A few feet from us stood a cool mist sprinkler. It looked like a snake that was frozen in a pose from a snake charmer, rigid and coiled. The head of the hose sprouted a fine cold mist.

"Cool" Ronni said, "I gotta get me one of these."

I had made up some fun gift bags full of candy and goodies for the kids, which also included summer fun things like bubble soap and blowers and sidewalk chalk. Ronni and I also brought a huge fruit platter with two different dips, one chocolate and one yogurt. The gift bags were a huge hit. Meghan loved gummi bears; they were her favourite so I picked up a special treat for her, a caramel and chocolate covered apple that was then dipped in gummy bears. There was a method in my madness, as the saying goes. I thought she may eat some apple while devouring this treat, and I was right, she loved it.

Across the poolside deck I watched Meghan. She was curled up in her dad's arms and nestled in beside him. Even when I write about it now my emotions run very deep. She looked so frail, and so delicate, like a wounded bird. He was her protector and the love shared between them was evident. They were in summer colours. Gerry wore a bright orange shirt, and Meghan so frail in her red bikini and cover up. The bandages were clearly visible on her chest, and one could see the scars as they covered her stomach and cradled her chest like angel wings. They sat in a big swing chair that had a shaded umbrella cover just a few feet from the edge of the pool; just the two of them. Beside Meghan was a plate of nibbled food, she hadn't eaten much, but was trying. My eyes were just fixed on the two of them as I wondered so many things. I will never forget this picture, never. I must have been lost in thought, as Mary tapped my shoulder, and had a drink for me.

"So glad you are here, and we love you." I hugged her, cried.

"She looks so sick, I am seeing her in a different light Mary; look at her, she…."

And with a gentle squeeze of my hand Mary said "I know, I know, and I am so sorry that she is dealing with cancer." How hard it must be for her to witness this, having just lost her son Michael, and to host this party was so brave, so strong, and so her. Mary, you are one incredible woman.

Meghan and Caitlin were still with their dad and Lanette this weekend, so I would be home alone tonight; never truly alone though are we? I have my dear sweet friend Ronni, and I have Jesus. The thing about Jesus is that I can completely break down with him. Yes and to be totally blunt I could totally lose my shit with him and I can cry as hard as I want, I can curse if I want, I can collapse and He would always be there for me. My deepest feelings were given over to him, and believe me; through this I have had some deep thoughts; things that I would never tell a living soul, but I would tell Jesus. Sometimes we just have to "shed our shit," pardon my language, but it describes it. Jesus then would turn it into fertilizer.

I got dropped off by Ronni early evening and headed upstairs for a hot, uninterrupted bubble bath. I poured myself an amaretto, lit a couple of candles and soaked while I thought of so many things. Since we got the news of this new horrible cancer, Meghan and I haven't really sat down and talked about it. It hasn't been that long, but we seemed to avoid the whole conversation. We just go through the motions of clinic visits, scans, tests, and play the waiting game again to see where we would go next. There was so much going on in that pretty little head of hers; how could there not be. Just when she thought everything was about to become normal; wham the nightmare became a night terror.

I closed my eyes even tighter and a few tears made their way down my cheek. I sank deeper into my bubbles as I sipped my amaretto. A taste that has never left me, salty tears and amaretto.

It was almost time to pick her up from her dads, I tidied up the car a bit, put some of my favourite tunes on to accompany me on my journey.

When I picked up Meghan she was withdrawn and I knew that something different and special needed to happen, something wonderful for this sweet girl. The first person I thought of who could make this girl smile was Glenn. He was amazing. He had known my girls since Meghan was five. I met him through a fundraising event that he undertook. It was a time in my life that I won't ever forget; the rewards to my heart were a Godsend. We never know how these special friendships come to be, and where they lead. I met Glenn in March of 1993. At that time in my life I ran a promotional company from home where I would set up trade shows or mall shows such as a boat show or car show and various arts and crafts shows. On a very cold and icy day in March there was a picture on the cover of the Burlington Post of a man in a kayak, covered in ice. I needed to find out more, why was this man in the lake and covered in ice, in March? I made a call to him that changed my life. He was training for a fundraising event that was going to take place that summer, as he was set to paddle from the east coast back here to Burlington, to raise money and awareness for cancer research. At that time, I just so happened to be running a boat show in the Burlington Mall, and offered him a prime spot to promote his marathon. I was touched by what he was about to do, and felt that I could help in a small way. I volunteered to be his promotional coordinator for his event, which we called *"The River of Hope Kayak Marathon for Cancer Research."* Glenn became a part of our family, and Meghan just adored him. I remembered when he went to her kindergarten class, with his kayak, to talk to the school about what he was doing. He smiled at her, teased her about how she was his little sweetie; she got to sit in the kayak at school. How strange that he would be raising funds and awareness for cancer so long ago and now here we were with Meghan. The same glow she had 10 years earlier sitting in his kayak returned as we pulled into his driveway.

I didn't tell Meghan where we were headed, I just let God lead me, and I knew that it was Glenn that could shake her from all that gripped her. Laura, Glenn's wife, put sunscreen on Meghan while Glenn got her a baseball cap and put it on her head. We headed out back towards the lake and Meghan froze in fear, "I can't, what if, it's too hard" her words seem to come out all jumbled and in one fast sentence. Then, in one scoop, he picked her up and carried her. Her frail body draped in his arms, her arms around his neck as he firmly

182

held her. She was secure in his embrace. Laura and I could clearly see how frail and sickly she was. But in his arms she was safe; fear was gone and she was like a little princess being carried off by her knight in shining armor.

He placed her in the kayak, a two seater; she was in front of him, and off they went. They were gone for over an hour, I was a little worried, as was Laura, but we knew she was in the best of care.

"Laura look," as I pointed to them coming in off in the distant and a sense of relief came over me. I know it was only an hour, but this was something so new, so different and a little scary for all of us. When I saw them come closer, I could see Meghan as she dangled her right hand into the water so serene and carefree. She let it trail behind her; something was different. She was transformed on the water in such a short time. I felt her spirit, light, renewed, alive.

Glenn scooped her up again, she giggled like a schoolgirl with a crush. Glenn was a fireman in Toronto, who had been on a calendar, need I say more! He carried her all the way to our car and then placed her in the passenger seat like the princess that she was. I hugged him, one of our famous long hard hugs. No words were spoken. I buckled Meghan in, and she broke down.

"Mommy, I want to tell him I love him for doing that." She whispered, "It changed me, it was the best thing I have done in my life."

My heart smiled. I knew my gratitude lay with the Lord, and also with Glenn for being a part of our lives. We were brought together many years ago, by Cancer, and who knew back then that he would be taking her kayaking to help her cope with her own cancer. We can never question why things happen, why people come into our lives, or why people leave our lives; but I like to believe things happen for a reason. Just accept everyone as a gift, for the moment, or a lifetime.

Chapter 17 – ICU

Chemotherapy started again, and Meghan would receive three different types, Methotrexate, Vincristine and I think VP16 or something like that. I just called them all chemo. Meghan ended up spiking a fever with her first round of treatment, and they have admitted her down to the ICU. I remembered there being an issue with the Methotrexate at Sick Kids, so I mentioned it to the ICU doctors; they were going to look into it, as it could be what caused this problem. Also, today was Meghan's 17th birthday, and she would be spending it in ICU. It seemed so unfair. She should be home doing teenage things. Instead of lying in ICU, hooked up to all kinds of machines and having chemo pumped into her. I brought in the big pink lizard that the kind woman gave me in Shoppers Drug Mart. When Meghan saw it she was terrified. I couldn't understand why, but then the nurse explained that she was on a lot of morphine and other drugs, and it looked different to her. Meghan thought it was a monster and not a soft toy. So it's bye bye for now to mister pink lizard, maybe she will like you later. We would celebrate her birthday when she was out. I sure was learning a lot, I listen, and I retain, and sometimes I spoke my mind which was not always a good thing, but I was my daughter's advocate.

"Monday August 14, 2006 - Today was a very full day at hospital. I came in with mom with the intentions of only staying a couple of hours. I talked to Dr. Posthma, apparently the only note that came to her from ICU was that Meghan was stable. I brought up the whole Methotrexate issue. (Meghan had a reaction to it in Sick Kids, and they took her off it). She seemed a bit annoyed or something, anyhow too much to get into and negative stuff, so anyhow again, I sent an email to Gina about my concerns of the lack of communication between hospitals and wards. ICU believes it to be an allergic reaction to the Methotrexate. They were to recommend to 3B that the cause was

185

anaphylactic shock, and it never got conveyed. So it's a good thing I spoke up. Oddly enough though, the nurses knew. I left about 6pm and Randy stayed with Meghan and watched a movie. She also got her morphine drip and was doing much better with pain management. Her mucositis and mouth sores have started, with only a few treatments, the horrible effects of chemo have begun."

Each day seemed to be harder and harder than the last as I watched my daughter experience so much pain. I sat by her bedside and held her hand as I have many times before. Yes she is alive, but when your child is suffering you want the suffering to stop. How do we as parents wrap our minds around how to feel in times like these? I didn't know, and all I could do was take one moment at a time, pray, and keep praying that she make it through. Meghan has a changed spirit that is for sure, she has found a gracefulness, never complains, does what is asked of her, and does it to the best of her ability.

"Friday August 18, 2006 - I brought mom and Auntie Helen in today in the morning, then I was to head back for a meeting with the pharmacist and two of the nurse practitioners.

I ran into Sonia in the hallway and she gave me the latest on Meghan. The dripping nosebleed isn't stopping, platelets aren't taking hold, and she is downstairs seeing an ENT specialist with Randy. I of course always jump to the worst, so I envisioned this nasty bleeding nose. She came back upstairs with her nose full of Polysporin and her spirits seemed good. "Polysporin in my nose now mom, who gets this done." She laughed.

I then met with Gina and she informed me that the Methotrexate was no longer going to be used and that they have an alternative chemo to use on her. I don't know if this is good news, any type of chemo can't be good. But the issue was addressed, and my concerns are gone with that particular poison. We went over all the drugs and I felt much better having talked to the pharmacist about all the medications she was on. It is going to be a long and hard journey for her but she can do it, with God she can do it.

I stayed the day with Meghan. She had lots of visitors, Rev. Steven Murray, Rev. Sandilands were in and Rev. Sandilands rubbed Meghan's feet at one point."

The mouth sores have started and so has the pain that goes along with it. Even though she hasn't had many treatments, the induction phase was usually strong and her poor little body was now a battle zone for the aftermath of chemo. I just held her hand, and reminded her that when she felt that she couldn't cope, to think of the time on the water with Glenn, to go kayaking in her mind, and maybe it would help. Sure they can give drugs to look after one side effect after another, but with each drug came a price. Morphine was a pain killer but it had an addictive element and caused hallucinations. Nothing in this journey was simple. It felt barbaric, and torturous, and my heart broke. I just held her hand, and cuddled her, and let her know that I was with her all the time. When I headed home late in the evenings, we had a thing we did, I held her left hand in my right hand and placed it over my heart, she held my left hand in her right hand and placed it over her heart, and then we would say "hand in hand and over our heart, together forever, never apart."

"Sunday August 20, 2006 - Meghan had a very hard night. She had fevers on and off most of the night. I went in after breakfast and she still had a fever. Her blood pressure was unstable again. They gave her more antibiotics and as the day went on she stabilized a bit. ICU was checking in on her and if things didn't improve she was going back down there.

God hear my baby's cry. Give me strength to pray with her again and strength for both of us to get through this. I

187

sometimes feel that we are at the end, that she isn't going to make it, and then poof she surprises me with an instant turn around, and surprises the doctors also. Meghan started to stabilize around 11pm, and that would have been when everyone at church was praying. God please don't take Meghan home yet, not for a long time, please. Blessings, she didn't have to go to ICU today. I am re-learning to take this one day at a time.

We were given a wonderful miracle today. Since Meghan hasn't responded to platelets, and they seem to dissipate in her, they needed to find a single platelet donor. My wonderful sister in law, Leighann is a perfect match for Meghan. She will be donating platelets on a regular basis. The hospital won't confirm exactly that her platelets are going to Meghan, but God has confirmed it. The platelets are her match; they are given to McMaster, and used when needed. It's just one miracle that we needed to help us all to feel that things are now moving in a positive direction. God in charge, well He always has been, I just lose sight of it from time to time."

If I have learned one thing in life it would be that I should never be afraid to lean on family and friends for support. So I did! Strange isn't it, how the timing of God works. Little did I know that only the very next day I would be using this faith, strong and deep.

"Thursday August 24, 2006 - I was heading into 3B today, heading to Meghan's room, which was 11, I got a call from Lanette. Meghan had spiked a fever so they were not going to do the LP, lumbar puncture, today. I let her know that I was just getting into the hospital and would be in 3B shortly.

As I arrived at Meghan's door, Sonia stopped me, gave me the latest on my baby. "Meghan is a very sick little girl." They are consulting ICU again. Her body keeps becoming unstable. Sonia has told me that they are now looking at the possibility of

188

the HLH being reactivated. I feel like a walking zombie today, randomly crying, and lost in this horrible living nightmare.

Both Dr. Posthma and Dr. Meado said something that really surprised me. Apparently with the liver biopsy in July, there were hystiocytes with the nodules on the liver. This is the first I have heard of this at all. I was in the lobby downstairs and I ran into Dr. Meado. I asked him about the hystio, HLH on the liver, and yes he said there was evidence of it around the nodules. Why on earth we were not told about this. Perhaps I was, likely I was and just didn't have it sink in. I just can't make sense of any of this. Meghan apparently asked Sonia to "Please don't let me die today." She is so scared. Meghan told Caitlin that she had a dream that we all gave up on her and didn't care anymore. God help her and all of us."

All of the nurses had developed such a special bond with Meghan, they loved her dearly and did all that they could for her. When Sonia told me what Meghan had said, I saw her as a woman, a mother, and a human being; who loved this child that wasn't hers, but was in her care. I believe she was one of those angels brought into this journey to hear those words "Please don't let me die today."

Back in ICU, with her vitals very weak, the team of doctors and nurses anticipated a harsh reaction to her treatments. Today I didn't feel like being the sweet strong mom, I felt like telling the world to go fuck itself. Meghan comatose in her bed. So many monitors and wires hooked up to her, she had the pink cooling blanket on again. It appeared as if it floated above her like a puffy pink cloud, it constantly ran with cool air, and it helped keep her comfortable during her fevers. I looked for someone who would update me on what was going on. I could feel my heart pounding in my throat. I saw nurse Christine walk towards Meghan's room.

Perfect I thought, *the nurse with a heart bigger than this entire hospital, and she is my Meghan's nurse today.* She must have heard me quickly trying to catch up to her.

"Hey," she said.

"Hey" I replied.

"She's pretty unstable again, huh?" I asked.

"Yes, but you know Meghan, she is going to surprise us all I just know it." She said assuringly. "She is one remarkable sweet girl" she said, and then told me what sort of treatments they were planning. "They will likely give her dopamine to help elevate the blood pressure. She is also on IV fluids to help stabilize her, and they will be putting in a special BP IV, (blood pressure IV)" she explained as she looked at monitors, and adjusted IV lines.

"Isn't your shift done now, its 7:30?"

"Yes it is, but sometimes I just stay on longer, for special people, so if it's ok with you I will be here until her procedure for the BP IV is done."

"Oh it's more than ok with me" I said, "Stay, I need you too and thank you" I said, and my heart filled with gratitude.

"Friday August 25 – Saturday August 26 - Friday seemed to run into Saturday in the blink of an eye. I had been here since Thursday at 10 AM.

Meghan was in pretty rough shape. They poked around and Meghan asked, "Why do you keep poking" – "We need to find the right spot." Meghan then began to pray out loud – "God please let them find the right spot – God please let them." She turned and said to Lanette and I (Lanette was also there with me) and said. Ha Ha I never prayed out loud before, and Lanette said, well it worked."

Nannie and I were in with Meghan today, and she had a turn around, yay for answered prayers. She was off the dopamine and the other heart medications. Her heart rate was good and the blood pressure was improving. Thank God for this.

Chapter 18 – God in Control

We're moving again, and yippy it's out of ICU; onward and upward, to 3B. They had moved Meghan last night while I was out, so it was a nice surprise, as nice as can be in a hospital, as we were still here with no sign of going home. When I got into the hospital this morning, the state of Meghan's mouth was somewhat shocking to say the least. I notice one of her doctors on the computer looking something up.

I casually said to her, 'Meghan's mouth looks terrible." The blood seeped out of the corners of her mouth whenever she opened it up; almost resembling a vampire who had just fed and not wiped up after. *It had to be more than just mouth sores* I thought to myself.

"Yes, we believe it to be something more serious," she replied. "Stevens-Johnson Syndrome," she added. "She could be dealing with a whole separate illness again" were words that I heard but cared not to. "Dermatology is coming to have a look at her." *Dermatology* I thought, how odd.

It was now confirmed, yes in fact she did have Stevens-Johnson Syndrome. It was due to the medications, the beta lactam family of medications were the cause (something like that at least). Chemo was now on hold now until she was better. Her platelets had been eaten up by fevers and were around 23. She was going to receive more today. Platelets were needed to clot the blood, her count was low. Meghan has had so many blood transfusions and platelet transfusions that she now had even more beads added to her previous ones. I'm so grateful that Leighann is continually donating platelets. I pray that her body starts to accept them. Meghan just hated receiving them. I remember one time while she was being transfused she said to me "mommy I don't like how they feel, it feels like my veins are going to explode inside me, please don't let them give me those." Her poor little battered and beaten body just didn't want it any more. Her reaction happened. She became violently ill temporarily. Will it ever end?

I was so very grateful that I had a counseling session before I headed off to the hospital. My therapist was amazing, and it's one place where I could just let out all my emotions. To my surprise, my therapist has offered to see me at no cost. Wow, God does provide. He said that this was the worst situation he has ever had to deal with and that the way I coped was remarkable. He was a father himself, and didn't know how he would be if he were in my situation. Being a single mom, having two children that both needed me, having a job and a home to manage, and having a very sick child that seemed to be going through one tragic illness after another. So to lighten the burden, he had offered his services to me at no cost so that I had a safe place to go to so that I could cope and heal. Dr. Glen had read about Meghan and how courageous she had fought all along. As part of my benefits through my employer I had coverage for counselling, my boss had reminded me and said "Ang, use the benefits provided. We want you to and if you need anything more, let us know." I needed more than visits to my pastor, so I decided to make use of those benefits. I began my sessions and it was amazing. I could just let it all out with no fear of upsetting or burdening any family member or adding any more stress to my strained relationship with Randy.

I had about a half hour drive to the hospital, so I put on some music, and was on my way in. My mom and Caitlin were already there, as Meghan had a CT scan set up for the morning and she wanted someone with her. I dropped them off earlier, and went to my appointment, and was now on my way back in to see her.

I met Meghan at the elevator; she had just come up from her scan when I got there at about 2:40 p.m. I could see some blood as it dripped at the corners of her mouth, and it almost looked like stringy membranes were being formed behind her lips when she spoke.

"It feels weird mommy, I don't like it." She mumbled when she spoke, and her mouth was swollen, it looked like she had been in a boxing match, with the cracks, the swelling and the blood.

I was so horribly shocked to see her this way and I looked at the nurse and said, "I don't like this."

192

"Neither do I" she replied.

"I think my mouth is bleeding more mommy" Meghan mumbled. We had just got back to her room, I washed up my hands outside and was about to enter her room. Mom and Caitlin waited in the hallway just a few steps behind me and were about to wash up as well. Arlene had wheeled the bed into Meghan's room; she didn't go down in a chair as it was easier to just take her in her bed.

All of a sudden I heard Meghan scream, "I'm bleeding, I'm bleeding badly help me" and then a long scream. Her screams were in a pitch that shattered my heart; I needed to get to her fast but was abruptly stopped.

"You can't go in, she is hemorrhaging" I was told as I was pushed away from the door. The screams from my daughter were horrific.

"Call code, call it now! Get them here she is hemorrhaging, do it now!" was the scream from Arlene. I turned to look at my mom, who was in the hallway with Caitlin.

"Mom, get her out of here, get Caitlin out of here; go to the waiting room out in the main hallway... NOW, go." I screamed at her.

"What's going on?" she said in a calm voice. "What is code blue?"

"NOW mom, go, just go." She looked confused and scared, but took my lead, she took Caitlin by the hand and got out of there just at the same time when a rush of doctors came charging up the hallway. Heads were peaked out of doorways to see who the code was being called for. Sonia was now in with Meghan and doctors ran up the hallways from all directions. Meghan's screams terrified me; it was the worst sound I have heard in my life. I was led over to the nurse's station by Karen, her physiotherapist. She got me to sit in a chair and had to hold my shoulders down to keep me seated in the chair because my whole body mind and soul wanted to be in there with my child.

"Let me up, let me go, I have to see her, please!" I pleaded and shouted. I could feel my hands as they gripped the side of my chair my nails dug into the imitation leather under the seat and broke through the fabric. "She's screaming, I have to go, I have to be in there" I cried out. Meghan continued to scream those loud terrified screams. I could feel the heat through Karen's hands and the grip of her fingers digging into my shoulders to keep me down. My legs would jump and my body trembled inside as I heard scream after scream. I couldn't cry at this point the fear I felt was overwhelming, my adrenaline had kicked in and I felt I needed to break free of the firm grip upon my shoulders. I watched as porters ran into her room with bags of blood that were being passed off to the nurses at the door and hung onto the IV poles.

A final scream from Meghan that sent chills through my body, "just fucking put it in I can't take it any longer." Anna called Gerry and Lanette, and someone called Randy. I waited for someone to arrive, it seemed like hours, but it was only minutes.

"Get me more platelets; get me suction, I need more packed cell reds, frozen fresh plasma" were the commands being shouted from her room. Every nurse on the floor was in her room working on her. Porters kept bringing in more bags from the blood bank. I got a glimpse of the room, and there were bags that even hung from curtain hooks as they ran out of room for IV poles.

"Just do it, just put the fucking thing in" she screamed again, "I don't care if I am awake just do it." Meghan was terrified, and brave, and I was afraid I was going to lose her this time for sure. Gerry arrived and I ran into his arms crying hard.

"They called a code blue, she was screaming and screaming, and her mouth just exploded and was bleeding, Gerry there was so much blood." My ears rang loud with the echo of Meghan's screams. "I wanted to be with her, but couldn't, the doctors needed to do their thing." Sonia came out of the room, and took off a face shield she had on. It was covered in blood, Meghan's blood. She just walked past me, and put her hand up. I knew she needed a moment alone. She was so close to Meghan, and she had to intubate her while she bled. She came to Gerry and me after a couple of minutes and said that Meghan was in critical shape. She was being put into a coma for a few days. Her mouth was packed full by the ENT specialist, and a whole team of specialists were on her case.

194

"That was the hardest thing I had to do" she said, but when Meghan said, "Just put the fucking thing in I thought, how brave and courageous of her so I prayed and intubated her while she was bleeding. I had to."

"It's okay," I said, and she cried.

"She is one special girl." Sonia said.

"Mom and Caitlin" I said to Gerry with a gasp. "Go down, I will get them and meet you in ICU."

"Did Meghan die, was that her screaming?" Caitlin asked, as my mom just held her hand while they sat in the family room and waited.

"There were so many doctors running down the hall. Were they all going into Meghan's room? What happened? It's all so fast and I don't understand" cried my mom.

"Yes, they were going to Meghan, she is in ICU now, her mouth had a bleed out that they couldn't control, so she is being put into a coma for a while." I informed my mom as I tried to catch my breath in between broken shook up words.

"She's going back to ICU? She just came out of there two days ago. I don't understand it, I'm angry. They should not have let her out with her poor mouth like that" mom replied in a way that I have never heard from her before. She normally kept her emotions to herself and never showed upset, but she was angry at this moment, and rightly so.

"I know mom, I am upset too, but we have to just be strong for Meghan now. She was terrified, and will wake with those same fears; I'm going down to see her now."

"Nannie, can we go to the gift shop? I need to get something for Meghan so she is happy when she wakes up." Caitlin asked.

We walked toward the elevators that lead to the first floor ICU, through the red zone, and into the yellow zone. The hospital was divided up into colours; we seem to bounce between the red and the yellow. We got to the main floor and mom took Caitlin to the gift shop while I braced myself to enter ICU once again. I didn't know what to expect after the code was called. I had been warned that her mouth was tightly packed. Randy had arrived and I was so grateful that I didn't have to enter the ICU on my own. I knew that Gerry was there with Lanette, but I needed my shoulder, my person to hold me up, and there he was. We were getting through this whole thing together and I was grateful that God had brought him to me. He was so amazing with Meghan, and maybe that's why God timed it this way, so that this man would be here to help me with my daughter.

"She was screaming so loud, it was terrifying, her screams are still echoing in me. Randy, she was screaming so so loud and I couldn't …"

He just held me, "Its ok, you are doing all that you can, let the doctors do their job" he said with as much reassurance as he could muster up.

"There was so much blood" I told him, as I felt myself shake and tremble against his body.

"What exactly happened?"

"Her mouth, it just burst, at first they thought she was throwing up blood, but it was the mouth hemorrhaging, it's all torn and. . ." I couldn't say any more. My eyes were now fixed on Meghan. She lay on her back, somewhat on her side, she was hooked up to so many machines and she had tubes going in and tubes coming out. Her mouth was packed and stretched extremely wide open, and completely packed with stuff. The ENT specialist decided that it needed to be done. Her platelet count was even lower, as she still reacted to them. They may have worked temporarily, but they are all used up now, and it's just a waiting game. Dr. Doyll was her ICU doctor, he remembered her from her two previous visits to ICU, and her previous code blue when she had the seizure.

"We are keeping her in a drug induced coma for a few days," he said to Randy and me. "We are concerned about what may happen when we take out the packing, but for now we have her stabilized."

When a doctor is concerned, their concern means that it could be a life or death situation all over again. I just stared at my daughter, the horrific way she had her mouth so fully packed, they couldn't move the dressing or disturb it, it needed to remain just as it was to stop and control the bleeding. She was hooked up to the artificial lungs that breathed for her.

"Is she in pain?" I asked, and Dr. Doyll assured me that she was under enough medications that she would not feel any pain.

"Randy, we know what happens when you pick a scab off a wound, it bleeds again. Look at her mouth. What is going to happen when they remove the packing?" I spoke to him in a whisper with tears streaming down and thought *is this the end, is she going to bleed uncontrollably. Her screams* I thought *would they be the last sound I would ever hear from her?*

"Thursday August 31/06 – Today I took Kate to the hospital with me. She was awesome, she prayed with Meghan and talked a lot to her. Even though Meghan was still in a comatose state, she still talked to her and filled her in on all the goings on in her life. I left the two of them alone for a bit, so that Kate could pray and have her time with Meghan, I waited in the family room just outside of ICU. When Kate came out we headed upstairs as I wanted to see Sonia.

We went to 3B and Sonia told me some things that surprised me. I talked to her about how Meghan wanted to do some special things, a bucket list of things she wanted to do, such as see the Northern Lights, and to see how gummy bears were made, and to swing on a tire swing tied to a tree. Sonia was different with me; she said things that freaked me out and had me upset for the rest of the day. She was confident that if they took the packing and the tube out that she wouldn't live. I was told that Meghan likely wouldn't be leaving the hospital ever, and that we should bring pictures of the Northern Lights to her, as she would likely not make it until Thanksgiving, and it would be her only way to see them. Also, that the chemo will likely be stopped now, and it won't be treating her cancer. Stunned and shocked that she would tell me these things, in front of Kate, and in an open setting where others could here as well. "Are you telling me that Meghan is dying." Kate and I

197

took a walk outside, "did they just tell me that Meghan is dying," I asked her with tears flowing. "Yes," and it was horrible how they did it." "Well I don't believe it, I can't, I don't feel it, so it can't be." "

I came back into the hospital and I bumped into Dave. The cool spiritual guy that did the PET scan and the gallium scan on Meghan. Well, he told me that he had just been in to see Meghan. He had prayed over her, and gave her a reiki treatment.

I was in tears. 'How was she? Did she seem to be responsive? Did she know you were there? Sonia just told me she was dying."

"Hold on" he said as he gently put his hand on my shoulder. "We are all dying, she is very much alive, don't lose hope, she is strong, and she isn't alone." Dave continued to tell me about the experience he had while he gave her the reiki treatment. He played a CD that had wolf sounds while he treated her, and I was so surprised.

"Wolves are her favorite, she loves the wolf" I told him with some excitement.

"Well wolves are family animals and stay together and they were calling her. Her spirit is connected to them." I knew in that moment that something very special had taken place; a special miracle was given to us. I forgot what Sonia said, and held on to the hope that I was given from Dave. I took Kate home, and asked her to keep praying, and to be strong

You see it wasn't important to me now that I had been upset. It didn't matter at all. I needed to see a bigger picture. My mind was still on Dave, how he came into Meghan's room and was probably performing his reiki at the exact moment that I had been upset. It just goes to show me, and anyone for that matter, that love conquers all. Dave told me that he said he loved Meghan, that he was her special angel and that he would always pray for her and would come treat her with reiki any time. I gave him the go ahead, that moment when we first met, that he had my permission, and Meghan gave hers also, that he could pray for her any time, and give her a reiki treatment. I believe it all ties in with the healing hands of Jesus. We are all gifted to heal, we just choose to do it in different ways. Some of us are doctors, some are teachers, some are preachers, some sing, some dance, and some simply are moms and dads who love their children more than life.

I stopped in to ICU to be with Meghan for a bit. As I sat beside her I gently held her hand, being ever so careful not to bump her at all. I gently kissed her hand. It was hard to look at her without completely breaking down. The soft pink air pillow blanket slowly rose and fell with each breath. It hovered over her like a magic carpet, but there was nothing magical about these circumstances, only in this delicate moment we shared. Her mouth still packed full with blood soaked gauze, a tube protruded out of the center of the gauze as they had to pack around the intubation. She also had a tube in her nose, likely to keep the stomach drained. But all I saw was love.

"You are amazing beyond words," I softly whispered when I kissed her hand. You are loved.

"September 1, 2006 - It's about 9:00 a.m. here at ICU. All the Doctors are in her room to do the first packing change in 3 days, 3 doctors in total, and two respiratory doctors, and her nurse Christine.

I've prayed already that everything go okay. That if it be Gods will, today, I am so afraid of what might be his will. Everyone seems to be on edge about the packing change. They wouldn't do it if her platelets had not improved, and since all counts are on the rise, now is the time. What if she bleeds out when the clot comes off? I am so on edge. Gerald is here, just sitting, not saying a word, he must be thinking along the same line of thought that I am. I can hear a lot of suction, and they have just put in an order for 5 bags of packed reds, and 5 bags of platelets. Time to take a break.

Packing change a success, there was no bleed out, and the feeding tube is still in, they haven't used it, as they don't want to run the risk of her throwing up, she isn't out of the woods, but being in a drug induced coma, and having her body heal and do nothing but heal is what is needed now.

Meghan continues to inspire and improve. Her counts are on the up, up, up, As of Sunday noon her white count was 9.4, her grans were 8.0 and her platelets have doubled on their own.

I have a cold now, so I haven't been in to see her for two days. Today I talked to her nurse and they were able to clean her mouth quite a bit. The feeding tube is still in.

Today is a total give thanks to God day. I know Meghan will make it through this, one day at a time. Jesus said He will never leave us or forsake us and I believe it. That's how it will be with Meghan, He will never abandon her through any of this.

Dr. Meado bumped into me in the hallway and had a big smile on his face. I showed him Meghan's counts for today, they are great.

Monday September 4, 2006 - Randy spent all day with Meghan. He helped the nurses turn her and comforted her. She had the tube taken out today. I am still sick and hopefully I can go in tomorrow, but the nurses said no not if I am sick. Her counts are fantastic; they are real pleased with her progress. I don't think I have seen her counts this good in a very long time."

September had arrived, the time to go back to school. It also happened to be cold and flu season which meant I could not see Meghan as I had caught a cold. However I did manage to go renew my driver's license as it was also my birthday. While in the line to renew the gal in front of me turned around and said "this is for you, it's all about love." She handed me a beautiful rose quartz necklace. She said to me "love is the ultimate power." I went home and with all the love in my heart I wrote a letter to Meghan which I faxed and a nurse will give it to her.

"Dear Meghan,

My sweet amazing baby girl. I miss you so very much. I have such a terrible cold that I have to get rid of before I can come in to see you. If I could be with you every moment I would, but that would be selfish of me. I have to put the health of you and every other patient there first. It would be very selfish of me to ignore that and to come in. Plus the nurses would probably drag me by the hair out of there hahah. Remember love is patient, love is kind, love is not selfish. It is because I love you so much that I am getting better before I come in. Actually Lanette and I both seem to have the same bug.

I call in several times a day and I am so proud of how amazing you are doing. You are the most incredible daughter any mom could have. You are my inspiration and I can't wait to hug you. Today is my birthday, but you will get this on September 6th. It's been a strange day – lonely without you and no one came over because they want to stay healthy so that they can see you, and I can't blame them. I had to go out to renew my licence plate, and get an emission test. That was a long enough outing, then back to bed. I am going to save my birthday dinner for when you are able to get out. How does tuckers sound. Kate wants to come see you again, but she has a tummy bug. When it is gone she will come for sure and hang out with you. We have a very very cool surprise planned for you but you will have to wait, haha.

I hope you don't mind me writing you a letter. I figured I could fax it, and maybe a nurse will either give it to you or read it to you. Boy I sure miss you. I tell all the nurses and Randy to make sure they tell you I LOVE YOU MORE. I hope you have been getting my messages. Caitlin as you know started school today. She was so cute doing her hair and makeup. I know she misses you and probably would love for you to give her some

201

make up tips. She let me wax her eyebrows if you can imagine. She actually asked me to do it.

What do you think of Randy's shaved head? He sure loves you, he tells me about his visits with you, how you held his hand and said you loved him. You cheeky thing, you made us both cry. Meghan I love you so very much, you are my life, you and Caitlin. You are the plan that God set out for me, to be a loving mother. You and I are never apart sweetie, find me in your heart. Hold your two hands together and imagine it's me right there with you. We will meet in your thoughts and in our dreams. And as soon as I am better the first place that I am coming is to see you my beauty. Remember when you feel anxious, think back to your special day, GO KAYAKING, take your mind there.

All my love and hugs xoxo
Mommy"

A good night's rest and I woke refreshed today, excited to be able to go and see Meghan. It had been five days since I last saw her and they were very long days.

Meghan was at the end of the hallway in a big room with her own bathroom and a nice large window. The view overlooked the main street in front of the hospital and mainly consisted of students as they walked about campus. McMaster was a teaching hospital and was part of McMaster University so there were quite a few students and residents. They always seemed to walk so fast outside hurrying off to somewhere, perhaps a class or lecture, or to be included in a medical teaching procedure. Not all the rooms had their own washroom, so I was pleased that she had this privacy. It was important that she felt that she has some sense of her own space in situations that are so private and personal for a young teenage girl.

I washed up just outside her room, gowned and then pushed open the heavy steel door. To see her beautiful face brought so much joy to my heart. We hugged and cried, boy did we cry.

202

"Hello beautiful" as I smiled,

"Hello mommy, I missed you and I just love you so so much."
Dear Sweet Jesus, thank you for this gem of a daughter you have
blessed me with.

"Mommy, it was so scary, I felt like I was in another world,"
she started to tell me.

"Well you probably were, in a strange way, a drug altered
world." I replied.

"I didn't like it, things were dark and scary, everyone was there,
but they looked distorted, and creepy. My feet still hurt, mommy.
What's wrong? Everything is getting so hard, I don't think I can do
much more."

I will make sure that no one touches your feet again, unless
you say it's ok, I promise."

"Can we go see Dave in MRI, Mommy? I want to thank him
for praying over me" she asked. *My gosh she is so sweet* I thought. I am
witness to such a transformation of a beautiful caring soul. Meghan of
long ago would never be so humble as to go thank someone for
praying for her. I was moved beyond belief.

It felt strange; as if daily I would see a new aspect of
transformation. Meghan had become brave but not bold, sweet and
kind, loving and tender, compassionate to the very core of her soul,
and had learned that in life we all suffer in some way, some more than
others, but faith and prayer sustain us and help us rise above it. She
knew the power of love, and when it was attached to words of prayer
it was the most powerful source of energy on this planet. That was
why it was so important for her to go see Dave. She too felt
connected to this man.

We as a family had reached the end of September. It felt like
this would never end, as we have been in here nearly two months now.
I do say we, because it is we. Yes I know that Meghan is the one
actually here, but it is where I am, where her sister is, where her dad
and step mom are, and where family was. I was beginning to think
that I won't ever get her home. The induction phase of her
chemotherapy was complete, and right now we waited. My baby girl

was still so very weak and required so much constant care. I didn't know if she had the strength to go on some days.

Oh, and speaking of constant care, I had no idea that a patient could qualify for PSW (personal support worker) care while in the hospital. One of the nurses brought it to my attention. She was quite upset that Meghan required so much care and no one had stepped up to even tell me, as her mother, that she could have full day PSW care in the hospital, so that I could get some work done, and take care of Caitlin and things I seem to have neglected. I started to think that I needed a clone of myself to get everything done. I constantly ran out of time and the energy to simply even cook a meal at home seemed impossible. So, the order for her PSW care was approved and from 7am – 3pm, Meghan would now have a personal support worker assigned just to her. She would have help with all her personal needs. Someone would be able to take her to tests if we are not here. Now don't get me wrong, I still plan to be here as much as possible, but it was good for Meghan to work with someone else. This was a Godsend for sure, and Meghan would be able to bond with new people.

I was so grateful for this help that had come to us, and it was because of that one special nurse, who took matters into her own hands, and demanding the proper care that Meghan deserved. Nurses truly are angels, their halo, a stethoscope. They seem to all be connected by the same spirit that lifts them naturally into a place that no one would understand, unless they are a nurse.

As Meghan built new relationships with other patients and with her PSW workers; I also built new friendships. Marilyn and I talked quite a lot, her son Brad was here quite often, he himself was dealing with cancer. Meghan and Brad visited each other quite often. Whenever he was an inpatient, he would always come in to see her, and her spirits seem lifted. I arrived one day and Meghan was grinning ear to ear, she told me about the visit that she and Brad had.

"He asked if I had a boyfriend" she said to me.

"Well what did you tell him? I replied with a smile.

"Well I told him no, I was ugly," she said and lowered her eyes.

'But then he said to me, "What? Meghan, you are HOT!" I could see the smile grow on her face as she fiddled with her fingers. Well, coming from a football star teenage boy, it was exactly what she needed to hear; a friend her own age, a boy, no less someone who was also going through similar things that she was going through. They understood each other in a way no one else would comprehend. Do I dare call it a blessing, when it involved the illnesses of two children? We saw blessings in everything. How was it possible for two moms to feel blessed that our children have struck up a very close special friendship, with the common ground being cancer? But it was what it was, and I will give thanks, not for the journey, but for the gift of people we have met through it.

Every child in here fights their own fight. We truly are not inside their minds, hearts and souls so we don't truly know what they feel. We witness the horror, absorb the pain in our hearts and feel things that are beyond even what can be expressed in written words. It can be heartbreaking, but we sit and watch and endure, and at times feel helpless beyond words. Chemotherapy feels like torture. They are tortured to be saved. My blessing, well she is my Meghan; her spirit so graceful and wonderful and can't be touched by any of this. I see the same bravery in so many of the kids.

I stood and fixed my eyes upon Meghan's beads as they hung strand by strand on her IV pole.

"Did you string up another necklace?" I asked her. "It looks like there are more beads hanging."

"Yes, I named the last one Tough Cookie. I've got eight of them now, mom." She was fed up.

"Well they look too heavy to wear now for sure" I answered not knowing what to say.

Then the idea hit me and I knew it was something that would help Meghan also. Together we designed a bravery bracelet, made with pretty glass beads, a bead for each treatment that would match the colour scheme of the beads that the kids received. That night I went to our local craft store and purchased some gorgeous glass beads. The red bead I chose truly looked like a droplet of blood. I also picked up elastic cord and some glue to secure the knots. I brought everything into the hospital the next morning. This was going to be a project for Meghan to use her hands and gain back some hand dexterity and movement; to use her fine motor skills while at the same time she would create something special for us to wear. The bracelets were so pretty and knowing what each bead stood for was a story in itself. The project then took on a life of its own. Nurses came in and as quickly as we made them we gave them away. We were both busy making bracelets; anyone who saw them wanted one. One mom ordered 10, we decided to sell them and give some money back to the hospital for the bead program so that they could keep it going and buy beads for the kids. I decided to write a poem about the bracelets, Meghan's Beads and right then at that very moment came the idea to write this book.

"Mom, you gotta write my story. No one else but you can write it the way it has to be told. Please mom!" she pleaded.

"Really? Meghan, I don't know if I can."

"Yes, mother you gotta do it, you just gotta, for me and for everyone."

Meghan loved her idea, so my journals and her journals with God's help had become what you are reading now. I also relive it as I tell it. It is both heartbreaking and therapeutic. My hope is that this book will be a blessing to anyone who reads it. It has taken years to write and rewrite, and there were times when I felt I could not do it and nearly gave up. Times arrived when I had to put it aside because it was too fresh and painful. I pray that it inspires and encourages.

"Tuesday October 3, 2006 - Bravery bracelets, looks like they are a hit. I didn't expect such a reply. They look great, and only cost about 4 dollars to make them. We will sell them with a nice card and my poem, and, then we will give money back to the hospital children's bead program. What a great thing to do. Meghan likes making them, that's the main thing. Maybe it is just beads to some people, but to these kids, it's a trophy, it's a

206

reward, it's a visual way for them to see just how truly brave they are. As a parent or family member we can now wear our own special bravery bracelet and feel strength from it in a very special inspiring way."

Meghan's Beads

I sit by her bedside as she's counting her beads,
She's threading them one by one.
Each one a colour, or shape that has its own price,
I think back to the day she had none.

Red for transfusions, green is for chemo,
Orange for a scan or test
Purple for bone marrow punctures,
A heart for the echo of the chest.

Some are real pretty; flowers and hearts.
A reward for what they go through.
Surgery, X-rays, losing your hair,
There's even a special one for ICU.

Days turn to weeks, it's become 8 months now,
I still look at her beads and cry.
So many green, red, purple and blue,
So much for my child; God why?

Meghan's beads tell us all a story,
Of courage, of faith, and of love.
Of grace bestowed upon a beautiful girl
From our Heavenly Father above.

With every step of this journey she's grown.
With every bead she's become strong.
I've watched with pride, the journey of my baby,
With her beads over 8 strands long.

With each bead came a blessing,
We were witness to each answered prayer.
Successful procedures, passed tests,
Just a little longer sweetie we're almost there.

There are a few more beads still waiting,
For the day they'll be in her hand.
She will thread them all one by one,
Creating that final strand.

One day soon, she will pick up that bead,
The one that says, Meghan you're done.
How perfect is it, that rainbow bead,
That says sweet Meghan you've won!

To my sweet baby,
Love mom. October 3, 2005.

Chapter 19 – Seeing Spots

As we continued to make bracelets I saw spots on Meghan's arm. Mom was with me, and I pointed out a couple of spots to her. I remembered my girls having had those very same type of spots before and my mom had told me back then. "Ang, your girls have chicken pox."

So, as I turned and said to my mom, "Ma, these look familiar, is it possible that they could be what I think they are?"

She nodded in agreement and said, "Oh, they look like it, but she has had them already" mom replied.

"Yes, but mom, the transplant, it wiped out all her immunities, she can get anything all over again," I answered and took a little walk around the hallway as I looked for someone to drag into Meghan's room. Meghan was set to try a new round of maintenance type of Chemotherapy and I needed to make sure she was okay.

"Sonia," I called out, "Meghan has some strange looking spots and they look familiar, I think she has chicken pox" I asked hoping I was wrong.

"Oh, no, not now," she immediately came into the room, had a look, and said, "Meghan, you have chicken pox, but we have to biopsy to confirm. Sure enough they sniped off a spot and down it went to infectious disease. Isolation time and no scratching were her instructions. She would have her own room, with a washroom and no visitors that haven't had the chicken pox, or a vaccine. The spots were everywhere and I thought of that Dr. Seuss book, Put me in the Zoo, you know the book about the big dog with all the spots. I used to read that book to the kids when they were little. Well, funny how I thought of it now.

"Put me in the zoo," I whispered to myself quietly.

"What?" Meghan asked.

"Oh nothing, was just thinking of the book I used to read you when you were little, you know the dog with all the spots?"

She smiled. "Don't even think about colouring my spots mom" Meghan laughed. I thought of how old she was for chicken pox and it hit me,

"Oh please God, with her being almost an adult, don't let her end up with shingles" I prayed.

When you go through a BMT (bone marrow transplant), you lose all of your immunities that you built up from childhood vaccines, and from being breast fed and any other life happenings that create immunity to disease. So basically she had become an open door to catch anything and likely would catch a few more things. Interestingly enough, when she would reach one year post transplant later in October, she would need to get re vaccinated all over again, just as if she were a baby. I hated the idea of that but would cross that bridge when we came to it.

"Wednesday October 18, 2006 - Meghan was great today. Interactive, happy, talkative, and she should be over the pox soon. Jessica, from Ronald McDonald House, was in with her and they had a great visit. Jessica came to us a few weeks ago, a young woman, maybe a year or so older than Meghan. She volunteers her time to build relationships with the children in the hospital. They do crafts together, and when the children are well enough to go out, they are invited to Ronald McDonald House events to socialize and try to feel somewhat normal again. They truly had a great visit. It's actually Thursday night now and once again I can't sleep, I write and every day seems a repeat of the last. Time ticks away, and my stresses eat away. No one understands, I don't even know how to talk to people sometimes about how all this is. God when does it end, I can't understand all of this. I need to let go and let God.

Thursday October 19, 2006 - I get angry at times and I seem to bite the head off of anyone around me. I get tightness in my chest that makes me feel like everything in me is racing away, spinning out of control.

210

Catch your breath Angela and slow down. Life should be sweet and fun and simple. This shouldn't be the way it is. What do I do when I feel like running away from my own life? Caitlin deserves more than I am giving her. I want to see both of my girls smile and be happy.

God, I need you so much. I need you to get me through this, stop the insanity. Please help heal my baby and bring her home. It's not fair, it's just so unfair that any child should have to go through even a bit of what Meghan has gone through. Someday soon, someday soon, smiles and laughter will ring again in my heart."

Now we were at one year post transplant. Today was about presents, cake and a new type of birthday. That was exactly what we did, I brought in a cake "Happy BMT year" and sang to her as I walked into her room with a big stuffed dog for her bed, and balloons.

Meghan was tucked in her bed and appeared a little flushed. Her skin was a soft pink. How I oddly adored her sweet little bald head; it felt odd in a way to celebrate a first year at her 17th year. She did like the cake and especially the soft fluffy oversized dog, something for her to cuddle with at night. The nurses loved the cake and made a big deal of this day for Meghan. Sadly many don't make it a year after their transplant. This was a huge moment; a day that we were not sure would ever arrive.

Sometimes it felt like we had been here forever as I remembered back to the start of this whole journey. What was supposed to be eight weeks has turned into more than a year. Certain people seem to have adopted certain tasks with Meghan's care. Her health aids are always making sure Meghan has her nails done, except for one finger which she has to wear a clip on to read her oxygen levels and heart info or something like that.

I mentioned to you before about the red chemo, Vincristine, it's the one responsible for the neuropathy pain. Well it was also responsible for her drop foot as they call it. The tendons in the back of her feet have lost their ability to function; so Meghan now wore splints on her feet. We didn't dare go near them as the pain was so severe with pins and needles in her feet. Meghan didn't like to have her socks changed or her toenails clipped. The PSWs aren't allowed to clip her toenails so it's up to the nurses or a family member. I tried doing it, but she cried so horribly from the pain that I could bear to hurt her, so I constantly bugged and pleaded with the nurses to please do it, please. However, it didn't seem to be a priority for them though, so I was just going to have to do it next time. They had to be maintained to prevent an injury.

That day came only a few days later when I noticed how long Meghan's toenails had become.

"Oh, honey, we have to clip them. It can't wait any longer." I told her as I collected a bowl and some foaming pump soap to soak her feet. "Maybe if I clip them in the bowl while you are soaking them in warm water they won't hurt so much" I assured her. I could see the anxiety and fear all over her face. She didn't want this done, but knew it had to be so. I let her soak her feet for a long time and then a nurse came in with some delicate little sponges that they sometimes use on the teeth when a tooth brush can't be used; usually in the instance of developed mouth sores.

"These will be good to gently wipe off the dead skin and you won't have to touch her very much," she said as she passed me a bag full of little blue sponge tipped swabs.

"Oh perfect, thank you" I replied as I took them from her. I gently clipped each toenail as I listened to her sob. I didn't dare look up as my heart broke a little more with each clip.

"Oh God, please just help us through this," I silently prayed as I began to gently brush off the dead skin from between her toes and under her nails.

"He he he," she giggled a little between her tears, "Mom, it actually tickles a bit when you do that, it still hurts, but at least I can feel a tickle and laugh" she commented.

"All done," I said, as I gently lifted her legs and let them lay to air dry on the bed.

"Don't worry, I am not going to dry them. They can air dry" I assured her as I held my hand up in a halt motion.

"Phew mom, that felt like a work out. Man, my heart is beating so fast. Glad it's done and those blue spongey things, we're keeping them" she insisted.

"I gotta step out to find a bathroom missy. I'll be back in a few, ok?" So I stepped out, not just to have a bathroom break, but to have a good cry in the lounge. I felt like I had just tortured my kid. I broke down and just cried with another understanding mom. Just one more day in the journey of this crap, but thank God for that moment of giggle. I will cherish it for sure.

Chapter 20 – Attitude

Gerry's sister, Karen, would come in every Thursday evening and read to Meghan, but lately she had told me that she didn't think Meghan was that interested. I encouraged her to keep coming in as it was good for Meghan to have a change of routine and try new things. Meghan seemed to just lay in bed and watch television or movies on VHS. I wanted her to have a variety of activities when here.

A comment was passed to me today when I came in. The nurse practitioner said that she felt Meghan has developed an attitude, and that she had been rude lately by not answering the nurses and seemed to just ignore people when they talk to her. She wouldn't even pull her call bell if her alarm on her IV pole was beeping.

"I know she is going through a lot, but her attitude needs to be addressed," she told me. Well, this didn't sound like Meghan at all and I let Sonia know that I would speak to her. On the other hand, I felt that this poor girl had every right to feel like ignoring people and situations.

As I entered her room Meghan was found in her typical position, sprawled out in her bed as she watched TV. I smiled at her as I came by to kiss her forehead. It was still a little difficult to see her with the feeding tube in her nose, but she needed it as she still wasn't eating enough. I knew she didn't like it and I let her know that as soon as she ate regularly and sufficiently that the tube would come out. Her skin had become quite raw and irritated from where it was taped down on her cheek.

"Just start eating well and that silly thing will come out," I assured her.

"I know, mom, I know." She replied.

"So, Meghan how did things go last night, with Auntie Karen, did you enjoy your visit?" I asked her as I sat on the edge of her bed.

"Meh, it was ok, she just reads to me, and sometimes I just end up falling asleep."

215

"Well that's okay; at least you get to sleep easier. I brought you in some audio books, something different than watching TV, or having someone read to you and you can just listen at your leisure." I said as made my way over to the far side of the room.

"What do you want to watch?" I asked her as I looked through the growing stack of movies. I didn't get an answer.

"Meghan, don't ignore me." I said as I looked through the movies. Still I didn't get an answer and so I turned around and said again, "Meghan, what shall we watch?"

"You pick one mommy, whatever one you want." I got an ill feeling about something so I turned my back to her and faced the TV.

"How about I put in Mrs. Doubtfire?" I asked, and still no response. So turned to face her as fear burned in the pit of my stomach, as I now knew what was going on.

"Mrs. Doubtfire," I said.

She smiled."Ya , I feel like I could use a laugh."

"Meghan, you can't hear me can you?" I asked with a soft voice.

Tears flowed, and she shook her head slowly side to side over and over again and said "No."

"Can you hear anything?"

"Not much mommy and I'm really scared" she blurted out.

"Why haven't you said something, and how come you know what I am saying now?" I asked.

"I can read your lips. I read a lot of lips, but some are harder, especially the ones with accents. I can read yours though 'cause I know how you sound."

Oh, God I thought, I felt, I feared, she has lost her hearing now.

"Don't be mad at me mommy, I didn't tell anyone because I didn't want any more things done to me."

"Oh my sweet baby, I am not mad and no one will be mad not one person will ever be mad at you. But I do need to tell the doctors and nurses, so that they can fix the hearing problem. Okay?"

I kissed her sweet cheek and brushed her tears away. "Okay" she replied. I popped in Mrs. Doubtfire and went to speak with Sonia.

216

"I'll be right back, ok? I promise." With one more kiss I left her room. When I ran into Sonia, she said she was also looking for me.

She began with "Meghan has been ignoring the nurses and they feel that her attitude has become so very rude."

"Actually, that is why I came to find you. Have you ever known Meghan to be rude?" I continued.

"No, but" she started to speak as I cut in.

"Never mind the buts. She isn't being rude, she can't hear."

The look on her face was that of complete shock. "What do you mean she can't hear?" She was worried.

"She has been reading my lips, and whoever's she can, but if a nurse asks her something and isn't looking at her, she doesn't hear her. I checked it myself, turned my back to her when I spoke, and she couldn't hear a thing."

Sonia immediately called for the doctor and came into Meghan's room. "Meghan," she called, and Meghan didn't answer. As she got a little closer she placed her hand on her leg gently as to not startle her. "Hi Meghan," and Meghan turned and smiled, and greeted her warmly with love and respect and genuine affection the way she always had greeted anyone.

"Hello, I'm watching Mrs. Doubtfire,.. Heellllllooooo, hehe" as she mimicked Mrs. Doubtfire with whip cream on her face popping out from behind the fridge door. This was the Meghan that everyone knew, the polite, sweet girl, who never complained, never judged, and was always grateful for anything and everything.

"I understand that you are having trouble hearing, so we are going to have a special hearing doctor test you and see if we can help you with the hearing problem, okay sweetie? Don't ever be afraid to tell us things, promise?" she said.

"I promise," she said, and offered Sonia her pinky "pinky swear."

"Meghan, how long has this been going on, the hearing loss?" Sonia asked.

"A long time," she said, "Almost since I got here, it's getting worse and worse."

"Oh, sweetheart, please tell us these things from now on, okay? We will have you tested tomorrow morning." Sonia was so apologetic to me, and I said, "hey, no need to apologize, she had us all fooled, me included." It's no wonder she hated it when her Auntie Karen came to read, she couldn't hear a thing.

The hearing test was scheduled for the morning to be done in the hospital, and then another appointment was made for the next day at another hospital, with an audiologist. We were allowed out for that appointment the next morning, and Randy took us. I think Meghan felt excited about being out, and the audiologist made it interesting and let her know that a hearing aid would help her to hear the sounds that she no longer could.

The cause of her hearing loss I found out was both due to chemotherapy and a combination of the antibiotics and antifungals that she had consumed. Apparently, when one has chemotherapy we lose our hair. We all know that, but we lose hair everywhere. It would all grow back except for the inner ear hair, that was where our hearing sense was from and that loss was permanent. It's very sad indeed, that her loss was so drastic, but we have hope again, she was going to have a hearing aid made special for her and it would be pink. So the process had begun to get her a hearing aid. It won't happen overnight, but at least she would be able to have some hearing ability.

It seemed like it was constantly one huge hurdle after another, but so far she had conquered each and every one, and continued to develop and grow into such a strong young woman. Her heart was being transformed into pure beauty. Her outer body has taken a horrible beating, but inwardly she was a blossom of heaven itself.

"Friday November 3rd, 2006 - This morning I went in early to see Meghan. Her feet were hurting her so much. A pain management team came in to see her. They will start her on Nortriptyline on Monday. Hopefully it will help her, the pain is so crippling for her. She was pretty good today, I know she is brave when I leave and wants me to stay over, but she is okay at night and knows I am always home. Caitlin and I went out for

218

lunch and also dinner. PD day today. She has Lauren sleeping over tonight. We had Chinese and mom came over and we made bracelets.

Oh, Meghan has a new room-mate – a 6 week old baby girl. She is so sweet. Sadly she has broken legs and ribs and a collar bone. Probably from abuse or an accident, I haven't heard the whole story, but I am led to believe that it's from abuse. Her little legs up in traction makes you just want to cry. Maybe she will be a little blessing for Meghan. I feel God at work in this situation. He has brought the pain team to Meghan as she was praying for her foot pain. Her body is being controlled by Him, as her chemo won't resume until He decides to release her to it. No more cancer has grown and other things on the CT are better. The spleen is better, the lungs are better. I feel good at this moment. I feel peaceful and feel Meghan is about to make good progress. She knows she has to eat and drink more and especially drink with the new meds for her pain. She will also eat better. It will come. God bless us all and keep us well. Amen."

Meghan's sweet little roommate had become an amazing blessing. The original reason she was put into the room was because of Meghan's hearing loss. If the baby cried, Meghan wouldn't hear it and wouldn't be disturbed. Well, it truly was God at work here and this angel baby was here for more than we realized.

When Meghan was first talked to about her HLH illness and how she would have to have chemotherapy, she was also told of the permanent horrific damage that it would do to her body, yes permanent; Meghan would not be able to have children. This news had over time set in with devastation for Meghan. I didn't have the words to comfort her then, but this little baby girl had taken care of all of that.

I walked into her room this morning and my eyes embraced the most incredible sight. Meghan was holding Taylor and feeding her. A nurse sat beside the bed and the smiles that filled the room were like beams of sunshine. Apparently Meghan had a calming effect on Taylor, and was the only one that the baby would allow to feed her. The nurses had tried numerous times, and on one occasion they let Meghan hold her for a bit; instantly she stopped crying.

"Quick get a bottle for her to feed her," and like magic, Taylor held onto Meghan's finger as she fed this beautiful little girl. Meghan knew why Taylor was there, but did she really? It wasn't just because Taylor happened to be the roommate for a girl who couldn't hear her cries.

"Look mom, I don't need to give birth, I can have a foster baby just like her, and love her just the same" Meghan said as she smiled with love and joy just beaming from her. I cried. What a beautiful sight and what a beautiful thought and pure truth. We don't love our children because we give birth to them we love them because it is our choice to love them as our own, to be a mother or a father.

Taylor was so beautiful, if you could imagine Snow White as a baby, well it would be her. Skin so soft and with just a hint of pink in her cheeks, raven black hair, not thick and messy, but soft and shimmery. She was beautiful, and her whole being just glowed. I can honestly say that I have never in my life seen a baby more beautiful. We decided to give her a nickname, it became ladybug. Ladybugs are supposed to be good luck, and this little ladybug sure brought that. Her birth parents were not allowed in to see her, and foster parents will soon be taking her home in a few days. Meghan continued to feed her, and helped the nurses dress her. It was a blessing for sure. I met the foster mom one after noon.

"I heard that you have given her a nickname, Ladybug" she said to me.

I smiled back and said. "Well she sure did bring us a lot of luck and joy."

"We are keeping her name as that, because she is our lady bug too." I could tell that this family was exactly the family that would be good for Taylor. The day they discharged Ladybug into the care of her new family was both a sad day and a happy one. Sad because Meghan knew she may never see this baby again, but happy because she was going home. Home was where Meghan wanted to be.

Ladybug's foster mom brought in a gift for Meghan, an Anne Geddes doll dressed in a ladybug outfit. They are cute beautiful dolls, some are bumble bees, some are flowers. Well this one was a ladybug and it was a gift that we will all cherish forever. Ladybugs now mean something special to our whole family, just as frogs have taken on a special meaning, so too has the ladybug.

I felt lost, so I began a letter to the paper as so much had happened since Meghan had come home from Sick Kids, I felt that I needed to update everyone on *our girl*. Christmas was not that far away and my daughter was still in the hospital. I wasn't sure at this point if she would ever come home and I began to lose hope fast. My letter to the paper was a way for me to reach out. Maybe if I reached out then another miracle would happen and my baby would heal and come home. So my letter became a plea in some ways, and a reminder to many that love truly is all that matters. I had a heart that loved my children and all those who suffer and I needed to just let it go. The paper ran my letter.

A mother's unwavering love – Angela Rush and her daughter Meghan share a painful journey together.
Nov 22, 2006
Editor's Note: *About a year ago The Burlington Post wrote a front-page story about a local teen, Meghan Rush, battling a rare blood disorder. Her mother, Angela, wrote to us last week giving an update on her daughter's painful journey.*
This is a heartbreaking story that only a mother can tell. However, it is also a story of determination, courage and wisdom. As the Christmas season is now upon us, the Post decided to run Meghan's story in its entirety and in her mother's own words.
* * *

She was the Post's "cover girl" early in December 2005. In April of that year, after weeks of flu-like symptoms, Meghan was diagnosed with a rare blood disorder called HLH.
This disorder was triggered by a virus and since that moment her world has been upside down. She had to undergo months of treatment similar to what a leukemia patient would receive. This was not cancer, yet she required a lot of chemotherapy. After six

221

months the disorder was not going away, and a bone marrow transplant was needed to keep Meghan alive.

Through many answered prayers a perfect 10 out of 10 match was found through the blood services bone marrow registry. A complete stranger -- a man from somewhere in this world -- was donating his marrow to save Meghan. On Oct. 16, 2005, she was admitted to the Hospital for Sick Children in Toronto, as that is where the transplants are done. Her transplant was a success; she received her new marrow and new start on Oct. 27. There were some pretty frightening moments in the five weeks that followed, but she pulled through them all. She was home and ready to begin life again.

LOW BACTERIA DIET

The months that followed were very strict for everyone who came near Meghan. Our home got a makeover thanks to my friends and family. We had to prepare a new sterile environment for Meghan. We painted, cleaned carpets, had the ducts cleaned, removed all stuffed animals, and purchased all new pillows and mattress covers. We had to have a dishwasher as the plates and utensils had to be so sterile. Hand washing stations were at the front door.

Caitlin, Meghan's sister, had to part with her guinea pigs as we could not have pets in the house. Meghan was on a specific diet for six months to a year. No fresh produce unless the skin came off. No salads, no honey, no meats or cheese from a deli, no seafood, no nuts or grains, no produce from other countries, no market purchased foods.

A low-bacteria diet they call it. What would normally be considered good healthy eating for us was a big no no for her. Frozen and canned foods with expiry dates were best. We had to cook things well, no pink in any meats.

She was also on so many medications -- steroids, anti fungals, antibiotics, special precautionary antibiotics for pneumonia, hormone pills, immune suppressants, medication to ease the stomach acid as the chemotherapy was so harsh during transplant. Time passed, and with only a couple hospital stays, one in December '05, and then in February '06 for pneumonia, Meghan was on the road to recovery and ready to tackle the world. She did incredibly well with her home school as she wasn't allowed to go out in public for at least six months.

222

We were registered for school, her hair had grown back, and she was gaining strength and had become the most beautiful striking young woman you can imagine. With new bone marrow, new blood type and a new outlook on life, she was ready to begin again.

In July we noticed she began losing weight and she complained of a sore hip and back. After routine CT scans and the close monitoring that follows a transplant we were called into the 3F clinic at McMaster Hospital where Meghan had weekly appointments. They found some abnormalities on the scan revolving around the liver and hip.

A biopsy was done, and we were then given the results about three weeks later. Meghan was now diagnosed with a very rare lymphoma, ALCL or Anaplastic Large Cell Lymphoma. The doctor said she was only the second case of this type of lymphoma that McMaster has seen. It is that rare. Oddly enough, the other case involved a child who also had HLH due to a virus, and then eight months later got the same cancer.

Devastation is the only word that I can use to describe the moment we were in. I will never forget as Meghan held the hand of her clinic nurse, she spoke these exact words -- "Please don't let me die."

I get choked up just thinking about it. I don't think I will ever be able to look back on that moment and make sense of any of it. After so much already, why did this have to happen to my daughter?

Meghan began her first treatment on Aug. 10; she ended up in ICU the next day, which was her 17th birthday. Since that day she has remained in hospital. She has been in ICU three times, and the last occasion was a "code blue"; she ended up in a drug induced coma for a week.

ONLY CHANCE TO LIVE

It's a long way back to recovery from something like that, but the whole team at McMaster is incredible. They stay ahead of things and are always amazing me with their ability to keep my baby alive and fighting.

Chemotherapy is horrible, but in Meghan's case it's her only chance to live. The fact that she has had a bone marrow transplant makes the chemo that much harder on her body. She *is a fighter and she is brave, just like all the kids I see daily as I go in to be with my daughter.*

It's just so unfair for any of these kids to go through so much. I have made some amazing friends through the hospital. Some are Burlingtonians.

When most teenagers walk through hallways they are greeting their school friends, planning weekends, exchanging grades and talking about their typical stuff. Meghan goes through her hallways greeting doctors. She is a common face amongst the medical world in McMaster hospital. She exchanges her news about her tests but they are things like CT scans, biopsies, blood counts and lumbar punctures. Her rewards for tests are bravery beads. She is about to begin her eighth strand. Her typical stuff is not what I would wish upon anyone.

We are in this together as a family, and I would not change places with any other parent for the simple reason that I would not want any child to go through what Meghan is going through. There may have been a time when I wished it could all go away, then I asked myself, where would it go? To another child. It made me cry, and I simply prayed. God, give us the strength to get through this together, help us bear this journey and spare anyone else from ever having to go through it.

Meghan has learned something so important through all of this. Every time we face something tough and her emotions and fears kick in, I hold her hand and ask her one question. "Meghan, what is the most powerful thing in the world? What is it?"

She squeezes my hand and says "love."

That's right, you keep holding on to love, the love from me, your dad, and your step parents and your sister and all your family, and especially God's love and you will get beyond this time of hardship and pain.

About a week ago Meghan got a gift, not a typical gift that you can unwrap, but a very unique gift. We call her ladybug. A roommate, a seven-week-old baby girl. She was medicine for Meghan's soul. My daughter fell in love with this tiny baby that brought her so much joy and healing.

That is something to keep in mind when we head into the Christmas season. Think of how much joy a baby boy brought to the world, think of the healing and the joy. I will think of it every single moment. It's all about love. Isn't that why God gave us the baby? It's all about love.

When I picture in my mind Meghan holding that gift, glowing and loving every moment of being able to share love and something special with a tiny baby, well, only God knows how grateful I am.

Chapter 21 – A Promise

It was late fall now the days were cool and the nights crisp. The air was like heaven to breathe in, I loved it. The leaves gave off a scent as they dropped from each tree; raining down in colours that brought a sense of peace to me. I knew that when things were stripped bare to the bone, or branch as this case may be, that given time it would bloom again. This thought gave me hope. Meghan had blossomed into a very incredible young lady. She saw life from her heart now and somehow she was able to see the blessing in every situation, which constantly amazed me. She became hope.

We often take for granted the beauty in the world around us as it is just right there for our very own eyes to behold. We can take a walk, and have all our senses awakened, sight, touch, taste smell and sound. They can become alive as a simple breeze blows through a cluster of trees and then like rain, the leaves fall and dance around. It's not just leaves falling, it's a song, a dance, a promise, and it's so much more that we take for granted. I knew I wouldn't after this fall.

One special day Meghan was blessed. Her health aid Johanna was taking her for a stroll in the chair, they ventured outside the hospital and into the University campus. They discovered a place that Meghan now called her special place. It bears the name *"the fountain."* It was a lounge with 20 foot ceilings. There were evergreens, a waterfall, plants, and windows that opened up, screened of course, but it allowed a breeze to come through. An oasis, a tropical paradise found that now became a place of refuge for Meghan. The front walls were all glass, and it overlooked the university campus grounds. Not only did this place let my baby experience a bit of nature, it gave her hope, it brightened up her day, she became energized when she woke up now.

"Can I go to my special place today?" became the first thing she asked each day and of course we took her. She tried harder, she got dressed faster, took more pride in how she looked, because there were students in this place, not just patients.

"December 1, 2006 - Dr. Meado is on for the month. The doctors take a month of rotation in the 3B ward, and I love it when he is on. Actually they all have their special qualities, but Dr. Meado is the one who diagnosed Meghan, and there is a special bond between them. He feels Meghan should be able to go home. She has been in hospital way too long.

I am so glad he is on this month. I know he is the best and he will do the best for Meghan. He passed a remark "Why do something for the sake of curiosity" I know he was referring to the lung biopsy. Dr. Posthma likes answers and wants to know everything whatever the cost.

A bone marrow test will be done on Meghan and they will know if chemo can be resumed. I was told that the cellularity should be at least 60% to tolerate the chemo. Meghan's last BM test was 20%, she needs some healing time before she takes another hit. I don't think she is even close to that percentage.

Many many prayers are being said, and I believe and feel God is bringing her home to feel love. God please keep me in your love and keep away fear and worry. Fill our home with love and light and laughter.

Tomorrow is a meeting with all of us and Dr. Meado and the team on 3B. Lord give me courage and strength to speak of your love and that now is right and time for Meghan to let her body become stronger and heal at home. I give her to you Lord."

Since hearing the words, "I think it's time for her to go home," there was nothing else on my mind other than getting her home. I want her home for Christmas, and it was my mission to do so. December had arrived and Meghan had been in here almost four months now.

228

I ended up writing an 11 page letter to further my request to have her home. The end result was that if I met certain criteria, then she would be discharged on December 18, 2006. Met certain criteria, "bring it on" I said to them. "Bring it on." I needed to learn how to insert the feeding tube and how to operate it as Meghan was likely to have to remain on it. Ok, task one done. However I also said to Meghan "you start eating now, and keep it up, pray about it, and when you leave here you will also leave this tube behind you. You will have two weeks to work at it"

Meghan was all for it, and the results were incredible. She would be going home so she put everything she had into this plan of action. With the boost that her special place gave her daily she was able to put so much into all of her tasks. She drank the required amount, and ate better each day. Amen, praise God, she put on a bit of weight. I had certain things to take care of on my end. Occupational therapy was going to come to my home to see if it was adequately equipped to handle her needs. I also had to complete five successful transfers in front of both her occupational therapist and physical therapist of safely transferring Meghan in and out of my car. I knew I could do it, with God, I could do anything. I had no fears and welcomed the opportunity to show them that me, my daughter, my family, my friends; we were all able and available to look after this child

"Why do something just for the sake of curiosity? It's time for her to go home." Those words inspired me to know that the journey was now in our control, if we passed the tests, this journey would continue then at home. Now that Dr. Meado didn't feel it necessary to just simply have another biopsy, they cancelled the lung biopsy. With everything they have done, what would it do now to go looking for more things to do and Dr. Meado, being a Godly man himself, knew it was time for Meghan to feel family, home and love.

"It's the medicine for her soul now" he said to me. We had dreamed and hoped that this day would come. We would continue to work together getting Meghan stronger, and getting my home prepared.

It was mid-December and the hospital was getting ready for Christmas. Various people have come by already to visit the kids. They have an area set aside out in the main family area on the third floor, just outside of 3B, where daily activities were planned. The kids were kept fairly busy with the entire goings on. Gifts arrived daily from so very many anonymous donors for all the children.

We were getting ready to leave for a walk to Meghan's special place, the Fountain, when a cart of very large gift bags was being pushed door to door and was almost to Meghan's door.

"Let's just wait to see what they have for me," she said with a smile and a giggle. "You know I love presents," she giggled again. The woman was short, and wore a Santa's helper hat.

She asked Meghan "how old are you?"

"Seventeen" she answered.

So she handed Meghan a bag that was marked, for a teenage girl.

"I have to open it now mom, I can't wait" as I wheeled her back into her room. We sat on her bed together as she opened the present. There were bottles of nail polish, and various cosmetic items, eye shadow, and a curling iron. Well, the tears flowed, and I had no words. A curling iron given to a girl who had no hair from her chemotherapy; mascara for a girl with no eyelashes.

Meghan threw the curling iron on the bed. "Stupid fucking curling iron" she blurted out. In that brief moment I saw the joy of a child opening a present instantly turn to heartache and sadness. Within seconds Anna, Meghan's child life guide, came into the room.

"Oh, for heaven's sake," she replied as she took the parcel, put the curling iron back into the bag, and said, "Meghan, I am so sorry, this is not your gift, I will be right back." She returned with a bright and very large gift bag that had the head of a giant white teddy bear peeking out of the top of it. Well, Meghan's eyes just lit up, and her smile returned. She may be 17, but her outlook on life was deep and meaningful like a wise elder yet her heart was that of a gentle happy child. This gift was perfect for her, an adorable, but large, stuffed teddy, white with a red bow, some CD's, and DVD's, and a whole assortment of cosmetics; a perfect gift. Her reaction still rings

230

through me, how horrible. Her remark clearly showed us that "Fucking curling iron, like what am I going to do with that?"

"I'm bringing polar bear to my special place," as she tucked the bear under her arm and seated herself into her chair. Meghan could move easier when she wore her splints during the daytime. It gave her piece of mind to know that her feet were covered and could not be bumped. They were a little difficult to walk in but one step at a time. We just had to get the pain under control and then work on desensitizing them a bit. Our hope was that she would walk again on her own with no splints. Movement would never fully return, but she would be able to walk on her own again of this I had no doubt.

One of the nurses from the hospital, and also a social worker were coming over today to check on the progress being made at home for some of the requirements for Meghan's impending discharge. Our home was now made wheelchair accessible with a ramp built out front. My dining room was turned into Meghan's temporary bedroom, until she had enough strength to manage going up the stairs, however with the foot pain, I didn't see that happening any time soon. A temporary shower area was also set up in the kitchen, with curtains giving complete privacy.

After I showed both of these women the progress that we have made in my home, we sat in the living room and had a tea.

"I am impressed with what you have set up here," both of them agreed.

"We are giving our stamp of approval, with happy hearts, that your house is safe. Meghan can come home."

"Well, I guess there is just one more test to pass the transfers from wheelchair to car, and car to wheelchair." I need to complete five of them in a row, with success and without strain from myself or Meghan, so that occupational therapy was satisfied that I wouldn't drop my daughter beside the car. I continued to smile while they collected their things.

"Alright then, let's head back to Mac, I am ready to bring my baby home" I said as we all headed out the door.

Everything was up to Meghan and I, and we had to do these transfers with ease, or she would not come home. When I got into

Meghan's room, I closed the door, and sat by her bedside. I knew she was anxious about all the tests and I told her that her home and new room were ready. She now had the whole entire main floor as her own. She could get in and out of bed, get herself onto her commode, wheel herself into the kitchen, and then wheel herself into the living room where her new TV, with closed caption waited. It was a larger TV and would be easier to read the captioning.

Today was discharge day, December 18, 2006. First things first, Meghan and I had to pass our five transfers tests set out by occupational therapy.

"Meghan, I need to know that you understand what I am saying, okay? So please let me know that you do, or ask questions. If you sense you are too weak squeeze me and I will kiss your cheek for you to hold tight for me to handle it."

She nodded and said "Okay mommy, we got this."

Physio and occupational therapy arrived shortly after, and we headed down to the underground parking, so that we could tackle this test. My car, a Ford Escort, was not a big car, and quite low to the ground, so it required a lot of bending and I made sure that I had on some good solid running shoes. Lifting Meghan from her chair wasn't so bad, but to lift her from the low seat in the car and onto the chair would be a bit more difficult. We managed fine and with the fourth lift could feel her legs getting weak. I needed her to help push herself up but I could feel her legs about to give way. So, I whispered into her ear as I kissed her cheek, "I got this one, save it for the last lift." She understood as she squeezed me to let me know right after I kissed her. Holding onto her, with a prayer steadfast in my heart, I lifted her properly, and transferred her to the wheelchair.

Then to my surprise for the last transfer she said "let me stand for this one mom, and you can just help me back into the car." She stood up, put her arms around my neck as I held her body and eased her back into the car. Both Andrea and Nancy looked at each other, "impressive" they said in unison and we passed.

We made our way back upstairs, to await our discharge papers. Home, we were finally going home. There was quite a bit of packing up to do. Meghan had accumulated so many things. She had some school things to collect from the hospital classroom. Yes, she took some courses while in hospital. Nothing really on a high school level, but it did give her routine to her day, and she loved going to class; a sense of normal for her in some way. I loaded up a double shelfed hospital cart on wheels with all of the things from Meghan's room, her VHS movies, magazines, clothes, gifts and the cart was full.

"Wait here for me, I am going to take this down and load up the back seat of the car, I will be back in a jiffy" and kissed her cheek. I took the load down and filled up the back seat. It was just Meghan and I today, Caitlin was at home with mom and Randy was there also as he was busy finishing the ramp. I grabbed a bag from the front seat and then went back for Meghan. When I arrived at her room I saw her crying.

"It's really happening mom, I'm going home." I kneeled in front of her, careful not to bump her feet.

"What's in the bag?" She asked.

I had made some special warm covers that were polar fleece to go over her splints.

"Wow, cool, and pink, they look like they are from the 70's, with the big flowers. I like them, nice job mom" she replied. I carefully slipped them over her splints so as to not hurt her feet; you would think she had the coolest boot slippers going. We made our way around the floor, so many hugs from so many nurses and from both Gloria and Johanna.

"Go on, get out of here," Johanna said as she hugged Meghan tight. Meghan would miss them both for sure.

Dr. Meado met us at the end of the hallway, he hugged me, shook my hand and reached out and touched Meghan's cheek. "You are a remarkable child of God" he said, "home is where you need to be," and we left with a smile and a grateful heart.

When we arrived home mom was there with homemade pasta and chicken, one of Meghan's favorites. This would be the first time for me to attempt the ramp that Randy had made for us. It wasn't perfect, but it was perfect for us. He had to rip out some trees in the front of my house to get it done and in order to have it fit properly, but it was ready and with one deep breath I wheeled her up the first level, along the front window and then up one more small level and into the front door.

"Home sweet home," I heard from the kitchen, as mom stirred the sauce, and then came out to greet us. Of course neither of us could contain our joy, and gratefulness.

"It's all yours honey, take a tour," as I led Meghan into the living room.

"Wow, all this space, I can wheel this thing around easily."

"Now don't get too used to it, you aren't going to be in that chair for much longer." I assured her.

"Just one step at a time mom, one step at a time" she replied with a smile that lit the room.

Meghan wheeled herself over to the couch, and then to my surprise she simply stood up and then let herself flop down on the couch and she burst into laughter.

"I've wanted to do that for so long, just flop down on my couch" she laughed and cried at the same time with her head tilted back and deeply sunken in comfort into the couch. The cushions were deep blue crushed velvet, with padded arm rests and high back extra cushions.

"Don't get too comfy, because you have your first physio appointment in about two hours." I smiled and gave her a wink. "But for now, oh my goodness, let's have some food, this smells amazing mom" I exclaimed as I went into the kitchen. "Yep, nannies pasta for Meghan and grilled cheese for Caitlin." For some strange reason this spaghetti tasted better than any other time mom has ever made it and it melted my heart. Enjoying your food is not just about taste, it's about who you eat it with and where you consume and share a meal. Home sweet home indeed.

We washed up, and Meghan got herself back into her chair, I could see she was exhausted and she wanted me to know that she would not give up. We continued to get ready to head out to her appointment and arrived shortly before 5:00 p.m.

"My feet really hurt mom, is he going to touch them?" Meghan asked in a tone of concern as we made our way to the reception area.

"I think today was just a meet and greet session." I replied.

"Hi Brian, nice to meet you, I'm Angela, and this is Meghan" I began.

"Hello Meghan, I've just been on the phone with Nancy, and she has filled me in on everything and is sending me your records to go over. What I wanted to do today is just a few base line tests, to see where your strengths lay and what would be a good starting point."

"Okay, but please don't touch my feet," sounded more like instructions and not a request.

"Deal," he replied with a smile. Brian checked things like how well she could stand on her own, how high she could lift her legs, how much upper body strength she had and a few other things. He would put together a customized program for her. "I will be working with her one on one three times a week for an hour each time and she will have some home exercises to do as well" he smiled and touched Meghan's hand. "She is quite a remarkable young woman, and it is my privilege to help her gain her strength back, we will have you ready to dance at your winter formal Meghan," and she grinned.

"Winter formal," wow, just around the corner, and I hadn't thought of it, but she may just be able to go. I think this gave Meghan a goal and maybe Brian said what he did on purpose to give her a goal to set; to dance at her prom.

"She has lost most of her hearing, so please if you can look at her when you talk she can read lips fairly well," I mentioned. We finished up the session and headed home.

A very special friend of mine from grade school and high school had come over, Karen. She, along with her co-workers, family and friends, had put together a special collection of gifts for my girls this year for Christmas. Every year Karen and her friends help a family instead of doing an office party and this year my family was that chosen family. I was moved beyond words, truly speechless. Karen arrived with so many gifts; I think the one that Meghan would cherish the most was the incredible soft blanket for her bed. It felt like being wrapped in heaven she told me. I wanted one for my bed. A mission for me now was to find a few more of those blankets. So many people have helped us through this journey, and I will be eternally grateful to each and every one of them. Various community and church groups had given us gift cards for gas or for groceries. I was just so grateful for so much that I didn't even know where to begin. Thanks God.

Today was December 23, 2006, and we were going to visit an amazing young man tonight. Marilyn invited us to their Christmas open house, so that Meghan would be able to see Brad. I knew Bradley didn't have much time left, and I think Meghan knew it also. His treatments were stopped before he was sent home in the fall and it saddened my heart to think that he would be leaving us soon.

Their home was a country home and not wheelchair accessible; however, with the help of Randy and Brad's father the two men actually carried Meghan in the chair right into the house; down the four stairs and into the basement. This was indeed a very special night for Meghan to see her best friend and confidant again. The bond between the two of them was special and will never be understood by anyone as they both battled for their lives daily and had for over a year now. Brad was hooked up to an oxygen tank, but could freely move around and enjoy all the company that had come to visit. Marilyn and I hugged; she understood the struggles, the suffering, the pain and the fears. We shared so many moments in and out of hospital rooms. She suffered from hearing loss herself, she knew Meghan's present condition and even assured her that things would be fine.

"I'm deaf too Meghan," she said to her, "and look at me, I am fine and life is great, you can do this my girl, you can do this and you will be okay." The thought of being deaf scared Meghan. We lived in a modern age now and with the help technology communication was now made easier for those who had any kind of hearing loss.

"Thank goodness for Facebook and for texting" I said to Marilyn, "our next appointment is coming up, and it looks like she will need a hearing aid," we hugged, cried and both knew that things could be a whole lot worse. My heart sank inside, I thought of things that this family must be facing, this will likely be their last Christmas together, and here they were sharing it with us. The feeling in my heart overwhelmed me, I hugged Marilyn tight and didn't want to let go.

"Thank you for sharing Bradley with Meghan and with all of us, we love you."

Christmas had come and gone. It was a quiet celebration at home with my two girls. Reverend Sue came over to give us a small intimate service at home, as Meghan has come down with a bit of a cold and I was not to take her out. We shared this service with my family, and had a Christmas Eve communion together in our living room, with the bread and wine and a special blessing for healing. It was beautiful and full of love and spirit. Thank you Jesus for the people in our lives who always amaze me with their love and kindness.

January 5, 2007 - Well it's been about 10 days since I journaled, and it's been busy. Point form is how it's gonna be here goes, and I will elaborate more later.

1. *Brad died December 29, suddenly, we weren't expecting it this soon. He went into a hospice on December 27th.*
2. *Went to the visitation on January 2nd, so sad.*
3. *Meghan couldn't go; she has a cold, and said that she wouldn't be able to handle it.*
4. *Meghan had a wish granted by the Children's Wish Foundation, a shopping spree at Mapleview Mall, just like Brad did.*
5. *Clinic appointment, counts are all good, platelets low, only 33, fevers and hot flashes can eat up platelet.*
6. *Meghan wrote to the paper, her article was in, grab copies.*

Brad's Visitation - We were probably the first ones there to get in the lineup of greeters and tears. Marilyn and her family waited as we all came to say goodbye to Brad. The grandmother hugged me and held onto me as if she knew me and didn't want to let go. I didn't know anyone except for Marilyn, Brad, and Stacey. Stacey is a friend of Brad's from school; she too had cancer, and would chill with Meghan and Brad. Then came the moment when I hugged Marilyn, we cried, sobbed, and shook, the emotions flowed between us, two moms, who knew that all they could do in this moment was cry and hold on tight. Brad lay in his casket; he wore a football jersey, and had on his high school football ring. He looked at peace. I still find it so hard to believe, and so fast to happen.

Meghan is dealing with so much right now. Her life frightens her, and yet at the same time she is so grateful. She has lost most of her hearing, and I can't imagine what it is like to look at us and not hear us, living so isolated. She is getting a hearing aid, and I sure hope it works. I myself keep praying for a miracle, that she will be able to hear, even with a hearing aid, that she will be able to hear again."

Meghan decided to write a thank you letter to the paper, as so many people have helped us in this journey, and she felt the need to express this openly. I gave her the email address for Jill, the editor of the Burlington Post, and she wrote. The letter was incredible, and it will speak for itself, and you will see just how beautiful my daughter has become.

The following poignant letter was written by Burlington teen Meghan Rush. It requires no further explanation. – January 05, 2007

* * *

Dear Burlington Post:

I want to thank you for putting the letter my mom wrote to you into the paper (Nov. 22, 2006). Lots more people began to pray for me and some very cool things happened.

I was supposed to have an open- lung biopsy on the Friday of the week the letter came out in the paper. It came out on Wednesday, and Thursday night the surgeon called my mom and said that whatever was in my lung was shrinking on its own and that they would be cancelling the operation.

I was glad because it was a pretty serious one. They were going to put me into ICU again after the operation. Also, I wanted to come home so badly, but I was so weak and had a feeding tube in. I was in so much pain with my feet from the chemo.

Well, more prayers were answered and I am now home. I came home on Dec. 18. I hope I don't ever have to go back. I just want to get better and be like all the rest of the teenagers. Well, I will never be quite the same because I've been through so much, but just to walk and go to a movie would be great.

I lost most of my hearing because of the drugs I was on, but it was either my hearing or my life. I'm still alive, and hoping that my hearing will come back.

When I came home from hospital, I began to feel the excitement of Christmas and what being home felt like. Christmas was being home. It was the best Christmas ever, to be able to be home with my mom, and my sister Caitlin. I've missed them so much.

I also go to my dad's; he always makes me laugh, and when he isn't able to see me I wear his high school ring.

My stepmom Lanette is cool, and Ian, my little cute brother, makes me smile all the time. Best of all, though, is sleeping in my bed and having my family all around me.

My soon-to-be stepdad, Randy, built a ramp for my wheelchair, and he and my mom turned the dining room into a bedroom. It's great to have four parents; it means four times the love. Randy helps me and my mom so much. He is goofy and we love him that way.

When people found out I was home I had friends visit that made me real happy. My friend Kate always came to the hospital and to my house. She even had a sleepover; it was fun.

My mom's friend Karen came over one night with gifts for me, my sister and my mom. We still cry about how generous it was for her to do that. She gave me a special DVD player that has adjustable headphones so that I can hear the movie. Just being able to hear a movie means a lot. People Karen works with helped out. They normally go out for a night, but this year they decided to give us a special Christmas, so I want to thank Karen, Ian, the girls and the people she works with and Karen's dad.

My mom has been so busy looking after me. She is just the best and I want to thank her and my sister. The most important thank you has to go to everyone who has prayed for me and for all the sick kids with cancer. Prayers help that is for sure. I am still here and I plan to keep fighting and stay here a long time.

Some people don't make it, but that doesn't mean that the cancer won, it just means that God decided to take over the fight and become the winner -- to take the pain away from the sick child.

Sometimes the answered pray isn't what we want, but it's what the child needs -- no more pain and suffering -- so God brings them home where everything is awesome for them. It's not about winning or losing a battle, it's about how you handle yourself through it. Like my special friend Brad (Campbell). He was a champion, and still is.

You will remember him because he was on the front page of the Burlington Post (Dec. 20) sitting on Santa's lap with his brother.

Brad was given his wish and had a shopping spree at Mapleview Centre. It was strange to see him in the paper, but it was a special gift to me -- a picture to keep and treasure.

Brad and I became like best friends. We understood each other because we were both fighting cancer. Brad went to heaven on Dec. 29. I cried so much and will miss him so much.

I will continue my battle with dignity and courage and always remember that it is how I handle myself that matters, so that I can help others, just like Brad helped me and lots of other kids.

Brad made everyone feel special. With everything that has happened to me, there are times when I just don't feel pretty. I have scars, stretch marks from steroids, and so many things that I don't like about how I look.

One day Brad said to me: "Meghan, how come you don't have a boyfriend?"

I said, "I don't know, not pretty."

He said, "What are you nuts? You are beautiful, on the inside and on the outside; actually you are hot."

I smiled and will remember that day always. Brad made me feel beautiful and made me take a good look at myself and realize that I am beautiful.

I went to see Brad on Dec 23; they had an open house. I couldn't hear, but I could see. I just wanted to look at him and let him know that he was my special friend who I love and who always gave me strength and courage. I admired him so much.

His mom, Marilyn, is amazing; she was in front of me right where I could see and hear her, or read her lips, and she said loudly, "I love you."

I remember smiling and it felt good. I smile when I am with that family.

My mom took a picture, which I am sending to you. In the picture Brad is over my shoulder, like an angel watching over me. If I could say one thing to him now I would say, "Brad, you will be my angel forever, and always be over my shoulder watching over me. I love you and I will miss you."

Oh, and Green Bay Packers rock, Philadelphia Eagles, they just roll...haha.

Love you forever, Meghan

P.S. Say hi to my poppie for me, he is lots of fun.

I look at my Meghan sometimes and think of things that I am so afraid to write about. I think of a day when it could be her funeral, and then I shake my head and shake the thoughts right out of my mind. I couldn't allow myself to think like that. She had pulled through so many things so far. Right now hearing loss was what needed to be faced and it scared me.

I knew Meghan sensed my fear and in her sweet wise way, she said to me, "mom, if Helen Keller can do it with no eyes or ears, then I can do it with no feet, and no ears, but I do need my eyes." How brave and how amazing was her attitude. I often felt ashamed of myself for feeling so worn out and afraid when truly all the things weren't happening to me, but to my daughter. Meghan was the one who would have to learn how to sign and live in a world of no sound. She was the one who had to rebuild strength, as best as possible, to one day walk on her own again. When I look at my bravery bracelet and rub the glass beads between my fingers I can't hold back the tears.

I don't think I would ever have been able to go through what she has thus far, I would have not had the faith or strength. Forgive me God for being so weak when it was the children who truly are being pillars of strength. So many people have said "Ang you are so strong to go through this." I am not strong at all; I simply don't have a choice, I have to go through this alongside Meghan and feel my insides rip open with each test, and just keep praying. My attitude at times had really sucked. I was not proud of some of my outbursts whomever they were directed at, at whatever time.

Being at home Meghan had progressed so much with the physio that I do believe when she has her three month assessment at the hospital they will be amazed. We had appointments set up for both a hearing test again and an eye test. Apparently the Stevens-Johnson Syndrome could damage the eyes also, and it was noticed that both of her eyes seem to be affected; they look almost cloudy at times and she said that she does have a hard time seeing. The membranes of the cornea have tried to seal over the eye. It was explained to me that it was like a person trying to look through a thick screen. The partial vision was obstructed by membranes that crossed over the cornea.

We went to the appointment, here in Burlington, at an eye surgeon's. Meghan was so excited to go for an appointment outside of the hospital.

"Why are you so excited?" I asked.

"Because normal kids go to the eye doctors like this" she replied. I got it, normal. When we arrived at the office it felt like a thousand pairs of eyes burned into the both of us. Here we were, and here sat Meghan in her wheelchair, in the winter with splints on her feet and my makeshift boots made of double lined polar fleece to pull over them.

"Can he fix my eyes?" She said loudly as everyone awkwardly tried to make an obvious stare not so obvious.

"Let's hope so," I replied, "You have had your fair share of things, so let's hope and pray."

"Well, I am thankful that I still have my eyes" and she giggled, "I sure have lost a shit load of things huh mom?"

I could see she affected the onlookers.

"Yes you have, but you have also gained more than anyone can imagine." We both knew that this was about her heart for God, the gentleness she felt for ladybug, the soft spot she held for her friends like Brad, and the hope that she had for all kids that one day no one would suffer any longer. Tears built in the eyes of many as I caught them look over at us. She amazed me with how she constantly saw hope and positivity in every single situation.

The right eye was the only one affected so far not both as we were led to believe. We were to continue to keep it moist, avoid bright lights and to rest it. It was of the utmost importance to keep both eyes lubricated; it could save the damaged eye and quite possibly prevent damage to the other eye. For now, we were given hope, hope that she would continue to see, but how well, and for how long, we didn't have an answer.

"I thought he could fix my eye," she said, as she cried so hard.

"He can't sweetie, it would require a cornea transplant, and he didn't think it would be successful, not with having the Stevens-Johnson Syndrome," I just didn't know what else to say other than to repeat again what the surgeon had said.

"Stupid fucking syndrome" Meghan blurted out loudly, "sorry mom" she added.

"It's okay, you have every right to swear, it's not pretty, but it's okay, as God knows I've done it lately myself."

Tomorrow is another day, and yet another appointment. We were going to get her hearing aid fitted, the mold was made and now it's was time to pick out what she wanted.

We arrived at the hospital and anxiously waited to be seen.

"Come right in Meghan." Wow, that was quick, barely a five minute wait, but I suppose given the situation, they rushed her right in.

After Meghan's letter was published in the paper, I received a phone call from a gentleman who worked for a hearing aid company. He was so deeply touched by her courage and was so saddened at the same time to hear of her hearing loss that he wanted to help. He was donating a very high tech hearing aid package for her. The works, whatever the works were as far as hearing aids were concerned he was going to give it to her. He let me know that he dealt with all the local hospitals and they knew him; so to simply let her audiologist know and he would set things up with her when Meghan's aid was ordered. How amazingly generous, I didn't have the words to even express my gratitude.

We were given the good news, and that we would have no expense at all with the purchase of the hearing aid.

"Can I have pink?" She asked.

"Whatever colour you want" her doctor replied.

"Yeah, pink, why hide the thing? I want a bright pink one, why try to hide the hearing aid, everyone will know I can't hear, so I want to show mine off."

Sometimes I didn't quite understand her thinking, but I knew she was going through this the way she was supposed to and that God constantly led her and held her every moment of this journey. So, pink it was, and in about a week or so, we would come back in to pick it up, and have a final test. In the meantime, I picked up this silly hearing aid thing from the TV store where sound was amplified, it works a little bit. I know we will all be taking ASL shortly, Caitlin and I have already talked about it and we are somewhat excited to.

Anna called; Meghan's child life therapist at the hospital. Every day at 4pm Anna would sit with Meghan for an hour until I got there. The PSW would leave roughly around 3pm, and then Anna would come and visit with her. She was one very special lady, her bond with Meghan was gentle yet strong, and I knew Meghan felt that she could confide in her almost like a big sister. I never asked what they talk about, it was their special relationship between the two of them, and I was grateful that God brought her to us. Anyhow, the phone rang and it was Anna.

"Hello?" I answered,

"Hey, it's Anna from Child Life, I have some wonderful news, Meghan is having her wish granted from the Children's Wish Foundation, so I need to speak with her, and find out what her wish is, have her think about it and then have her call me, okay?" She said.

"Wow, a wish granted can you email her?" I asked.

"Absolutely, I feel just as silly asking you to have her phone me, I'm so sorry" she replied in a tone of remorse.

"No need to apologize, it slips my mind all the time" and I hung up.

"Who was that, Mom? I saw you on the phone, and you looked pretty intense." Meghan asked.

"It was Anna, she is going to send you an email."

"My Anna from 3B, why?"

Without hesitation, Meghan waited for the anticipated arrival of Anna's email.

"Woohoo, I am getting my wish granted!" she screamed with excitement from the living room as she nearly sent her laptop flying when she threw her hands in the air. Meghan wanted the same wish that Brad was granted, a shopping spree, so that she could give her family and friends a lot of cool stuff.

Within a few days I received a call from the Children's Wish Foundation, from a sweet gal named Angela. Angela wanted to make this wish extra special for Meghan and asked what some of her favorite things were and what sort of music she liked.

"Well, she listens to CHUM FM, Cory Kimm is her DJ of choice, and she absolutely loves Elmo," I told her. Together with the mall management, we all worked to have this day be magical for Meghan. She would be treated like a celebrity with a red carpet, a stretch limo, and the works. Before long the day would arrive and it was something that would both connect her with Brad, and bring a smile to her face. I just hoped that the weather would hold up, it had been stormy and being mid-January we never knew what to expect.

Wish day was set for January 16th; the local paper was going to accompany us by sending a reporter and photographer. It would be as if Meghan would have her own paparazzi. They were set to arrive at the house for a pre-interview at 9:30 am. I had also arranged to have both of her PSW workers, Johanna and Gloria arrive and surprise her in one of the stores and have lunch with us. The day was all set, and joining us would be Meghan's friend Kate. I chose Kate because she had done so much for Meghan and I knew her excitement would be contagious with everyone. There were other friends that I wanted to ask, but I left it up to Meghan and she only wanted Kate to come.

"Mom I just can't have everyone, so I am only picking Kate, she has been there so much."   Kate had put on the spaghetti dinner and had come to see Meghan in ICU, and had even slept over in her room at the hospital a few times. It was a very difficult decision for Meghan to make, to choose only one friend, and I knew it weighed heavy on her heart. I simply put it to her, don't think of it so much, just for a moment, choose one friend quickly, and without hesitation, she said Kate because of so many things. Kate may not have been her best friend in previous years; they had only reconnected through Meghan's illness, but the faith and prayer that the two of them shared was a bond that God placed and it was His choice really that Kate share this day, not Meghan's.

"January 16, 2007 - Today was the granted wish day. It was so amazing. The Post arrived at about 9:30. Lisa the photographer and Jason the reporter.

Jason talked to all of us, and I wrote notes so that Meghan knew what was going on.

"What does it feel like to have a wish being granted," he asked. She smiled and said with eyes bright, "like a kid on candy."

She was so funny and chatty, it was great to see. Jason said to me that he could feel her fighting spirit.

The limo arrived – A white stretch. Meghan had the brightest smile on her face. We bundled up, and her paparazzi took place to capture all the moments. As I wheeled her down the ramp, and up to the door of the limo, she tugged at my coat and pulled me close. "Mom, I am afraid to get into the limo, it's not like our car, I don't think I can do it. "Goodness me, you aren't doing it alone, I will help you in just as I always do, and when you are inside, stretch out if you like, you are the star for the day, and shine bright you will my dear.   With all her fear and

246

anxiety, together we did it, and as I helped her sit down, and buckled the seatbelt across her, I kissed her cheek softly, as she kissed mine back. "I love you momma."

We all got into the car, and the driver headed on down the Guelph Line, and then pulled into Burlington Mall. "Huh," Meghan said, "I thought we were going to Mapleview." "We are I assured her, he just got a little confused." Shortly after we arrived, Let the shopping and memories begin."

There were so many greeters with signs that waited upon Meghan's arrival. The marketing manager for the mall met us at the limo and insisted on being the one to wheel her along the red carpet. Yes there was a red carpet set out for her. She was an instant celebrity. So many greeted us with signs written in big bold letters. *"Welcome Meghan," "Enjoy your day Caitlin and Kate."*

A very handsome young man - okay a super-hot guy, who is kidding who – a totally hot guy came over to Meghan and gave her two dozen long stem red roses. He also had a sign that someone held for him saying *"Im Matt, your model escort for the day."*

What completely captivated Meghan wasn't the handsome, extremely hot model; it was something red and no not the roses either. Elmo. Yes, Elmo. He skipped his way over to Meghan's chair and gave her some balloons.

"For real mom, I'm shopping with Elmo, awesome," she squealed with delight and giggled. "This is amazing," she added, "Look Caitlin; Elmo is going to shop with us."

She started the day at Total Image with a free makeover and a free wig; a short and sassy blonde one; which matched her mood today. I loved her carefree spirit. Cory Kimm, her DJ from CHUM FM was also there to greet us. He had a bag of gifts from the station for Meghan. Cory was awesome, he took part in the makeover and Meghan laughed when he was putting blush on the stuffed lion that the Children's Wish Foundation had presented her with. Once her makeover was complete, we were ready to shop. We started in a perfume store, one of Meghan's weaknesses was Ralph Lauren

247

perfume; when we were in the shop she got all nervous as we have never spent money like that before.

"Meghan, it's a granted wish, buy whatever you want, for whomever you want" I assured her.

"Okay, then I will take Ralph for me, Gucci for my mom and step mom, Burberry for my dad and Randy, Caitlin can pick whatever she wants and oh, Matt, what do you like?" She turned and asked him.

Surprised, he said, "well I like the smell of Angel, a girl I knew wore it" he replied. "Okay, I will take Angel and you can spray some on me so I smell pretty too" she insisted as she leaned back for a spritz. She was so cute and frisky, and she was having no trouble falling into the role of celebrity shopper. We had mall security with us also and they would collect the packages she purchased and take them to the mall office. I stayed behind in each store and settled up purchases. The stores were so generous. When I would take the cards up to pay, some of them said, "It's on us," and some said, "We are only charging you our cost." It was amazing, she was given gifts, and given special prices, and treated like a princess. I had never ever seen her smile so much.

When I caught up to her in the next store, she tugged my sleeve, "mom, I'm nervous, how much did I spend there on all that perfume and what is left?"

I smiled, "well, you spent 800 bucks, faster than anyone I've ever seen, but not to worry, I doubt you can spend the rest of this in one day" I challenged.

"What? Oh I'm so sorry I didn't think it was that much." She felt terrible for having spent that money.

"Meghan, its ok, it's a wish, you are supposed to spend and spend, and follow your heart, so here's the thing; I doubt you can spend the rest of it in one day, so have fun, don't ask again what is left, because I won't tell you and enjoy every moment." I replied and kissed her cheek softly.

Her next stop was a toy store, because she wanted to pick up some things for Ian. We also had to stop at a sport store and pick up a Green Bay Packers jersey for her dad. The morning went by fairly quick, and it was time for lunch at our favorite, East Side Mario's, where she would absolutely order three cheese capaletti; after all it was her favorite. While we shopped from store to store, the photographer snapped hundreds of pictures. We were followed by both the reporter and the photographer. Today she was a celebrity. My sister, Pam, Jill (the editor of the Post), Mary (Michael's mom), and the rest of us were all treated to a fantastic lunch. Pam brought Meghan a bouquet of flowers. Meghan presented me with a beautiful ring that she purchased in a jewelry store. While she was in the jewelry store she was able to try on some pretty incredible pieces. At one time she had a ring on each finger and won't even tell you the value but it was over six figures. Boy did she smile in that store. Matt had got down on one knee and had a huge diamond in his hand and made like he was proposing to her. Meghan giggled and giggled; then he kissed her cheek. I have never seen her like this, and Caitlin came up alongside of me and held my hand.

"Pretty cool day huh momma?" She said.

I looked down at her, "absolutely." I had no other words. She shopped in almost every store in the mall. Meghan purchased a camera, and we immediately put it to use. I have never seen anyone shop so much, it became confusing as she just couldn't think any longer and bag after bag was escorted to the mall office. We all lived the phrase "shop til you drop" that day. It came time to head home; the limo was waiting and security started to bring all the parcels to us. I looked at all the bags, and in unison both Lanette and I said, "How are we all going to fit in the limo with all of that?"

"Wow, that's a lot of stuff," Meghan said as she giggled.

We managed to fit it all in, and also packed ourselves in all nice and cozy. Lanette had called Gerry to meet us at my house, he was anxious to see everything and hear about our day. We unloaded everything, with the help of our wonderful driver, Ahmad, and Gerry arrived shortly after.

"Come on in dad, if you can find the couch." Meghan was overflowing with joy and giggles. A lot of what happened in the day I missed, as I was busy paying for things in each store as she journeyed on with her hot new friend and shopped in the next place. Here are a few things she said at home that pretty much summed up her day.

- "When they say shop till you drop, I did."
- "My feet hurt so much you think I walked on them all day and I was in a chair."
- "I've never shopped like this in my life, and never will again, it was amazing"
- "Favourite Mall, Favourite Restaurant. Favourite Day"

That last line, actually, the last two words, favorite day, well I knew that Meghan truly had a wish granted. It was her favorite day, but not because she shopped, but because she felt the love. Matt promised to keep in touch with her and he gave her his cell number. He said that he added a texting plan that day so that she could text him any time she wanted, and it was just for her.

I tucked her into bed; she had her cell phone beside her on vibrate as she waited for Matt to text her back. They had an instant bond and special connection from the moment they saw each other. I had an on-air interview at about 7pm with Cory Kimm from CHUM FM to talk about the day. The interview was live, and afterwards I thought, *holy crap, Meghan couldn't even hear it,* so I had him send me the recording so I could type it out for her.   We all wound down slowly, and enjoyed the memories that this day created and we will never forget. As I tidied the living room, and sorted through some bags, I heard the vibrating sound of her phone, and could feel her smile from another room.   Then, tick tick tick, she would text to her new friend.

"Thank you God," as I looked upward, "You truly are amazing."

"Sunday Feb 4, 2007 - I picked up Matt at the Go Station and he spent the day with us. When we got back to the house, Meghan looked beautiful. She had a bit of makeup on. Even mascara and eyeshadow, which she never wears now because of how her eyes bother her, and lip gloss. It was so sweet to see Meghan with some girliness going on. Kate had also come over, to help break the ice for when Matt came in.

Matt is so gentle and nice. I know he has found a new family to be a part of and also I know he has a special soft spot for Meghan. They have been texting nonstop. He is about three years older than she is, but she is having the time of her life. Tonight he was taking her to the movies, they would see 23, and Meghan said to me on the way there, (as I was driving them), that she didn't care if she couldn't hear, she was with the hottest guy in the theatre.

When I picked them up, it was so cute, I saw Matt wheeling her about in her chair outside the theatre, up and down the ramp. My heart skipped a beat, as I thought about what if she fell, or bumped herself, but I knew he had her, he would not let her go. She was giggling, and knew that all eyes were on the two of them. It was a good day. I watched as he kissed her on the cheek again, and I know she felt as though she were a pretty girl again. She is so beautiful, maybe this is the guy to help her through this. He has a new name for her, and he said as he kissed her, "my lil angel."

I drove Matt back to his place in Etobicoke, as I didn't want him to have to take the train and this way he was able to stay longer with us. We shared some memories, Caitlin came with me, and Kate stayed with Meghan, so they could girl talk.

"She is one very special girl, and I love her very much," he said to me.

"Matt, you are an incredible young man, taking the time to be with her, to lift her spirits, and make her feel so beautiful, thank you" I said.

"No, thank you, she has changed my life, she is so brave, strong, gentle, and has an incredible heart, she is my lil angel." I smiled, and was glad to have him as part of our family.

"Oh, and by the way, I am taking her to her prom, if that's ok," as he smiled. "Even if all we do is go in and come out, that lil angel of mine is going to her prom" he insisted.

251

"Okay, I won't argue with you on that one, and I bet Meghan is thrilled" I answered grateful, feeling his genuine love for my girl.

I spent the next day shopping, I had to surprise Meghan with a prom dress, something that would make her shine in the room, not that she would need any help shining; I knew that she would just glow with being able to go with Matt and have an actual prom date who in her words was hotter than hot.

I found two dresses; one was black and white with a lot of shimmer of light silvers and glitter. It was so pretty and elegant, a sweetheart neckline and very soft shoulder straps that were slightly gathered. The other one was in shades of pinks, well more like coral and salmons, almost a type of ombre effect to the gown, and it too had a lot of sparkle. Both dresses were the same style, but because of their colours, they looked completely different.

The sales gal asked "why two?"

"Well because she is just that special and can have both" I answered. She put them into a garment bag, and I headed home. I entered the house to find Meghan in her favorite position on the couch watching an episode of Friends. She squinted to read the closed caption and I thought immediately of the Stevens-Johnsons Syndrome; *please save her eyes* I thought silently in prayer. I would hear a delayed giggle as she would finish reading each caption. I tapped her leg gently to get her attention.

As she turned to face me she had the biggest grin, *oh how that smile melts my heart every time* I thought.

"A little birdie told me you have a prom to go to so I brought a couple of dresses home for you to see. If you don't like them, I will go get more, and you can see which one you would like," I said as I held up each dress and removed them from their garment bag. Caitlin was all excited and helped us with the dresses.

"Mom, is Meghan going to the prom, who with, how?" She asked as she helped unzip each bag.

"Well Matt is taking her," and I heard Meghan giggle, she couldn't hear me, but could read my lips.

"Lucky" Caitlin added with excitement.

"We are going with a bunch of people too," Meghan blurted out, "Jackie and Chris, Heather and Kim, and a bunch of them from school, but Matt is sitting with Jackie and Chris and I."

As Meghan looked at the dresses she cried, "stupid stretch marks," and began to sob even harder. I knew she was worried about the stretch marks on her upper arms and chest.

"Oh, don't worry about those, the way these dresses are cut, you won't see anything on your upper body, and we are going to get you a very pretty white sweater to wear over."

"Really mom, you would do that? Oh thank you" as she hugged me.

"Absolutely, I would do anything, I've seen some pretty cute little cotton shrugs that would be perfect, or maybe a silk shawl; we can go out tomorrow and look for that together, we still have some gift cards still left from your shopping spree you know."

It was quiet at the mall and we could shop easier, and take our time. I didn't want to stay out long, it was cold and I always felt safer just being home on those brutal winter days. We found an adorable little white cotton knit shrug and a matching purse that was silver and white that could go with either dress. As for shoes, well that was a whole other issue. Meghan didn't wear shoes; she wore these splints on her feel to help with her drop foot.

"Well, it looks like I am going to have to sew you some white silk covers for your splints," and we laughed. "How about I make you a white fur cover and wrap for your wheel chair, and you can look like a queen?" I said to her forgetting for a moment about her hearing loss.

"What, I didn't catch all of that?" She replied, "mom you gotta speak slower for me to read your lips." It was hard remembering that she was recently deaf and I felt bad when I would speak without thinking.

"Sorry," I replied.

"No biggie, can we go home? I'm tired and want to rest" she said.

"Sure, whatever you need honey," and I leaned over and kissed her softly on the cheek. *"I love you Meghan,"* as I looked in her eyes.

"I love you more mommy," and she kissed my cheek softly.

Chapter 22 – Home

The one constant medical struggle we always seemed to have as of late was in regards to Meghan's platelet count. They wouldn't come up on their own to where they should be. The hospital medical team tried everything and they only increase from a count of 5 to 7. She was in a very serious situation with counts. The number one priority for Meghan was to increase her platelet count now. Her gums would lightly bleed and she had a sore in her mouth that had now clotted over and the clot seemed to get larger and larger. I spoke with one doctor at McMaster, and he advised us not to touch it. We were to just leave it and if it comes off rinse with ice cold water. If it continued we were to get her to emergency pronto. I was so worried because of the code blue we experienced when her platelet count was higher than it was now. I knew this was different; it's because of the platelets and not the Stevens-Johnson Syndrome. With her counts being so low this was so very dangerous and also very scary.

Easter was just around the corner and I was praying for a lot of things, miracle healing was on top of that prayer list. "Dear Lord, don't let her bleed, let her heal, amen."

"Sunday March 10, 2007 - I woke at 3am to the sounds of Meghan screaming. Ran downstairs, her clot had come off. It scared us, she sucked on crushed ice. Thank goodness for the magic bullet. I crushed ice cubes. The bleeding was not clotting and scary. I called Randy and he took us into the emergency at McMaster. We pretty much waited until morning when her own team of doctors were in. So, by 8am we went up to clinic. Meghan was given platelets and as previously, she reacted badly to them. Her body is rejecting them, it has built up antibodies to them, and she reacts violently when she gets them. "Mom, it feels like my veins are exploding," she cried out. She had severe

diarrhea, that was almost black, and vomiting.   Her vitals became unstable, and the ICU team was called in.   Needless to say she was admitted, and not happy about it.   I was pretty upset also, maybe even more than Meghan was.   My fear was taking over. I didn't like it at all. I stayed all day with her, and slept by her side all night. We shared some very special moments, and Meghan said how much she loved me.   I prayed, and called mom to put the word out to all the prayer chains that we need prayers for her bleeding to stabilize, for the clot to come off and for the platelet situation to be resolved.

God was at work for sure, already the big clot had come off 2 hours after my email and now prayers were being answered.

I woke around 8am, so tired, I didn't sleep much as I was so upset.   I heard talk in the hallways about giving her more platelets.   I confronted the doctors, and pointed out that the last round nearly killed her, and that her count didn't even come up one point. It frightened me to think that they would give more platelets and risk her vomiting with such a low count.   I was assured that they would not be giving them unless she was actively bleeding.

I have missed Caitlin so much. She is at her dad's for a couple of days and also horseback riding. I can't wait to see her in her first horse show.   If it weren't for Ronni, I don't know what I would do.   Thank you God for such an incredible friend.

We are home, Thank you Jesus. We also got great news from the last bone marrow biopsy, which are done regularly. No lymphoma in the bone marrow, and she has the producer cells needed for platelets. Steroids are now being given for 2 weeks to help them come up by suppressing her immune system. Oh, God I pray this works."

Each and every week seems to be a repeat at clinic. We head to finger poke to establish her counts; then head upstairs to the 3F clinic to wait for results. Today the counts were all fine except platelets, and so we went home. We also got news that her bone marrow production is at 20%. I am not sure what that meant exactly other than it was slowly producing and they would definitely not give any type of chemo at all with it being so low. Their decision for treatment was made long ago and by God, not by them. By God I mean that whenever there was a plan to initiate chemo, it failed. We were already given the news that there was no lymphoma detected in the bone marrow, so that to me was the biggest relief. Healthy blood cells were coming from the marrow slowly; but they were coming. Good that we had new hope finally.

"March 20, 2007 - Great news today. Elsbeth, Meghan's math teacher, called me and MMR is going to graduate Meghan. With a high school diploma. She will get her grade 12 diploma. It was so amazing to hear such awesome news. "Meghan, you are going to graduate, I screamed, and then realized. Damn it, she can't hear." I apologized to Elsbeth, and said I had to write Meghan a quick note, and would be right back. She held on the line while I delivered the news. Boy was Meghan excited. "Mom, I'm gonna walk across that stage."

Sunday March 24 ish. (I think) - Saturday night was just Meghan and I. Caitlin went to sleep over at Lauren's house. So, we watch movies, chatted, and cuddled. We have this thing now where we talk at night and share things. She lay on her side, and I would spoon in behind her and cuddle up with her. "Mommy, I want to just talk, ok, and I know I can't hear, so if you want to say something, just tug my hair and I will turn over to read your lips, but I just want to talk tonight." So it began, as I lay with my arm around her, holding her close with all the love in my heart for my baby. "Don't let me go mommy, don't let me go anywhere. I don't want to go anywhere mommy, just

257

don't let me go, ok," It took everything in me not to lose it. I tugged at the little tuft of hair at the back of her head, she turned to face me, and I said "where do you think you are going to the moon, heck you aren't going anywhere," and I kissed her forehead. She rolled back over, and I began to cry thinking she could not hear, so I just let it out. "Mom, you're crying, I can't hear you, but I can feel you, please don't cry."

That moment will never be forgotten. I know she was talking about dying, we both knew it, but we stepped far away from it. I didn't want to think it, but from time to time, it did pop into my mind. Who wouldn't think it when their child has cancer. But you choke the feelings and fears away, and hang on to the hope and faith that all will be OK. I stayed by her side all night, not wanting the moment to go, to feel her in my arms. Her skin so soft just like when she was a baby, and she was that, my baby, but 17 years old.

"Friday March 30, 2007- Today we will get results. I was a nervous wreck, and even though we don't see eye to eye a lot of the time, I was glad Gerry was also in clinic as he wanted to sit in on the results. We waited for over an hour, then finally met with Dr. Manners, as Meghan calls him.

The Results – nothing on the liver , or back, or spleen, everything normal.

In simple terms – cancer free, from what we see, she is cancer free.

Being that he has a heavy accent, Meghan couldn't read his lips, but we all smiled, and cried, and I turned to Meghan and said. "Cancer free." Her face lit up, she cried, her hands went up in the air. "Cancer free, baby, got that shit out of me," were her exact words, and became her Facebook status shortly after.

On the way home from the hospital, I took my usual route, leaving the hospital, and making my way through Dundas and *along York Road, and then along Plains Road. I stopped in at the office of a very special family friend. I needed to tell someone, and so did Meghan, she said, "let's stop and tell Bill."*

He came out, and she said it to him exactly as she did in the hospital. "I'm cancer free, got that shit out of me." He laughed, hugged her, and asked us to wait a moment, he came out with a gift, and handed her a sand dollar as he just came back from vacation. How cool is that, a perfect ending to this day, the gift of a sand dollar."

Our instructions from clinic now were simply to keep her on the steroids and hope that the platelet count would come up. We were on the road to recovery, cancer free, oh how those two words are like music to my soul. Our next appointment was for Friday April the 13th. Gerry and I were both going to clinic, and then he was taking her for the day to a Toronto Raptor's game. A special night planned for her, to celebrate being cancer free. Her platelet count was still quite low, she didn't need to be admitted, we just needed to be careful with her. I knew he would be. She was so excited to be going to her first basketball game and to be treated so special by everyone. This was her night. She loved the game but loved the special time with her dad more.

Lanette brought Meghan home the next day, Saturday, just before dinner. She was complaining that her leg was very sore and I noticed how her feet looked swollen in her splints. Looking at the sore spot on her leg, it was quite pink and warm, I called Lauren's mom Angela to come over. She was an oncology nurse in Oakville.

She drew around the area that was pink and said "keep an eye on it."

"I will" I answered, "I was planning on taking her to the clinic on Monday, as her body seemed to be retaining fluid so I will have them look at it."

Monday morning, April 16, 2007, my Meghan was extremely down today when we arrived in clinic. She said she was just fed up of everything, and this pain in her leg was the worst pain she had ever felt ever. We had a CT scan and x-ray; no clots were found. When we went back upstairs to clinic, the doctors and nurses said that they felt she should be admitted.

"We want to admit her," I heard more than once. Whenever I heard this, I heard the voice of God, not out loud, but within, but it was loud. I didn't want to have her ever be admitted again, and whenever the word "admitted" was uttered, I would hear *I'm taking her home.*

I would argue with the doctors, and said to Gina, "I can't ignore God speaking to me, I've done it before, but this time it's loud and clear He wants me to take her home, and that's what I am doing." This went on for hours with various doctors and nurses, as they all tried to convince me to have Meghan admitted. After talking with Dr. Winthrope, and she said that she wanted to admit her, I heard the voice again; *I'm taking her home.*

I looked upwards, "God what am I to do? Everyone is against me, yet you want me to take her home." I pleaded for direction.

"Call Randy," said Dr. Winthrope.

"Why?" I asked "Why would I call him?"

She replied, "Just as you are getting your message to take her home, I got one to have you to call him" she insisted. So, I did, while she listened in, and then I passed the phone to her. They spoke, and then she passed it back to me.

"Ang, they are going to admit her, but not keep her more than two days, they won't poke and prod her, they won't go looking for new things, they will simply get her fluid off her, and get her a little more comfortable," he spoke to me in a comforting voice.

"Ok, fine, and then I'm taking her home, because that's what God wants" I insisted. We all had an agreement in place; I would allow her to be admitted only to get the fluid off her feet and legs and to get her more comfortable. They would not go looking for new things to treat and it would only be overnight. Gerry was on his way back to the hospital while I went home to get Caitlin and to also get a change of clothes for Meghan. They had already moved her into 3B and when I arrived about 2 hours later, the ICU team was in with her. Dr. Winthrope was also in with her, apparently the pink mark on her leg had spread and deepened in colour. Gerry was with her, and Meghan seemed to be giggly and giddy, she didn't seem bothered by any of the fuss going on around her.

As I walked into the room, I watched as they hooked up something to her IV, and I yelled out in a fast and furious tone. "If that is something from the Beta Lactim family, or whatever, don't put it in her, she will hemorrhage because of Stevens-Johnson Syndrome."

Immediately they clamped it off, and the Dr, said "Good call mom."

"Good call, my ass!" I screamed. "Don't you read the charts? Don't people pay attention to what she can and can't have?" I didn't know what to think or feel. I was so angry and so scared and my words let everyone know it. Luckily I got there when I did, nothing had entered her system. I then apologized because I knew my outburst was not all that polite, I was just on edge so bad.

I spoke with Dr. Winthrope, and said "Meghan doesn't look good, what is going on?" I asked.

"We are trying to get the fluid off her, yet her vitals are unstable, so we need to give her fluids to bring them up, it's a double edge sword at the moment," she spoke in a tone of sadness.

"It seemed like it's always a double edge sword with her, doesn't it?" I muttered. Caitlin waited outside the room and was doodling in her notebook.

"Pass me the bowl dad, I feel like I need to puke" Meghan said with her arm stretched out as he handed her the blue plastic spit bowl. This was the moment when things for me became very real, and messages that were given to me just a few hours earlier had been misread. Meghan vomited blood. I watched in terror and left the room as my eyes overflowed. Randy had just arrived, and I told him what had happened.

"She is throwing up blood, and her platelets are 3."

The doctor from ICU shouted his orders "move her to ICU now."

We followed without hesitation and the tears wouldn't stop. I entered the ICU, and felt numb; it was then that I was hit with the reality. Meghan was bleeding internally and they were not exactly sure from where. The discolouration of her skin was so evident, not just a warm pinkish skin tone, she was a deep red and almost the shade of eggplant. The bleed was spreading all over her legs and lower body. It was fast and the swelling from fluids caused massive blistering that was the most horrific thing I have ever seen. I played over the last few hours of the day in my mind.

"I'm taking her home, "I'm taking her home, "I'm taking her home." It ran over and over in my mind, my body, my heart. I looked upward for a moment and with tears streaming down I said, "I misunderstood, forgive me, YOU are taking her home." My heart pleaded, "Oh God why, she is cancer free, why are you taking her home?" yet I knew that it could not be stopped He was taking her home. It all became clear; God had told me that he was taking her home. This would explain Meghan's carefree attitude, she felt no pain; she didn't seem to care that she threw up blood; she had no fears or any pain of any sort. It was as if the Lord had protected her precious soul and mind and she was peaceful beyond words. Her fear of needles had vanished as she was being poked and prodded.

"We need to put her into a coma to treat her effectively, we need access to some main arteries and we need her still and resting; there is a lot going on and it is very serious" was what we were told.

I then heard from the same voice that only hours earlier had said "I'm taking her home," that same voice now said two words "three days," as the soft whisper penetrated my soul. "Three days."

"Do whatever you have to, you have three days" I shouted. "What?" The Dr. said.

"Never mind, yes, just do whatever you need to," I repeated. We were gathered in Meghan's room; they brought in platelets and were about to sedate her.

"Whoa, are they giving me butterscotch again? Mom, make sure they give me extra to put me out because I don't want to feel those going in me ever again" Meghan said with eyes wide as she pointed to the platelet bags.

"You heard the little lady; give her what she needs to not feel anything and don't touch her feet, she feels it." I instructed in a shaky voice. I looked at Meghan, and pointed to her feet. "I told them all that they are not to touch your feet either, Okay?"

She smiled, "Thanks mom, I love you more. Can I have a popsicle when I wake up because my mouth tastes like shit?" she smiled.

"You can have anything you like." Her eyes closed and I died inside. I knew I would never ever see her beautiful blue eyes again.

Dr. Winthrope had arrived, and came straight down ICU. She had heard that Meghan had taken a turn for the worst and wanted to come straight here.

I sat her down, and said to her, "Remember our conversation yesterday and how I explained to you that I heard a voice say to me, I'm taking her home, and I thought I was supposed to take her home?"

"Yes," she said, as we held hands.

"Well, I misunderstood and almost disobeyed Him" I cried broken hearted. Her eyes filled up with tears, "Meghan is going home, He is taking her home." I said.

"No, no don't think that, she can fight, she always does, she will pull through" were her words as she tried to comfort me and offer me hope.

"No, it's not His plan; He is taking her home" I stated. "She is bleeding internally now, and it's spreading through her whole body, her platelets are three, and they are doing everything medically possible, but she has three days, just like Jesus did."

I continued and thought *three days, just like Jesus."* I let her go see Meghan, and I prayed and prayed, and wandered the halls. I called Kate, Jackie, and Matt, they were the only friends who I knew Meghan would want there.

I could feel her telling me, "mom, don't you dare call anyone else, I don't want them to see me like this." I called my family and a couple of friends, Ronni and Karen. People came and went, and there was a lot of praying going on. Nurses came from 3B and were in tears. Meghan had become somewhat of a light house to all; she was that beacon of hope amidst the storm we called cancer. She had

263

survived five code blues, and seven drug induced comas. Now here we were and I was the wandering ship, lost and alone. The light in the lighthouse was soon going to be gone. Meghan would then follow a new light on a new journey home. Only I knew of what happened only hours earlier, how the Lord spoke to me and told me He was taking her home. Hour by hour her situation became more serious. Platelets were not working; surgery could not be done to stop the bleed in her stomach as it was now determined that it was coming from there. Her whole body, except her precious face from the shoulders up, had become affected as her entire body succumbed to the internal bleeding; the rupturing of her veins along with the stomach bleed. I watched this terrifying episode of her life, her final three days, become something I never in my life imagined. Fluids were being pumped into her to keep her vitals up and they had nowhere to go but to form blisters on her precious body. Her body was torturing itself, it was no longer her; it was a torture chamber.

"Oh, God, please don't let her feel any of this," and as the moment my prayer went out, I felt peace. I knew he had already calmed her, she would feel no pain; it was taken care of as we saw before they induced the coma. The hours melted into each other; I was given an intern's room to catch the odd hour of sleep, as I had no plan to leave the hospital. I said nothing to Gerry, or Lanette, or Caitlin about my message from God. Only Randy and Dr. Winthrope knew of this message and Randy was at a loss for words to comfort me. I was numb and knew that by Wednesday April 18, she would journey home. Dr. Winthrope was having a hard time, as she understood now what I had heard and she too watched it unfold.

We were all called into a meeting on Tuesday late afternoon. "We are doing everything we can, but it is not looking good" the team told us. "We aren't giving up, not yet, but there may come a time when we can't do anything more." I knew we had one more day, God was in control, and He would decide when the time was exactly right for her to go home. It would be at a time when the doctors could do no more, and all machines that supported her life would be turned off.

It was now Wednesday, about 3:30 in the morning. I wandered into Meghan's room, and heard Christine, her nurse, talking with her.

I smiled. "I remembered her from the first time she was in here almost two years ago," she said. "I know she is deaf, but she is spirit too, and her spirit can hear" she continued.

"I'm so glad you are on shift today" I told her.

"It's today you know" I said.

She just nodded, "yes, I know." I believe God revealed some things to her also and placed her there for me, to comfort me.

"What are you doing?" I asked.

'Oh, just cleaning her up a bit, with a sponge bath I guess" she replied.

"Can I do it, please? I gave Meghan her first bath; I would like to be the one to give Meghan her last bath." I pleaded as I reached for the sponge with a trembling hand and heart. We cried, and she told me what to do, and how to be very careful around all the injection sights where IV's were. I took my time, washed her slowly, while Christine helped to move her so I could get the back of her. I was shocked at how badly the internal bleed had spread. Her legs were dying and had lost all circulation; it was also believed that she had a bleed in the brain as she was unresponsive to things. I am not sure of what was happening, all I knew was this was my last day with her, that she would be going home today. I felt so very alone, no one was here but me, and I just slowly bathed my baby for the very last time. I would not hear her voice, or dry her tears, or feel her hug, she was on the last day of her journey, and the biggest fear of my life was unfolding before my eyes. I didn't want to think my Meghan was dying. Meghan was going to heaven, to be with our Father.

I had called Randy to come to the hospital by about 11:30, he was at a job site. He arrived at about 12:30. We were called into a meeting at about 1:00 p.m. We were all told that "we have done all we can, her blood pressure wasn't responding to medication, the bleeding was everywhere. She won't make it through this, and we need to let you all know that ultimately she will go."

At 1:30 we all stood around her bedside, holding hands, and the machines were turned off. I was at the head of the bed with my right hand on Meghan's head, my left hand was holding onto Caitlin's hand. Then there was Randy beside Caitlin; Lanette and Gerry were on the other side. We were told that we would hear her breathing, but that it wasn't really her breathing, it was gasses coming from her as her body shut down. Something came over me and I knew I had to pray, so out loud, I prayed over Meghan. I laid my right hand on her sweet little head and as we all held hands around her I said. "Meghan, it's okay, you can let go. Get up and walk, you've wanted to walk for so long. Feel the sand in your feet, the wind in your hair, and go to Jesus and Poppie. It's ok, you can go. This isn't your body any longer, it can't keep you."

"She left at that moment. I felt something strange, her spirit, I suppose leave her body, a gentleness for just a moment as it went right through me."

I will never forget how I felt a pull go right through my right hand, right through the palm of my hand; I felt her leave through me. It felt like she was holding my hand and then she was gone. Things became a blur; I remembered hearing her dad sobbing and say "she's gone."

Caitlin was holding onto Meghan's head not wanting to let go, not wanting to leave her sister, she ran out of the room, and I started after her. Randy stopped me and wanted me to go back in with his girls.

"Please, not now, I have to find Caitlin. Meghan just died, and I don't have the strength to go back in there again to relive it, I have only enough strength to find Caitlin" I said to him in sorrow as I ran out of ICU to find my baby.

I ran out of ICU and found her sitting on a bench down the hallway. I brought her to the butterfly room. I thought she was going to pass out. She was trembling and her heart raced so fast, she was as white as a ghost; I didn't know what to do. I knew her pain

266

was different than mine and I knew that in that moment, my life was for her, Caitlin and I had to continue this journey now and help heal each other, with the help of God and family, we would make it. In that moment, the only thing that mattered was to hold my Caitlin, and cry together. I don't know how long we were in the butterfly room, I just held her and we cried. When we came out, everyone was gone. Randy, his girls, my mom, Gerry, everyone; they were all gone. It was just Caitlin and I. We headed back to ICU, and I met Anna, I asked her if she could please collect for me all of Meghan's last beads for these past three days, that I wasn't going to leave without them. Anna helped me to select those last beads for here final strand.

"I am going to have to name this one I suppose" as I tasted the salty overflow of tears roll past my lips. "Rest in Peace is what it needs to say." I said to Anna as she picked out the letters with shaky hands. One of her longest strands was now in my hand as Caitlin and I decided it was time to say a final goodbye. I walked back into the room where a single blue sheet lay over Meghan exposing only her beautiful face. I kissed her cheek and felt an odd sensation of cold. She was truly gone, and this was now only the battered frozen shell that once held her beautiful spirit. "Rest in peace my sweet baby girl" I said as I blew her a kiss from the hallway knowing that I would never see her again.

It was now after six, Caitlin and I walked hand in hand down the hallway. I clenched that final strand of beads tightly in my hand and could feel every single bead dig deep into my flesh. Together we entered the underground parking. Caitlin got into the front seat, where Meghan usually sat. We cried again, and then held hands, I started the vehicle and we journeyed home. The drive was long and lonely, and very scary. We both knew that we would never see Meghan again; that our lives now were forever changed and it scared us. *How am I going to do this*, I thought. I didn't even remember how to properly drive; but I had to get us home safe. Holding hands was something Meghan and I did all the time, she wanted to feel me with her always as her loss of hearing scared her. Whenever I drove anywhere with her, we held hands. Now I had another hand to hold, Caitlin's, and together God would get us through this pain.

I arrived home and shortly after friends appeared with flowers. A lot of it was a blur, I don't think I even saw faces, just heard the hum of voices and the hugs that followed.

The phone rang, it was Randy.

"Where are you?" He asked.

In a snarky voice I replied, "Well at home because you called here and I answered didn't I?" I knew he must have looked for me everywhere when I ran after Caitlin.

"I will be over soon," he said.

I felt angry at everyone, and everything. We were all broken hearted now. "I need to take a hot bath and just have a few moments to myself, okay? I will be down in a bit." I seemed to just tell it to the air as I have no idea who was even in my home or whom listened as I headed upstairs. I filled the tub, lit a candle, climbed in, and cried a guttural cry. I made no sound, just tears that rolled down like a waterfall that burned into my cheeks. I had an ache inside me and I knew it would never ever from this moment on be the same.

My mind screamed, "How could this happen? Just two weeks ago she was cancer free, and happy. How can it be? I don't understand why you took her home God; I don't like it at all" I thought as I lay chin deep in bubbles and tears.

Randy had arrived and helped me out of the tub; I suppose I was in there for a long time as I felt dizzy and weak. Karen was in the kitchen and made tea and Meghan's friends had arrived. I didn't know what to say, my house rapidly filled up with flowers. I checked my email and the Burlington Post had sent me their condolences. I slowly got dressed into some comfortable clothing; black rugby pants that Meghan loved as they were loose and baggy and a big flannel shirt. I needed to wear clothes that I felt wrapped in as I needed to feel as much comfort as I could. If I took a breath the wrong way I would either pass out, or throw up, I was on the edge of something that I have never felt before nor do I want to again. As I sipped my tea and let the tears flow, I felt a calm come over me.

"Turn and look outside" Randy said. I had never seen him cry. As I turned around to look out the front door I froze in what I saw; hundreds of teenagers, with candles, with flowers, in tears. They filled up the street. Cars in the distance would drop them off. I could see up the street and how so many kids walked through the field. I thought of the movie Pay It Forward and was moved to tears. I went outside, lil man, Jackie, Heather, Natalie, Marissa, Matthew, Cori, Karen, Kim, Jenna, Chris, Ryan, oh, and so many more. I can't even begin to name them all.

I started to speak. "Wow, I guess Meghan got you all moving to get your butts over here," they smiled and some giggled through tears.

"Her spirit is real, and is touching each and every one of us as we stand together tonight" I began to speak in a shaky voice. "Thank you for being here, this means more to me than you will ever know." I looked upon tear streamed faces and then began to speak.

"Meghan did not die of cancer and yes she was cancer free. She won her battle against cancer" I began, "She was completely cancer free." If any of you have any questions, please ask me, I am here to openly answer anything." I continued as I felt hands holding onto mine to give me strength.

"First, I feel the need to speak freely on the use of drugs and I know that some of you may have, or still may be, experimenting with them. Please stop, I beg you, and so does Meghan. It's the drugs that she had no choice in taking that caused a lot of her problems. Her spirit is here now with us and she is wiser for having gone through this journey; she would tell you that it isn't worth it. It's not worth the damage to your health, to your body, mind and soul to take drugs. Some cause hearing loss, some cause infertility, some may kill you, some cause bleeding. Please stop." I pleaded as I felt this message had to be given.

"Okay, that's enough of my lesson on drug abuse" I smiled and even heard a few giggles again. "Seriously, if anyone ever wants to talk to me, please do. I am here for each and every one of you, just as you are here for me tonight. I want you to ask questions, don't be shy."

"Was she in pain, did she suffer?" a voice from within the crowd said.

"No, she wasn't in pain, to look at her you would think so, but something bigger than we can imagine took control. Meghan was carefree, lighthearted, and acted like she had no worries in the world" I assured them.

"If she didn't have cancer, what caused her death?" was the question from the other side of the street.

"Well, she had to take a lot of drugs and had to receive a lot of transfusions and over time everything took its toll on her body, her cause of death was internal bleeding." I replied with a heavy heart. "Her poor little body just couldn't come back from all the treatments; some because of chemotherapy and some because of other drugs; it was simply her time to go, as God knew her suffering, and He took her home peacefully."

"What kind of cancer did she have?" another asked.

"It was a blood cancer, it may have been related to her first illness, HLH, which wasn't cancer, or it may have been caused from her chemotherapy and drugs after her bone marrow transplant." I responded and was glad that the questions were being asked as it helped me also.

"You mean people can get cancer after having chemotherapy? I thought chemo killed cancer" was a concerned and confused voice in the darkness.

"Yes, it does kill the cancer cells, but it will alter healthy cells also, and they have a chance of becoming cancer cells, especially in the blood, like leukemia or lymphoma. Meghan had lymphoma." I responded

"Did she know she was going to die?" someone asked with a choked up voice.

"No, I don't believe she did because she asked if she could have a popsicle when she woke up."

"What do you mean when she woke up?" "Well," I replied, and took a deep breath. "Things were becoming very serious; her body was very unstable, and she was put into a drug induced coma so that they could perform various things to try to save her. She needed to be in a comatose, calm state. She said to me as they hooked up the IV to her, mom, when I wake up, can I have a freezy, so she went to sleep, happy, and imagining an icy cold freezy, probably a red or blue one, when she would wake up."

"We never got to say goodbye, how come?" one of her dear friends asked as she sobbed and sobbed.

"Well, that was a hard decision and when I thought it over I could feel Meghan's spirit say to me, "Mom, don't you dare let all my friends come see me like this, I want them to remember me how I was, not what I look like here." I cried, and said sorry to all that were listening. "Please understand that it was a very hard decision, only a couple of people, and family were there, and some didn't even go in because of how horrific things were. It would not have been fair of me to allow anyone to see what was happening to her poor little body, and I pray that you will all understand, and remember the Meghan that each and every one of you knew, please forgive me."

"She seemed so strong through all of this, how did she do it?" came another question from the crowd in the dark.

"She didn't do it alone, she had faith and her faith grew through her journey. Her strength was amazing, yes, and her faith was why it was so. She found Jesus, not that he was ever lost to her, she always believed in Him, but she learned how to trust the faith that grew. Meghan learned and shared openly a love that was bestowed upon her and within her. Her journey taught her as I hope it will teach all of you. Have faith, don't be afraid, and just be nice to each other."

It was then that I shared a special saying that Meghan had. "She had a saying, "It's not about how long you live, it's about how you live your life," and "I think she lived a life very full in these past two years, yes they were full of suffering also, but in all the suffering, this little gal of mine would discover a blessing. I don't understand how sometimes, good God she amazed me and always will, but she would find a blessing in everything. Like when she lost her hair. Oh, well, no more tangles, and she would giggle. Or when she lost her hearing, it's cool I can read lips now mom and I think that I feel more inside. She had a favourite song, I don't think many of you know it, it's a Christian song that she and I would sing a lot, Testify to Love."

As I continued to talk my legs trembled and I could barely stand up, but the strength of these kids kept me going.   All of a sudden, Karen and a couple of others began to sing.

"Oh my stars, you know that song, how on earth?" never mind, I smiled and said, "Just keep on singing."

It was a cool crisp night on this night of Meghan's journey home. The sky was clear the sun was setting with a fire glow. An opening in the clouds with the most spectacular rays burst through almost as if a portal to heaven had opened especially for Meghan. I have never in all my life witnessed such a spectacular sky, and knew it was my Meghan's fiery spirit in the sky, as her friends gathered around with candles lit; wax had melted on the driveway and sidewalk, and many had flowers in hand.

As the girls continued to sing on the sidewalk I summed up my talk with saying, "I have only one thing to ask of each and every one of you and that is that you can't leave here without giving me a hug." So, one by one, they approached me and I was able to share some time with each of them. I stood on my front lawn with Heather, Chris, Marissa, Natalie, Jackie, Matt, and of course Caitlin and Randy. As I hugged each one of these amazing friends and cried with them, I felt strength grow within me. Certain hugs that I will always remember and to this very day stand out in my mind are so treasured. One hug in particular came from her friend Matthew, I can remember how I used to drop Meghan off at his house and they would hang out, play pool, and chill. I told him during our hug that I was going to write a book, that Meghan had asked me to do so and that it would one day God willing; it would be her story for everyone to share.

"I want that book he said, as he hugged me, she will never ever be forgotten, and you are an amazing mom." I felt his love for her in his hug, just as I felt it in the hugs of so many others. Each one of these special kids had their own unique relationship with Meghan. Her childhood friends, Natalie, Sharmane, Marissa, Virginia, along with her high school friends, Heather, Jackie, Chris, Kate, Katie, Karen, Cori, Cam, Jessie, Courtney, Kyle, Mitch and Little Man. One by one I met each kid, we hugged and cried together, and I shared in a special moment of memory with each of them. This night, her first night of passing had become something I could remember with both joy and sadness.

I may not ever know the whys and the hows, but one thing I will always know is that this journey, it wasn't just Meghan's it was all of ours, she touched lives and will continue to do so. Thank you Lord for giving me my Meghan for the 17 years that I had her. My life will be forever changed and from this moment on I will always remember that:

> *"It's not about how long you live; it's about how you live your life"*
> *- Meghan Rush*

Chapter 23 – Testify to Love

I felt numb for the days ahead and we had a lot to do. Lanette, being a funeral director, looked after a lot of things and I was so very grateful to her for that. We had some special requests that Meghan and I had discussed. She said to me, "mom, when I die, someday, I want everything white, white casket, white car, and colour, nothing black." I took a mental note at that time and hoped I would never have to act upon them. I didn't want to plan this, I hated every minute of it. I think the only thing that kept me going was clinging to the fact that Meghan was watching and I had to do this to honour her wishes. "The casket has to be white, and so does the coach car." I instructed Lanette.

An open casket visitation was planned and there was one thing I felt strong about, Actually, I felt like Meghan was asking me to do it. "Mom, please do my makeup, everyone will see me and I don't want to look stupid with some guy having done my makeup crappy."

So I asked Lanette. "Can I please do her makeup?"

Lanette's words to me were "kudos to you Ang, I don't know of anyone who could do this, but yes you can do her makeup and I will be right there with you." I met Lanette at the funeral home, and she led me down the hallway, down a few steps where we waited outside a room. She entered first and made sure that things were okay for me to come in. I unzipped my bag of all her favorite things; even her perfume, Ralph. I carefully applied her soft pink shades of eyeshadow with a bit of glitter on her eyelids. A beautiful shade of soft peach and brown was applied to the mid area of her eyelid; a single coat of mascara on her beautiful long lashes and a touch of eyeliner to finish up the eyes. Her foundation was a gentle dusting of power that had a delicate shimmer to it and then a hint of bronze colour for her cheeks. Meghan never wore a lot of makeup, but always wore it soft and delicate, very classy. I tried not to think of anything other than to get this right; I had to do this the way she

275

would want it to be done. "Oh God please let me get this right", I dabbed on her favorite lip gloss over her full pink lips as tears filled my eyes. I did my best not to cry over her, afraid that if I got her makeup wet it would be a disaster. Her skin was very tight, and it felt more like I was putting make up on a mannequin, not my daughter. I knew that this was just her shell and believe that her spirit was with Jesus now yet it was still the shell that all would see tomorrow and I wanted her to be so pretty. She looked beautiful, flawless and priceless. I felt in my heart that she was happy and that it was important to her that her friends see her looking beautiful and peaceful. It also allowed me to connect one more time with my baby. I needed to feel that I was able to do all I could in her death and to plan her funeral was the very last thing I could do.

The funeral home was right across the street from the hospital and it was easiest to hold it there so that nurses and friends could come to say goodbye. I also didn't want it close to home, in Burlington, because I knew that every time I would drive by the funeral home afterwards I would be reminded of my daughter's funeral, so having it in Hamilton was the best and only choice.

Before the guests arrived we had a small intimate family viewing where we could say goodbye to Meghan on our own. I stood at one end of the room and just stared at the casket. From where I stood it felt like she was miles away and I was looking down this long horrible path I was about to walk. I didn't want that moment to arrive when I had to walk towards her and say my final goodbye. She was my baby, we had so many more things that we needed to share. In that moment I froze and thought of all the things we would never be able to do as mother and daughter, I would never see her graduate, I would never help plan her wedding. I thought of the things that she never got to experience in life and how terribly wrong and unfair all of this was. She never got to travel, fall in love, have a child, or drive a car. She never experienced life how she should have, but she did find love and peace in God. I began my walk towards her with tears melting into my soul. *How do I do this Lord, how to I continue without her?* With each step the sadness and pain deepened. The reality hit hard. I allowed myself to be consumed by it because it was the only way I could take another step. Consumed by the pain, I managed to touch her beautiful face. I touched her hand and whispered in her ear "hand in hand and over our hearts together forever and never apart".

I wandered around to look at her life's celebration that everyone had worked so hard to put together. We created special boards of pictures and brought in some of her favourite things. Tables were set up with things that had become dear to her. We even had a can of spaghetti out; it had to be her favourite kind as she would eat no other. Also, a fantastic video of pictures that we played the entire two days. It was a wonderful slideshow of her life, her friends, her family, and it played along with her favorite tunes. Finding a white casket wasn't easy. We had an auto body shop paint a casket white. We had three rooms full of memories of Meghan; it was truly a celebration of her life. At the end of the long third room was her casket, she lay in this beautiful glistening casket with her white and orange top. Her hands gently crossed over each other and she lay peacefully with the face of an angel. She looked beautiful, just as she had wanted to look. On each end of the casket were two enormous bunches of balloons standing tall as pillars bright and colourful. A table was also at each end of the casket and on each table was a beautiful crystal vase full of colourful Sharpie markers. We were going to write our messages to Meghan, and send her off with them. As friends started to arrive the tension began to build. The kids were full of fear to go and see their dearly departed friend, unsure of why there were markers there. Sadness was deep and thick and spread throughout the entire building like a fog that was unseen but felt.

I took the hand of Meghan's little brother Ian, whom I just adore and I said "let's go and draw a picture for Meghan."

"What, on that?" He pointed to her casket.

"Yes absolutely on that, she is in a gift box and going to heaven, so we need to send it off with lots of pictures and love." He picked up a marker and began to draw. I too grabbed a few markers and created a rainbow with hearts. Matt, who was also quite an artist, drew a dolphin with a special message to his lil angel. He wore his orange shirt today also, the one he was going to wear to take her to prom. One by one each family member, friend, relative, nurse and neighbor we all took turns as we adorned her casket with special messages and pictures. I enjoyed reading the messages and asked one of the funeral gals to please take pictures of every message so that I could have them to cherish forever. It was a long two days of greeting people, and saying goodbye. I took a few breaks during these days to quietly work on my speech for Monday.

"How do I do it, how do I get up and talk about any of this?" I asked God as I sat on one of the pews in the funeral home away from everyone I just bowed my head and quietly sobbed. I felt a hand on my back; it was my friend Angie. She was the mom of Meghan's childhood friend who lived across the street. I needed this moment to hug an old friend and to be able to just cry. My neighbor Ed was soon by my side also. I hadn't spoken to him since Wednesday when Caitlin and I arrived home from the hospital on the day Meghan died. He hugged me tight and cried with me then just as he hugged me now here at her visitation. We talked about how Meghan was just a wee little thing when he moved in next door to us.

"She was a cute wee lass just getting ready to start school and the other wee one would run around on the front lawn in her wee little booties and a diaper" he recalled in his Irish accent.

"She's not suffering any more missy, she's with your da" he whispered as he hugged me tight.

"But she's not with me" I sobbed, "She's not with me" as my tears soaked the shoulder of my kind neighbor.

Monday arrived; the day of Meghan's funeral was here. We had a few things to still arrange. We had ordered hundreds and hundreds of balloons for outside the church; they were going to be let go when we would all say goodbye outside. Gerry wanted to ride with Meghan in the coach car on route to the church. They drove by the high school and he was able to see hundreds of kids, as they paraded from the high school to the church, all wearing pink. The church overflowed with people, we set up an outside area with video for those who could not fit inside the church. Hundreds upon hundreds of guests were there to say a final goodbye to a very special girl. Also, Meghan had wanted to attend her prom in a firetruck. This wasn't prom but it was her graduation into heaven. I had arranged for a

278

firetruck to be outside the church as a surprise for her dad and others so that it could escort the white coach car to the crematorium. With Glenn's help the firetruck arrived quietly while we were in the church.

Seeing the casket closed with the cloth over it was very difficult for me. Up until this point I always had a visual of Meghan, now she was truly sealed and to be delivered, just as I told Ian, like a present being sent to God. Inside I felt like I wanted to open it up. I even visualized myself doing this, just to get one last look, but I knew I couldn't, still in my mind I wanted to open it up for one last look and kiss on the cheek. Music played and the church overflowed with people. Rev'd Sue was running the show, and Rev'd Steven was going to give the eulogy. Rev'd Steven was always there for Meghan, as a youth pastor in Randy's church he had a way of connecting with the kids and I wanted him to speak to them today. Steven had visited Meghan many times when she was in hospital.

The time came for me to speak; I was numb and Randy stood with me so that I could feel the strength and warmth of someone beside me. My eyes were fixed on her casket that was now covered with a white cloth; it wasn't the cheerful and colourful message scripted casket that was at the funeral home; it was now draped as she was being put to rest in God's home. I didn't like how this looked in front of me; I liked even less how I felt inside. I still wanted to open the casket and keep her and beg her to be back with me. I clenched the papers in my hand and took a deep breath as I choked back tears. Looking out into the crowd I knew that what I had to say had to comfort and impact many of her young friends, to teach them about love, courage, faith and about who Meghan had become for all of us.

So I began:

Wednesday, early evening, Caitlin and I were coming home. It was the most difficult drive we ever had to make. We had just said good bye to Meghan at the hospital and we were now "Going Home."

We cried so much, and held onto each other's hand all the way home. We shared some very special moments together in that drive.

One of the things that strongly stood out in my mind was that Meghan too was "going home." I cried out in tears, "God, how am I going to do this," feeling such an ache for Meghan, and so much for Caitlin. I then felt a subtle reminder of something of something I use to tell Meghan.

In my heart I heard her saying...."remember mom, love is more powerful." I said, OK, we can do this. Love will be the way. I prayed for strength and courage, and my prayer were answered. Friends and family that had been with us since Monday were still carrying us. Thank you and God bless you.

Late Wednesday night I was summoned from a hot bath. "Angela you have to come down here, some kids are here to see you." I went downstairs to find a few kids inside with flowers, Randy was so broken up and said, "turn around and look outside."

What I saw was the most beautiful thing. Over 300 kids stood outside my house with candles. It took my breath away. You guys have no idea of how much you gave me and Caitlin. You welcomed us home with LOVE and with LIGHT. And I know it was all because of Meghan. Because of my beautiful baby and how her spirit touched all of you and inspired you to do what you did.

280

Standing out front with you, talking, sharing, crying, remembering, laughing. It was wonderful, and I could feel Meghan with us.

I know and understand better now what it means when I read "those who believe in me will have eternal life." Meghan's spirit, her eternal life touched all of you and has continued to do so with; wear pink for Meghan, the bbq, the pasta night and all the plans that I am sure are still brewing in your cute little minds. Thank you so much for hearing her spirit, and following your hearts. You bring gifts to all of us in what you do in her honor.

I loved talking to you, and the hugs you gave me were amazing. Some of you wanted to ask me questions, and I am glad you did. If any of you have anything to ask, come to me anytime, come to my house, and I will answer it. I will put my email on facebook, Caitlin will have to teach me, and then you can ask me privately anything you want. Deal.

Thursday arrived with little or no sleep. My mind was all over the place. I tried to write a speech over and over but was stumped. I had questions, feelings, fears, and so much that only God could understand. One thing I asked was WHY, why did we get the news, Cancer Free, and then have her leave us. Why give us hope, and then hit us so hard. I didn't like how I felt, I was angry, and it felt crappy. I began to pray for an answer, and later it came loud and clear through someone very special.

The news "cancer free," it wasn't for me, it was for Meghan. God asked me, how did Meghan feel when she got the news. HAPPY. I said. He said, it was her news, her answered prayer. She was happy happy happy, and she didn't lose any hope at all, her happiness was more important, it's all she wanted.

One of Meghan's prayers daily in her journal was to be happy again. These last few weeks she has been the happiest that

281

she has ever been. God took her cancer, and gave her a huge dose of happiness.

Now I understand I said to God, Being cancer free she still wasn't out of the woods, and she knew it, we all did, but she got back her happiness. We got to witness her being happy, she did have her prayers answered.

March 24th she wrote in her journal. - overall my day was pretty darn good. I am so happy today which is even better. Thanks mom and Caitlin you are the greatest. I love you both so much always remember that. Most of all Thank you God for helping me have a good time and thank you for helping me realize and noticing the good and positive in life, Good nite and amen xxoo ☺

March 25th - Today I woke up in a wonderful mood - I had a good sleep. Mom made home made pizza; -- I had 4 or 5 pieces Darn steroids.

March 26th - Today was awesome, You know it makes me feel really good inside when I have good days, and it doesn't matter who it's with. Today it was with dad. He took me for my bone scan – 2 hrs ugh - But the day was worth it. We went to walmart. Can you believe Kraft Dinner was only 57 cents. Then toys r us – then mount royal – I love that place – indigo to see grandma and grandpa – I could spend hours there.

March 30th - Today is quite the day I must say. OH NO I forgot to write last night. Hahaha So last night my new great friend Jaclyn came over. We watched a movie – the pursuit of happiness – maked cookies.. mmmmm chocolate chip, very sweet.

Ok, back to Friday. Clinic – I get my scan results back. Mom, dad, and Randy wer there. We got called into a room with the Dr. Best results ever "Im cancer free." Got that shit- out of me. I still can't believe it. 2 years and poof. Dr. gave me 2 thumbs up.

Mom was so happy, she's been crying all day. It just made me laugh and smile all over, inside and out. To see her so happy like that makes me happy.

It became so clear to me after that. Her Cancer free news was for her, to bring her happiness, and I am so glad that I don't feel the way I did a couple days ago about it. Her happiness was always the most important thing to me, and always will be. We will always have hope, Meghan never lost it. She left this physical world happy and journeyed home happy. She got her prayers answered, God new what she needed. She got her happiness.

We are celebrating Meghan's life, remembering her as she grew into the most beautiful girl you could imagine, both inside and out. She and I grew very close over the past 2 years. She went through so much, more than anyone could imagine. She rose above each and every thing she encountered and in it she always found God's blessing.

Meghan loved babies, and she had a 6 week old roommate at mac for a while. We named her ladybug. Meghan loved her so much. Ladybug went home into foster care. And I remember Meghan saying. "Mom its ok that I can't have kids, I can be a foster parent and love my kids just as much, or adopt."

She just always continued to amaze me with her courage, strength and love. The simplest things made her so happy. She always made her best effort in everything. She had a style about her that someone once said to me was "the picture of grace." This is so true, she is Gods Grace.

One of the things Meghan lost was her hearing. She didn't let it get her down. Actually I think it probably upset me more than her because I just couldn't bear to see her go through anything more. One night she caught me crying, she couldn't hear me, but she figured it out pretty quick. She made me tell her what was wrong. I said that I was just so sad that she had to go through yet another journey. She said to me. Mom, if Helen Keller can do it with no eyes or ears, I can do it with no ears, I still have my eyes. Besides sometimes it's nice not to hear, haha.. I knew she was referring to the times I was disciplining 2 arguing sisters that were both teenage girls.

She became quite a chatter box after losing her hearing. She had the cutest sense of cheekiness. We had a shopping day about a week ago. She so badly wanted a lazyboy chair. So of course we headed out to Lazyboy. She tried a few, and then found the ultimate lazyboy chair.. it had a remote.. well Meghan then started working the salesgirl. "ya know, if I had this chair mom would have more free time, she wouldn't have to keep helping me in and out of a chair, and most important, she wouldn't hurt her back, since I am on steroids I have gained more weight, and I don't want her to hurt herself." The sales gal was sold, It was funny to watch Meghan in action. Randy said to her, Meghan you know why they are called lazyboys right, 'cause they make you lazy.   ... "Well grandma Gina has one and she isn't lazy"....I think we lost that battle, and were probably going to get a lazyboy.

My most treasured times with her were at night. I would snuggle in beside her and play with her hair, and caress her neck. She and I would talk. Meghan would say "Mom I can't hear you so I will just keep talking. 'cause I love talking with you. When you have something to say, just tug my hair, or poke me. I will turn to see you. Some nights we both talked, some nights I just listened. She was so incredible to talk to. She had patience and an understanding when we shared our special time.

Meghan, I know you can hear me now, and I want to say a few things to you sweetie. I miss you so much, and my heart aches for you. But I know you are in a place where you can run *along a beach, hear the laughter of little kids your favorite sound. You have no pain, no scars, and your long beautiful hair. You are happy, I will make you as proud of me as I am of you and be the best mom and friend to Caitlin. She is my precious gem, and you are her angel. I will live by your example and always remember. "it's not about how long you live, it's about how you live your life"*

Meet me in my dreams sweetie, give poppie a hug from me, and when god calls me home I will meet you at the rainbow. For as long as I shall live I will testify to love.
I love you more."

A few others got up to speak. Meghan's friends Jackie and Chris they got up together and spoke about their shopping day with Meghan to the dollar store and how they had sword fights in the aisle. Hearing her friends laugh was comforting, and I knew how hard it was for them to get up and talk today when all they truly wanted was their friend back.

Ronni got up and spoke about how she found courage in Meghan's battle. As someone who battled many illnesses daily, Ronni found strength in Meghan and was grateful for having been able to be a part of her life. It touched me deeply to know that my daughter had helped Ronni to continue to fight her battles and to face them with more courage than she was able to before.

Glenn got up and spoke. He looked amazing and was in complete uniform as a firefighter. Meghan would have smiled knowing that he was speaking at her funeral. In fact, I know that she was. Meghan always looked up to him as her hero, but today, she was his.

Gerry spoke last, his words were so sweet, and I wish I had an actual recording of the funeral service. I wish I could remember more of what her dad said. I know he talked about how the name Meghan meant courage, and that she indeed embodied courage. She was daddy's girl for sure, they shared a special bond. Cheese heads when

285

they watched football together.   Meghan was his peanut.   His pain today broke my heart, I was glad that he had Lanette to help him through this. I worried about her little brother Ian, he was so young. How would a loss like this affect such a young child? Of course my heart broke for Caitlin. They have lost their sister.

Kate had written a song for Meghan, and for the first time I heard the voice of an angel sing about her dearly departed friend. This friend who had changed her life forever; the song was about my daughter. Silence filled the church as we listened to Kate on guitar. Beautiful words that truly came from her heart filled the entire building and echoed outside and then fell onto the hearts of every person there. Here are the words to that beautiful song. Meghan, here it is one more time for you...

Meghan's Wings

I know an angel
I met her in real life
I know she's an Angel
Because I watched her take flight

I've witnessed a miracle
God blessed her to my life
I've seen beautiful
I saw it in her eyes

She taught me what it means to live
She showed me what it is to give
There is a girl who watches over me
And that girl lives in my memory
It's that girl's bravery that carries me that sets me free

I've seen the unbelievable
Her strength never compromised
I've seen the unattainable
Her courage never subsides

I am going to meet an Angel
She's waiting right beside
I know she's my angel I can feel it inside
There is a piece of my heart that will never die
Because she's found her wings and now,
Now she flies

She taught me what it means to live
She showed me what it is to give
There is a girl who watches over me
That girl she lives in my memory
It's that girl's bravery that carries me, that sets me free:
I know an angel; I met her in this life
I know she's my angel I feel her by my side.

It was that time, the time for all of us to meet outside; to leave the church and say our final goodbye to Meghan. Her favorite song was now being played and sung by all, loudly, proudly, and with tears flowing. The girls from the funeral home met us outside and handed us candles, and packages of seeds; purple forget-me-nots. The balloons had arrived, and the sky was filled with colour, just as Meghan had wanted. We were all handed a few balloons; I was handed quite a few. The casket emerged from the open doorway of the church. It was carried by Gerry, Matt, and a few others and was being put into the back of the white coach car; at that moment the balloons were set free, soaring high, just as her spirit was.

I remembered hearing Gerry say, "She got her firetruck."
I went over to him when I heard him and hugged him. "Is it okay? I wanted this to be a surprise at her funeral for you" I said as we embraced in tears.

"Yes, it's absolutely ok, she is getting the royal treatment today, escorted by a firetruck" he replied as he sobbed. Her body was now at rest, inside a box, wrapped with words of love, admiration, gratitude, and sadness. The white clothed coffin slid into the open back of the white coach car; the door was closed and in that moment I knew that any bit of strength I had in me now had to be given to her friends. I prayed silently, soar sweet angel, with all the colours of the rainbow, and all the voices in the wind, let your spirit soar and with God's help I would continue here on earth to love and comfort, grow, and live a life that would make you proud as you looked down from heaven.

My eyes wandered the crowd and I caught a glimpse of Matt. He was one of the pall bearers that helped slide her into the car. Matt stood in the middle of the street, looking lost and about to crumble. I felt his heart, I made my way over to him and we hugged while we cried together and I said. "Matt, you are stuck with us now, so don't even think that you are alone in this, little sis needs you too."

"I'm not going anywhere, you are my family, and you will see lots of me, I am going to need you guys too" he held me tight.

The firetruck started to pull away and position itself in front of Meghan's coach car. The driver closed the doors behind her casket, made his way to the driver side and entered the vehicle. Hundreds of balloons still drifted overhead while a firetruck so silent and strong escorted my daughter away. Everything in me froze.

That's it I thought, *She is gone now forever.*   I didn't know what to do in that moment. Part of me screamed in silence "come back" and part of me wanted to run after her. I was frozen in this moment as I looked around I realized that so was everyone else. I held Caitlin close, squeezed her little hand and kissed the top of her head. There was too much sadness in the air and to change things up a bit I whispered to Caitlin "let's go and see what goodies the ladies from church have put together for the reception." I didn't feel anywhere close to being able to taste anything other than salty tears that made their way to my lips, but I just wanted to get out of the thick sadness that rest upon the entire crowd outside.

"The ladies from my church have put together a reception downstairs for everyone" I shouted, "please come and join us as we remember and share our love for Meghan together."   It was a beautiful gathering and I received so many hugs; which were desperately needed.

A few days had passed and even though I had said my goodbyes when I let the balloons go, there was however one story to share. Family, immediate only, were gathered around her plot at the cemetery. Gerry and I both carried her urn with the ashes up a carpeted walkway toward the hole where we laid them while a few words were being said. Gerry was hunched over as he reached inside the hole after we had put Meghan's urn down inside. I wasn't sure what was going on.

"Are you okay? Is it your heart or something? What's wrong? Why aren't you getting up?" I questioned oh so quietly so no one would hear. We were there a fairly long time and silence fell upon the family.

"I dropped my bank card; it fell out of my pocket" he whispered as he continued to stretch deep into the dug hole.

"Oh, crap," I muttered, "Can you reach it?" I could hear people mumbling, as they wondered what on earth was going on and why we were be both crunched over and still bent into the hole.

"I guess she wants to shop," he said quietly to me so no one else heard "and is taking my bank card with her." Well I couldn't hold it in, that cracked me up and I began to laugh loud and hard. "Ah, got it," he said as we then stood up and he flashed the card to them.

"She wanted to take my bank card in case there are malls in heaven." Well everyone laughed so hard. I still to this very day laugh when I think of it; it was the perfect moment to lighten up that day as putting her ashes in the ground was something I could not even bring my mind to deal with.

I suppose it was Meghan's way of saying, "lighten up, it's cool up here, we can even shop if we like. Hey dad, mind if I have your card?"

We had one last big event to get through, graduation day. Meghan was, as you know, supposed to graduate with her class. Well, she still was, but Caitlin and Ian were going to walk across the stage, dressed in pink and accept her diploma on her behalf. Before that day arrived, we had a few things to prepare. A bunch of Meghan's friends, Kim, Heather, Kate, Jackie, and a few more, were going to come over to make pins for all of the graduating class and teachers to wear. We had printed off a bunch of tiny pictures, and were hot glue gunning them onto pink foam cutouts of wings and then of course add glitter. Pink had become a colour of representation for Meghan.

Her high school even held a Wear Pink for Meghan day and they wore pink to her funeral; so we thought that a pink wing pin with her picture was appropriate. I brought the finished pins to the school days before the ceremony, and also had them dedicate a song for the graduating class.

Matt arrived on the day of graduation and we met up in the gymnasium. The two front rows were reserved for our family and of course we all wore pink. To see every single faculty member and every student wear a pink wing badge, was overwhelmingly touching and in fact every moment of the ceremony was special. Chelsea, one of Meghan's friends, had composed a song that she sang and played piano. It was beautiful. One by one, each student crossed the stage, shook hands and then came down the front steps close to where we sat; many made a detour to hug me. The moment arrived, "Meghan Rush," her name was called out by the presenter. The entire gymnasium went crazy, a standing ovation, clapping and whistling as Caitlin and Ian hand in hand walked across to accept Meghan's diploma. I didn't expect it, the support and love and cheering. *Good golly, my girl is smiling down from heaven now*, I thought. As the ceremony came to a close her song that I dedicated to all of her classmates played. I thought to myself as I looked over a sea of pink hearts and tear streamed faces. I knew in that moment that life would go on and that the lives of all those kids were forever changed as was mine.

Chapter 24 – Chill and Spill with Meghan

I will share with you some of Meghan's thoughts from her journals. I know she would love for you to get to know her and to know her does not mean that she has to be here, she is spirit and she is love. Meghan kept many journals during her struggles, and I know that after you read some thoughts and feelings in her own words you may feel touched. I have selected a few questions and answers that are personal to me and I hope you feel blessed.

Imagine a place in your mind that is special to you, where you feel safe and free. Describe this place.

- A place special to me is an open field with a weeping willow tree that has a tire swing. I would be the only one there.

Imagine you are a small seed that has been picked up by a bird that takes you away and places you somewhere. Tell us about this journey.

- I'd become an orange lily and I would grow tall with lilacs surrounding me because they remind me of my mom. My grandma would discover me and tend to me.

What are your talents and strengths and what bothers you?

- Well, I am very strong and was once good at soccer.
- Needles really bother me, and also being in a lot of pain. Also, if I catch someone lying.

What advice would you give someone in the same situation?

- The advice I would give them is to close your eyes and count to 10 slowly. Or close your eyes and go to your favourite place.

What things are you most proud of?

- I'm most proud of the fact that I've come this far and also that I've been able to handle a lot of pain.

If you could change the world in one way, what would you do and why?

- If I could change the world in one way then no one would ever get sick, because I would not want little kids to go through what I went through.

With the prompts I want, I need, I fear, I wish, I hope, I expect, I am and I love, write a few statements for each.

I WANT – to go home, to be strong, to be better.

I NEED – my mom, my dad, to eat better, to be stronger.

I FEAR – falling, getting sick again, losing my hair again, having to stay in the hospital over Christmas, not getting strong.

I WISH – I never got sick, I never lost my hair, I could have said goodbye to my poppie before he died (I think I'll write a note, attach it to a balloon and let it go)

I HOPE – I get to go home soon, the pain in my feet goes away soon

I EXPECT – people to be honest

I AM – a girl, 17 years old, strong, honest.

I LOVE – my family, friends, the doctors and nurses, ME!

What does it mean to cherish yourself?

- By caring for yourself, understanding what's going on with the good and the bad and most of all to be happy even if times can get rough.

Do you believe it is true that you are responsible for your own happiness? Why or why not?

- Yes, because if you don't try and be happy it's harder and harder to see the good.

What can you do to make your life a more joyful one?

- Don't do too many things at once that could easily stress you out. Space out your time and put the harder things first then relax with the smaller things in the end.

What is one lesson you have learned from pain?

- There's different kinds of pain, such as emotional and physical. When you have emotional pain you have to learn to be strong and not hold onto it, you must move on. When you have physical pain you must keep a positive attitude.

Think of a couple of quotes that fit your life?

- Don't judge somebody when you don't know them.
- True beauty lays in the eye of the beholder and also within yourself.

Write about a time you gave something to someone else that did not cost money. How did it feel?

- I gave my best friend Heather a glove stuffed with cotton balls because she wanted to hold my hand while I was in the hospital but can't visit. So I gave her a hand to hold.

Make a list of things you are grateful for.

- Having such a caring and understanding family.
- Prayers from people
- Friends who are there for me now more than they were before
- Learning more about myself from this disease.

Why are you grateful for those things?

- In a way I am grateful that I got this disease because I wouldn't have learned about myself more, about others, about having a bigger belief in faith. I have more friends now that are closer to me. I have also had prayers answered and I never had that before.

When someone loses themselves, how do they find themselves again?

- Go with your gut, say no to things and follow your path, it's simple.

What morals do you have that help you set boundries?

- I tell the truth, therefore I speak my mind. If something does not look right I say so, or it does not feel good, I say so. If I need help, I ask. The truth has many ways to come out. It's not just about talking, it's also asking for things. Like I said, if someone needs help then they have to ask it, that's the truth.

Can you think of a time you were upset about something that now seems funny?

- I used to get so upset and nervous about getting my dressing changed on my arm, but now when I look back, it's just tape and I've gone through a lot worse.

Do you ever feel like life won't start until something happens?

- Life isn't about the past or the future, it's about the ride.

When life challenges us it is easy to lose faith. How do you explain things that happen in the world that appear to be unfair and senseless?

- I don't everything does happen for a reason. If nothing happened, then there would be no reason for something to happen.

Describe Faith?

- Faith is who I am, where I live and how I live my life. It means believing in something you want to happen. It keeps me relaxed and calm when things get tough. It feels like a safe feeling, having something good surround you.

Describe a moment you needed emotional support?

- I needed a shoulder to let some tears out on and there was my mom, right when I needed it.

What about you is heavenly?

- God lives within.

Some of Meghan's Actual Journal Entries:

I've typed them exactly as she has written them, didn't want to correct anything. God Bless you Meghan for being so sweet ☺

Friday September 2, 2005
"Today I had to get up earlier than usual because I had to have a CT scan. A CT scan is where they scan your whole body and take pictures, then I had to get a dressing change on my arm ... not afraid of those much anymore... and finally got more pills... then off to home. My mom and I got some lunch from McDonalds and brought it home then I had to pack for my dad's. When we got to my dad's we had to go and pick up Ian at day care. He drew a picture for me ☺ Then we had our Friday night tradition ... pizza and wings. Hehe Then I went to bed earlier than usual because I had a small headache and had a long day at MacMaster."

Tues. Sept 27/05
"this morning I woke up at 9, had breakfast and pills then watch the "Maury Show," on how husbands abuse and control their wives. The teacher was supposed to come today but did not because we had a meeting at Sick Kids hospital in Toronto. It was a long meeting about the BMT (bone marrow transplant). He told us the good, the bad, the rules of what to eat etc. I won't go over everything cuz its to much. Then we got a tour of my area of the hospital it is huge! The main floor looks like a food court. By that time it was 6pm we had a sub to hold us off til dinner at nannies Its been a veery long and stressful day."

Tuesday October 5/05

"Today I woke up from my new bed, it was very comfy. Then I had a toasted tomatoe sandwich for breakfast yet again. Then the teacher came and helped with math, then I had lunch, then mommy is going to pamper me... hehe. Well mom gave me a bath, clipped toe nails and helped me with lotion for my stretch marks. After all that mom gave nannie and grandma a call. We went to Mother Tuckers for dinner. I was very stuffed, but it was very good. It was a nice treat out since I won't be able to eat out for a year. Then we came home and Randy got her and we watched House then mom laid with me in bed till I fell asleep."

Thurs Oct 20/05

"Today was a hell of a day. Okay, first when I woke up I went pee, then mom came with breakfast ... an omlette. Then the teacher from the hospital came by and I did some math for a bit. Then I had a lung test that was an easy one, I got perfect ☺ After that I had to go down and get a chest x-ray once again a very quick east test. Then mom and I came back up for lunch. I had the make your own taco, it wasn't the greatest so mom went down and got me a sub from Mr. Sub. After lunch I was hoping to have a nap, but no, person after person came to talk so I didn't get to have a nap. The doctor came, kidney person, dietician and more doctors. They came and told us I had to have a CT scan because they saw something, a shadow (tumor). So I went down, got the scan, got the results ... found out it wasn't , it was just puss (liquid) sitting there. So now I have to get it drained tomorrow, thank goodness I'll be put to sleep and hopefully not have a chest tube or any other tube in me. While I was getting the CTG scan I felt something rubbing my feet and legs and moms voice saying "relax just relax Meghan" turns out mom was on the other side of the room nowhere near where she could touch me and was praying out loud. It was kinda cool kinda like touched by an angel. Then we came up for dinner. I had chicken frided rice and carrots. It was Ok. Randy and Courtney were coming up to visit. We went down to the lounge and played a game of pool. Now I'm on MSN having a snack n watching TV then going to bed ☺"

Sat Nov 12/05

"todays the day after step down. I'm in my new room now. I've been very emotional with everything from happy ... to sad and to just feel like crying. The one thing that got me upset the most is seeing myself in the mirror for the first time in a while. It made me really upset, I did not like it. Then I soaked in a nice bath later, mom help me. It was scarey getting out because my legs were weaker and it was a lot harder, but mom was there just like she always been. Then it was time to take it easy and ready for bed. The next morning was a bit easier. I went for a couple of walks, had a few naps. Mom has just gone out for dinner and will be back by 7, I can't wait, I miss her already ... "

Weds. Nov 16/17? I forget / 05

"Today was an ok day. I wasn't so emotional. Daddy was here and I enjoyed that cuz I really missed him. He gave me a back rub, put lotion on my head, legs and feet, it was nice. But yesterday was funny because he put bum lotion on my head. Hehe. I also slept today, I was really tired. Only a few more days til I do come home, yay!. I think I'm going to go and get some rest, maybe watch an movie, Goodnight til next time. Love you all!"

July 25,06

"On July 25, 2006 I found out some pretty shocking news. The whole family had to meet with the doctor at McMaster hospital. The doctor had the results of my liver biopsy. He told us they found some kind of lymphoma, it's a rare type of cancer. I did not like the news, neither did anyone else. They have the treatment all ready for me. I can do this because I'm not a quitter, I'm a fighter!"

March 24/07
"Today I had a pretty damn good day! This morning I woke up veery tired actually, drove to clinic, finger poke then dye injection and then my counts. Good, cept platelets are pretty slow. After that we picked up Nannie for lunch and heady to Philthys, best restaurant ever! Food was awesome☺. After lunch we went to Mapleview Mall to shop a bit. I think we over did it on the movies... of course not! But we got "Look whos talking" best movie ever, and other ones too. Then we went to AE I got a shirt and belt. Too bad we had to leave so soon cuz of math. But we didn't even do math, hehe. We watched a movie ☺ while Caitlin was at a school dance ... so cute, hehe. So then we had subs for dinner and Caitlin and I watched movies, it was fun. Mom had a bath though. Overall my day was good and I'm happy today, which is even better!!
Thanks mom and Caitlin, yu guys are the greatest. I love you both so much always remember that ! Most of all thank you God for helping me have a good time today, I really needed it. And thank you for helping me realize and noticing the good an positive in live. ☺
Time for bed for me, good night and Amen xoxo "

Friday March 30, 2007
"Today is quite the day I must say! Oh no, I forgot to write last night, ha! Ok, so last night ... My new great friend Jaclyn came over ☺ we watched a movie .. "The pursuit of happiness," sad, but good. After we baked cookies. Mmm chocolate drop cookies! Very sweet. I had a god time, it was fun!. So that was last night.
Now today. This morning it was clinic and to get my scan results back. When mom, Randy and I got there, dad showed up, which

was nice☺. Then we got called in a room with a doctor. ... BEST RESULTS EVER !!! I'm cancer FREE BABY! ALL FUCKING BETTER. I still can't believe it's been 2 years almost and "poof" it's gone and I'm better. Doctor gave me 2 thumbs up !!

Mom was so happy, she's been crying all day. It just made me laugh and smile all over inside and out to see her so happy like that ... makes me happy. Then we went to tell Mr. Swybrous .. he was very happy and went to get me a gift from his office. He gave me a sand dollar, which was so cool. Then we went to see grandma ... no one home. Then to nannies, also no one home. So we went back home for math and lunch. Teacher was very pleased. Tonight we celebrate, me, Randy, mom, Caitlin, Lanette and Ian are going to Red Lobster for dinner. Then hopefully to the mall for a short while. Then I am going to dads after for some time to spend with Lanette which should be nice. Caitlin didn't come home after school. God please don't let anything happen to her, its been almost 2 hours, Please bring her home safely."

   Friday April 7/07

"Today's exactly 2 years since I first got sick with HLH and went into a coma at McMaster hospital. But other than that my days been okay. Jackyn came by around 11 or 12 and we baked tons and tons of cookies ... 60! Before we knew it, it was 5 oclock. So we ordered pizza for dinner then watched a movie. After the movie we went back to finish decorating the cookies then watch TV. Im kinda having a sad and hurting night. I feel really fat and ugly ☹ my tummy is getting bigger so fast and it upsets me a lot. It hurts too because its stretching. Then there's my eating controls, it's so hard God, ... Why? Why do things have to be so hard? Why do I get so afraid of such tiny things? Why can't I be more brave? Why can't I be more like other people and not be so afraid? Why don't I think I'm pretty? Why have I lost old friends? Why did I have to get sick?

Why did God pick me? Why can't things be easy? Why do people like me better now than before? WHY WHY WHY?

"Challenges is what makes life interesting . . . Overcoming them is what makes life meaningful"

"It's not about how long you live . . . It's about how you live your life" "Why Why Why, so many questions begin with why but nobody can ever answer them . . . Only God knows . . . But he won't tell you."

This was Meghan's last note. Nine days later she was put in an induced coma and never opened her beautiful eyes again. She passed away on April 18, 2007. Such powerful words of wisdom.

"It's not about how long you live.
It's about how you live your life.

"Why, Why, Why, so many questions begin with why but nobody can ever answer them… Only God knows… But he won't tell you."

Life truly is a timeless journey of endless love. Have faith and remember you are loved. Hand in hand and over my heart, together forever, never apart.